Social Justice Among the Women

About the Editors

Nazish Bano (Ph.D.) is working in the Department of Psychology, Sant Vinoba PG College Deoria, U.P. She started a career from 2-8-1995 as Lecturer and now she is Associate Professor. She did her Ph.D. from Gorakhpur University in 1993. She has published three papers in journals, six chapters in books and two chapters are under publication. She has presented 21 papers in national seminars.

Aradhana Shukla is Professor and Head of Psychology at Kumaun University, SSJ Campus, Almora and Dean (Arts), Kumaun University, Nainital. She is serving in this University from last 35 years and before joining this University she was UGC fellow at DDU Gorakhpur University, Gorakhpur and Assistant Research Officer at Department of Paediatrics, IMS, BHU. She has guided 52 Ph.D. students completed, 4 major research projects from UGC and ICSSR. She has written and edited 15 books and developed 15 psychological tests. More than 150 papers written by her have been published in the journal and books of National and International repute. She has co-edited four volume series on Mental Health: Psycho-Social Perspectives, Volume one 'Issues and Intervention' (2015), Volume two 'Multigroup Analysis' (2015), Volume three 'Strength of Human Resources' (2017) and Volume four 'Therapeutic Applications' (2017). Her major areas of interest are cross-cultural psychology, health psychology and psychological intervention.

SOCIAL JUSTICE AMONG THE WOMEN

Edited by
Nazish Bano
Aradhana Shukla

CONCEPT PUBLISHING COMPANY PVT. LTD.
NEW DELHI-110059

ISBN-13: 978-93-86682-93-2

First Published in 2019

Published and Printed by

Concept Since 1974

Concept Publishing Company Pvt. Ltd.
A/15-16, Commercial Block, Mohan Garden,
New Delhi-110059 (INDIA)
T: 91 11 25351460, 91 11 25351794
E: publishing@conceptpub.com; *W*: www.conceptpub.com

Cataloging in Publication Data--Courtesy: D.K. Agencies (P) Ltd. <docinfo@dkagencies.com>

Social justice among the women / edited by Nazish Bano, Aradhana Shukla.
pages cm
Includes bibliographical references and index.
ISBN 9789386682932

1. Women—India—Social conditions. 2. Women—Violence against—India. 3. Sex discrimination against women—India. 4. Social justice—India. I. Bano, Nazish, editor. II. Shukla, Aradhana, editor.

LCC HQ1742.S63 2019 | DDC 305.40954 23

Acknowledgements

Social justice is a phenomena that not only leads and challenges people to increase the quality of their life but also provides the true path of life. In India women are seen victimized in almost all areas of life that hampers their behaviour and future as well. This volume is a question mark on their status and the contributors have done a lot to aware the female fraternity about their rights.

Keeping these views in consideration this piece of work is planned and it deals with social justice in women. We have taken ample support and co-operation from many people. We are thankful to them and want to place our gratitude on records.

We are grateful to the contributors who supported us by giving their articles and waited patiently to get it in shape. We are thankful to Mr. Abhishek for doing the tedious job of the systematization of the articles.

We place our thanks and regards on record to Mr. Ashok K. Mittal, M/s. Concept Publishing Company Pvt. Ltd., New Delhi to shape this book.

10 February, 2019
Basant Panchami

Nazish Bano
Aradhana Shukla

Contents

Section C
Consequences of Social Justice in Women: Existing Status and Promoting Psychological Health

---

Social Justice and Indian Women

Nazish Bano and *Aradhana Shukla*

In recent years, a social justice movement has emerged in which psychologists have started to become agents of social change, working to alleviate oppression through activism and systems-level interventions (Goodman *et al.*, 2004; Vera & Speight, 2003). This approach moves beyond intrapsychic intervention to address the interpersonal and systemic origins of racism and race-related stress. For example, Bryant-Davis (2007) have highlighted the importance of transforming both individuals and society to dismantle the systemic sources of racism.

Social justice is a matter of thought and implementation. It is the base on which a frame of ideal society can be formulated and the responsibility of this ideal formation depends upon the advocates of legal and social affairs and the professionals of psycho-physical healthcare. It is a firm belief in the equality approach which defines that the concept of a utopian society can only be successful when equal distribution of wealth, opportunities and privileges within a society can be maintained. It means to say that social justice states the equal distribution of rights among every sort of social strata. It also believes the proper and fair administration of laws confirming to the natural law that all persons irrespective of ethnic origin, gender, profession, race, religion, etc. are to be treated equally and without prejudice. It can also be defined in terms of personal rights acquired by an individual by being a citizen or resident automatic entitlements to contain freedoms or conferred by law or custom.

In this way, it is surely fair to say that the concept of 'social justice' is primarily based on the idea that all human beings are equal in society without distinction of religion, race, caste, sex, colour or creed. It also means the absence of privileged class in the society. Harold J. Laski says, "The more equal are the social rights of citizens, the more likely they are able to utilize their freedom in realm worthy of exploration...The more equality there is in a state, the more use in general we can make of our freedom".

Women : The Natural Portrait

It is a common saying by St. Thomas that man is the origin and end of the women, but, how it can be proved or advocated, cannot be verified. Inviting writers to write something about women and speaking as a member of that half of the species whom no international organization have yet thought fit to assign a whole decade, as was done for females, one cannot but feel how women is a different species.

Men and women are equally important for a social setting and women in certain cases especially the tenderness and warmth of heart which have always kept them emotionally superior to men, can be called as the pulse of a country's life but it is rather unfortunate to say that the researches that have been done during the last fifteen years have lost the most important element of society, i.e., the woman.

The old dictum "There is a great woman behind every great man" was never a reality in the present patriarchal society where woman hold an inferior position to a man in physical and mental capacities. Man has always been a privileged class and woman a subjugated one. The position of women almost in different schools of philosophy had remained inferior to men.

Women and Justice—The National Commission of Women

The Government of India has redeemed itself by setting up in January 1992, the National Commission for women, which is the first of its kind. This fulfils a long-felt need expressed repeatedly at every forum by various women's organizations in the country. The Commission has an enormous task for the production of any document relating to the cases it hears. Besides, it is obligatory on the part of the government to consult the Commission on all major policy matters concerning women.

One of the priority areas for the National Commission for Women is to examine the various legislative measures enacted for the welfare of women and get the loopholes plugged.

Fundamental Rights of Women

The fundamental rights of women only are achieved by the women when necessary opportunities are available to the citizens to develop their personality. For this, some fundamental rights have been guaranteed to citizens in Part III of the Indian constitution. This fundamental right has special status in the Constitution in the sense that any law which contravenes or takes away or abridges any of the fundamental rights shall, to the extent of contravention, be void. Speaking about the importance of fundamental rights Bhagwati, J. observed that "these Fundamental Rights represent the basic values enshrined by the people of India since the Vedic times as they are calculated to protect the dignity of the individual and create conditions in which every human being can develop his personality to the fullest extent. They weave a pattern of guarantee on the basic structure of human rights, and impose negative obligation on the state not to encroach on individual liberty in its various dimensions".

Part III of the Constitution of India provides for various Fundamental Rights, such as,—Right to Equality, Right to Freedom, Right of Personal Liberty, Right against Exploitation, Right to Freedom of Religion; Cultural and Educational Rights and Right to Constitutional Remedies. These rights are equally available to both men and women. They are given below:

(a) Right to Equality

The Constitution guarantees the right to equality to every citizen of India. Article 14 of the Constitution of India embodies the general principles of equality before the law and prohibits unreasonable restrictions between persons. It provides that the State shall make the protection of the laws. Both these expressions, 'equality before the law' and equal protection of the laws', aim to effectuate one of the objectives i.e. equality of status, enshrined in the Preamble of the Constitution. These expressions have also been used in Universal Declaration of Human Rights. The basic purpose of this right is that the law should be applied to all equally and there should be no discrimination between one person and another.

However, Clause (3) of Article 15 of the Constitution empowers the state to make special provisions for the protection and welfare of women and children as they require special treatment on account of their very nature. According to Munshi's draft submitted in the Constituent Assembly regarding prohibition of discrimination on the ground of sex etc. and special provisions for women, "women citizens are equal to men citizens in all spheres of political, economic, social and cultural life and are entitled to the same civil rights and are subject to the same civil duties unless where exception is made in such rights or duties by the law of the Union on account of sex."

In *Dattatraya* Vs. *State,* the court held that the reason for empowering the State to make special provisions for women was that "women's physical structure and performance of maternal functions place her at a disadvantage in the struggle for subsistence and her physical well-being becomes an object of public interest and care in order to preserve the strength and vigor of the race".

Such special treatment for women does not violate the principle of equality as the concept of equality does not mean absolute equality among human beings which is physically not possible to achieve. "Equality before the law means that among equals the law should be equal and should be equally administered, that like should be treated alike".

Keeping in view the Article 5(3), various laws have been made, such as establishment of educational institutions by the State exclusively for women; reservation of seats for women in educational institutions; special maternity relief to women workers, special treatment for women in matter of granting bail; special treatment under Factories Act and Mines and Minerals Act; authorizing service of summons on men only; and special treatment to women on considerations of public morals and rectitude, e.g. Section 497 and 354 of Indian Penal Code. Likewise in pursuance to Article 15(3), other laws have been made by the State to provide special treatment to women which are considered not to be in violation of Article 15(1).

Similarly, Article 16(2) of the Constitution provides that the State shall not discriminate between citizens on the basis of religion, race, caste, sex, and place of birth, descent, residence or any of the matters of public employment. Article 16 embodies the particular application of general rule of equality laid down in Article 14 with special reference to appointment and employment under the State. Thus, no discrimination can be made in matters of public employment merely on the basis of sex. A provision in service rules requiring a female employee to obtain the permission of the Government in writing before her marriage is solemnized and denying right to be appointed on the ground that the candidate is a married woman was held to be discriminatory against women and, hence, unconstitutional.

The provision providing for special treatment to women have been justified and upheld on the grounds of public morality and morals and necessity of the weaker sections of the citizens. The Constitution provides no less opportunity to women than to men. However, it does not mean that men and women are equal in all occupations and in all situations and do not exclude the need to pragmatism where the requirements of particular employment, the sensitivities of sex or the peculiarities of the social sectors of the handicaps of either sex may compel selectivity.

It must be borne in mind that a law providing for special treatment to women as to that of men citizens is permissible only if the differentiation on the basis of sex regarding the application of that particular law is demonstrable; and there is some relation between the law and subject. In this context, the submission is that a law providing for special benefit to women and discrimination only on the basis of sex regarding standard deduction under Income Tex Act is not just and proper as there is no rational relation to subject (women) and the object sought to be achieved by the Statute and, therefore, contravenes the rule of equality.

(b) Equal Political Rights

To effectuate the principal of equality of status in the Preamble and Article 14 of the Constitution, some political rights have also been provided by the Constitution itself. Article 325 of the Constitution provides that no person shall be illegible for inclusion in special electro roll on grounds of religion, race, caste or sex, Similarly, Article 326 provides for the elections on the House of the People and to the Legislative Assemblies of States to be on the basis of adult suffrage. Thus, it is clear from the above provisions that the Constitution has provided equal political rights to men as well as to women.

(c) Right against Exploitation

Article 23 of the Constitution prohibits traffic in human beings, meaning thereby selling and buying men and women like goods and includes immoral traffic in women and children for immoral or other purposes. Under Article 35 of the Constitution, Parliament has been empowered to make laws for punishing acts prohibited by Article 23. In pursuance of this power, Parliament has enacted the Suppression of Immoral Traffic in Women and Girls Act, 1955 and in 1986 to make the prohibition under Article 23 effective by providing punishment for the acts which result in traffic in human beings.

(d) Right to Constitutional Remedies

Article 32 of the Constitution, which in itself is a Fundamental Right, is nothing but an effective machinery to the enforcement of Fundamental Rights. It provides that if any of the Fundamental Right is taken away or abridged by the State, a person can directly move to the Supreme Court (or High Court under Article 226) for the enforcement of his/her Fundamental Right. This right is available equally to men as well as to women.

Directive Principles of State Policy

In addition to Fundamental Rights given under the Constitution, there are provisions in Part IV of the Constitution dealing with "Directive Principles of State Policy" which are meant for certain socio-economic, cultural and educational objectives for the State. These Directive Principles are the ideals which the Union and State Governments must keep in mind while formulating policy or enacting a law. The directions, which are mainly related to the welfare of women and their social and economic upliftment, are as follows:

Principles of policy to be followed by the Sate for securing economic justice—Article 39 specifically requires the State to direct its policy towards securing the following principles:

- (a) Equal right of men and women to adequate means of livelihood; ....
- (d) Equal pay for equal work for both men and women.

In pursuance of Article 39(d), Parliament has passed the 'Equal Remuneration Act, 1976'. The Supreme Court in *Randhir Singh* Vs. *Union of India* opined that though the principle of 'equal work' is not a Fundamental Right, it is certainly a Constitutional goal and, therefore, enforceable under Article 32.

Similarly, to secure social justice, Article 42 of the Constitution provides for just and human conditions of work and maternity relief for women workers. Thus, the enactment of the 'Maternity Relief Act, 1966' by Parliament, providing for maternity relief for women workers, is the step towards securing social justice.

Fundamental Duties

Part IVA 21 of the Constitution, containing a single Article, namely 51A, dealing with 'Fundamental Duties' declares ten duties which are binding on every citizen of India. Out of these Fundamental Duties, a duty which is directly related to the women is that it shall be the duty of every citizen of India to renounce practices derogatory to the dignity of women. The legal utility of the Fundamental Duties is similar to that of Directive Principle with a difference that the directives are addressed to the State while the duties are addressed to individual citizen without any legal sanction for their violation. The duty, as such, is not legally enforceable in the courts but if the State makes a law to prohibit any Act or conduct in violation of any of the duties, the court would uphold that as a reasonable restriction on the relevant Fundamental Right.

Thus, if we go thorough and analyse the above mentioned Constitutional provisions, we can easily conclude that the Constitution treats both men and women equally. In the eyes of Law, status-wise a woman is no less than a man in any sphere of life. Moreover, where it was seemed necessary to promote the interests of women, to develop their personality, to secure social justice, to ascertain upliftment of weaker section of society and to provide for just and humane conditions for female workers, special provisions are made keeping in mind the special physical structure of women. It is to be submitted that there are sufficient laws for the welfare of women. The need is that the women should make a balance between herself, heavily duties and social responsibilities so that a better understanding social justice can be made, the emancipation of women will not damage the family, on the contrary, it will benefit family-life. Interestingly, possibilities are envisaged for the redistribution of familial functions and the new pattern of family-living that emerges will make richer companionship in the family.

References

Basham, L., (1989). *The Wonder that was India,* New Delhi: Rupa & Co.

Basu, D.D. (1991). *Introduction to the Constitution of India,* New Delhi: Prentice-Hall of India.

De'Souza, A., *Women in Contemporary India—Traditional Images and Changing Roles,* New Delhi: Manohar.

Desai, L.P. (1985). *Caste, Caste-Conflict and Reservation,* Delhi: Ajanta Publications.

Good, L.A., Liang, B., Helmns, J.E., Latla, R.E., Spanks, E. & Winterbug, S.R. "Training Counselling Psychologists and Social Justice Agents: Feminist and Multi-cultural Principles in Actions", *The Counselling Psychologist,* 32: 793-837.

Krishan Iyer, V.R.K. (1986). *Human Rights and the Law,* Indore: Vedpal Law House.

Prasad, A., (1991), *Reservation Policy and Practice in India,* New Delhi: Deep and Deep Publications.

Prasad, I. (1986). *Reservation—Action for Social Equality,* New Delhi: Criterion Publication.

Rao, K. S. (1974). *Social Justice and Law* (IPCS).

Report of Mandal Commission, New Delhi, 1980.

Report of the Backward Classes Commission (K. Karlekar, Chairman). Government of India Press, 1995.

Shelly, K.P. K. (1969). *Fundamental Rights and Socio-Economic Justice in the Indian Constitution,* Chaitanya Publication House, Allahabad.

Singh, P. (1985). *Equality, Reservation and Discrimination in India,* New Delhi: Deep and Deep Publication.

Vera, E. & Speight, S. (2003). "Multicultural Competence Social Justice and Counselling Psychology: Expanding Our Roles", *The Counselling Psychologist,* 32: 253-272.

Wasserastrorm, R. (1977). "Racism, Sexism and Preferential Treatment: An Approach to the Topics", *Loss Angles Law Review.*

List of Contributors

Dr. Anubhuti Dubey, Associate Professor, Department of Psychology, DDU Gorakhpur University, Gorakhpur, Uttar Pradesh. **E-mail:** *anubhutiddu@rediffmail.com*

Dr. Anupam Nath Tripathi, Professor, Department of Psychology, D.D.U. Gorakhpur University, Gorakhpur, Uttar Pradesh. **E-mail:** *anupamnath.tripathi@gmail.com*

Dr. Aradhana Shukla, Professor in Psychology, Department of Psychology, Kumaun University, Campus, Almora, Uttarakhand. **E-mail:** *aradhana.shukla5@gmail.com*

Asha, Research Scholar, Department of Psychology, D.D.U. Gorakhpur University, Gorakhpur, Uttar Pradesh. **E-mail:** *swarha07@gmail.com*

Garima Singh, Research Scholar, Department of Psychology, D.D.U. Gorakhpur University, Gorakhpur, Uttar Pradesh. **E-mail:** garima.keepintouch@gmail.com

Dr. Hemant Kumar Gutam, Assistant Professor, Department of Education, H.R.P.G. College, Khalilabad, Sant Kabir Nagar, Uttar Pradesh.

Dr. Manju Mishra, Associate Professor, Department of Psychology, H.R.P.G. College, Khalilabad, Sant Kabir Nagar, Uttar Pradesh. **E-mail:** *drmanjumishrahrpg@gmail.com*

Dr. Nazish Bano, Associate Professor in Psychology, Sant Vinoba P.G. College, Deoria, Uttar Pradesh. **E-mail :** *nazish786.93@rediffmail.com*

Niharika Tripathi, Research Scholar, Department of Psychology. Deen Dayal Upadhyaya Gorakhpur University, Gorakhpur-273009, Uttar Pradesh. **E-mail:** *tulika2461988@gmail.com*

Dr. P.S.N. Tiwari, Professor, Department of Psychology, D.D.U. Gorakhpur University, Gorakhpur, Uttar Pradesh, **E-mail:** *tiwaripsn@rediffmail.com*

Dr. Pratibha Singh, Department of Psychology, DDU Gorakhpur University, Gorakhpur, Uttar Pradesh.

Pratima Kumari, Lecturer, Department of Psychology, Kalpadevi Ramdev Rai Balika Mahavidyalaya, Sant Kabir Nagar, Uttar Pradesh.

Dr. Priyanka Pathak, Assistant Professor, P.G. Department, VKSU, **E-mail:** *priyankapathak456@gmail.com*

Dr. Purnima Awasthi, Associate Professor, Department of Psychology, Banaras Hindu University, Varanasi-221005, Uttar Pradesh. **E-mail:** *awasthip9@gmail.com*

Ravi P. Pandey, Research Scholar, Department of Psychology, Banaras Hindu University, Varanasi-221005, Uttar Pradesh. **E-mail:** *rppandeypsy@gmail.com*

Dr. Ruchi Chandra, Assistant Professor, B.B.D. College, Lucknow, Uttar Pradesh.

Dr. Rupali Joshi, Department of Psychology, Government P.G. College Ramnagar, Nainital, Uttar Pradesh. **E-mail:** kashi.bhu@gmail.com

Dr. Shagufta Afroz, SRF Department of Psychology, D.D.U. Gorakhpur University, Gorakhpur, Uttar Pradesh. **E-mail:** shaguftaafroz78689@gmail.com

Dr. (Smt.) Shilpi Singh, Lecturer, Department of Psychology, H.R.P.G. College, Khalilabad, Uttar Pradesh. **E-mail:** *shilpikhalilabad@gmail.com*

Dr. Shoaib Hasan, Assistant Professor, St. Andrews P.G. College, Gorakhpur, Uttar Pradesh.

Shobhna Joshi, Professor, Dept. of Psychology, BHU, Uttar Pradesh. **E-mail:** *getshobhna@yahoo.com*

Sunil Kumar, Director, EMS School, Almora.

Dr. (Mrs.) Sushma Pandey, Associate Professor, Department of Psychology. Deen Dayal Upadhyaya Gorakhpur University, Gorakhpur-273009. **E-mail:** *sushma_35gkp@rediffmail.com*

Sushmita Upadhyay, Assistance Profesoor, Department of Psychology, Gangotri Devi Girls P.G. College, Gorakhpur.

Dr. Swaran Lata, Assistant Professor, Department of Psychology, Faculty of Social Sciences, Banaras Hindu University, Varanasi- 221005, Uttar Pradesh. **E-mail:** *swaran80@gmail.com*

Section A

Social Justice in Women: Concept, Retrospect and Prospect

1

Women Empowerment and Justice in India

Hemant Kumar Gautam

"You can tell the condition of a nation by looking at the status of its women". —**Pt. Jawaharlal Nehru**

The status of women in India has been subject to many great changes over the past few millennia. With a decline in their status from the ancient to medieval times, to the promotion of equal rights by many reformers, the history of women in India has been eventful. In modern India, women have held high offices including that of the President, Prime Minister, Speaker of the Lok Sabha, Leader of the Opposition, Union Ministers, Chief Ministers and Governors.

Women's rights are secured under the Constitution of India—mainly, equality, dignity, and freedom from discrimination; further, India has various statutes governing the rights of women.

Why we talk about women empowerment only and not men empowerment? Why women need empowerment and not men? Women make almost 50 per cent of the total population of the world. Then why this substantial section of the society needs empowerment? They are not in minority so as to require special treatment. Biologically speaking also, it is a proven fact that female race is superior to male. Then the question arises that why we are debating the topic 'Women Empowerment'.

Need for empowerment arose due to centuries of domination and discrimination done by men over women; women are the suppressed lot. They are the target of varied types of violence and discriminatory practices done by men all-over the world. India is no different.

India is a complex country. We have, through centuries, developed various types of customs, traditions and practices. These customs and traditions, good as well as bad, have become a part of our society's collective consciousness. We worship female goddesses; we also give great importance to our mothers, daughters, sisters, wives and other female relatives or friends. But at the same time, Indians are also famous for treating their women badly both inside and outside their homes.

Indian society consists of people belonging to almost all kinds of religious beliefs. In every religion women are given a special place and every religion teaches us to treat women with respect and dignity. But somehow the society has so developed that various types of ill practices, both physical and mental, against women have become a norm since ages. For instance, *sati pratha*, practice of dowry, *parda pratha*, female infanticide, wife burning, sexual violence, sexual harassment at workplace, domestic violence and other varied kinds of discriminatory practices; all such acts consists of physical as well as mental element (Joshi & Joanna, 1985)[1].

The reasons for such behaviour against women are many but the most important one are the male superiority complex and patriarchal system of society. Though to eliminate these ill practices and discrimination against women various constitutional and legal rights are there but in reality there are a lot to be done. Several self-help groups and NGOs are working in this direction; also women themselves are breaking the societal barriers and achieving great heights in all dimensions: political, social and economic. But society as a whole has still not accepted women as being equal to men and crimes or abuses against women are still on the rise (Prema, 2012)[2]. For that to change, the society's age-old deep-rooted mindset needs to be changed through social conditioning and sensitization programmes.

Therefore, the concept of women empowerment not only focuses on giving women strength and skills to rise above from their miserable situation but at the same time it also stresses on the need to educate men regarding women issues and inculcating a sense of respect and duty towards women as equals. In the present chapter, we will try to describe and understand the concept of Women Empowerment in India in all its dimensions.

Women empowerment in simple words can be understood as giving power to women to decide for their own lives or inculcating such abilities in them so that they could be able to find their rightful place in the society.

According to the **United Nations**, women's empowerment mainly has five components:

- Generating women's sense of self-worth;
- Women's right to have and to determine their choices;
- Women's right to have access to equal opportunities and all kinds of resources;
- Women's right to have the power to regulate and control their own lives, within and outside the home; and
- Women's ability to contribute in creating a more just social and economic order.

Thus, women empowerment is nothing but recognition of women's basic human rights and creating an environment where they are treated as equals to men.

From ancient to modern period, women's condition-socially, politically and economically—has not remained same and it kept changing with times. In ancient India, women were having equal status with men; in early Vedic period they were very educated and there are references of women sages such as Maitreyi in our ancient texts. But with the coming of famous treatise of Manu, i.e. *Manusmriti,* the status of women was relegated to a subordinate position to men.

All kinds of discriminatory practices started to take from such as child marriage, *devadasi pratha, nagar vadhu* system, *sati pratha* etc. Women's socio-political rights were curtailed and they were made fully dependent upon the male members of family. Their right to education, right to work and right to decide for themselves were taken away. During medieval period, the condition of women got worsened with the advent of Muslim rulers in India; as also during the British period. But the British rule also brought western ideas into the country. (Sharma, 1987)[3]

A few enlightened Indians such as Raja Ram Mohun Roy influenced by the modern concept of freedom, liberty, equality and justice started to question the prevailing discriminatory practices against women. Through his unrelenting efforts, the

British were forced to abolish the ill-practice of *Sati*. Similarly, several other social reformers such as Ishwar Chandra Vidyasagar, Swami Vivekananda, Acharya Vinoba Bhave etc. worked for the upliftment of women in India. For instance, the Widow Remarriage Act of 1856 was the result of Ishwar Chandra Vidyasagar's movement for improving the conditions of widows (Basu, 1991).[4]

Indian National Congress supported the first women's delegation which met the Secretary of State to demand women's political rights in 1917. The Child Marriage Restraint Act in 1929 was passed due to the efforts of Muhammad Ali Jinnah, Mahatma Gandhi called upon the young men to marry the child widows and urged people to boycott child marriages.

During freedom movement, almost all the leaders of the struggle were of the view that women should be given equal status in the free India and all types of discriminatory practices must stop. And for that to happen, it was thought fit to include such provisions in the Constitution of India which would help eliminate age-old exploitative customs and traditions and also such provisions which would help in empowering women socially, economically and politically.

India's Constitution makers and our founding fathers were very determined to provide equal rights to both women and men. The Constitution of India is one of the finest equality documents in the world. It provides provisions to secure equality in general and gender equality in particular. Various articles in the Constitution safeguard women's rights by putting them at par with men—socially, politically and economically.

The Preamble, the Fundamental Rights, DPSPs and other constitutional provisions provide several general and special safeguards to secure women's human rights. The Preamble to the Constitution of India assures justice—social, economic and political; equality of status and opportunity and dignity to the individual. Thus, it treats both men and women equal. The policy of women empowerment is well entrenched in the Fundamental Rights enshrined in our Constitution. For instance:

- Article 14 ensures to women the right to equality.
- Article 15(1) specifically prohibits discrimination on the basis of sex.
- Article 15(3) empowers the State to take affirmative actions in favour of women.

- Article 16 provides for equality of opportunity for all citizens in matters relating to employment or appointment to any office.

These rights being fundamental rights are justiciable in court and the Government is obliged to follow the same.

Directive Principles of State Policy also contain important provisions regarding women empowerment and it is the duty of the government to apply these principles while making laws or formulating any policy (Pande, 1999).[5] Though these are not justiciable in the Court but these are essential for governance nonetheless. Some of them are:

- Article 39 (a) provides that the State to direct its policy towards securing for men and women equally the right to an adequate means of livelihood.
- Article 39 (d) mandates equal pay for equal work for both men and women.
- Article 42 provides that the State to make provision for securing just and humane conditions of work and for maternity relief.
- Fundamental duties are enshrined in Part IV-A of the Constitution and are positive duties for the people of India to follow. It also contains a duty related to women's rights:

Article 51(A)(e) expects from the citizen of the country to promote harmony and the spirit of common brotherhood amongst all the people of India and to renounce practices derogatory to the dignity of women. Through 73rd and 74th Constitutional Amendment of 1993, a very important political right has been given to women which is a landmark in the direction of women empowerment in India (Ramusack, 1999).[6] With this amendment women were given 33.33 per cent reservation in seats at different levels of elections in local governance, i.e. at Panchayat, Block and Municipality elections.

Thus, it can be seen that these Constitutional provisions are very empowering for women and the State is duty bound to apply these principles in taking policy decisions as well as in enacting laws.

Here is the list of some specific laws which were enacted by the Parliament in order to fulfil Constitutional obligation of women empowerment:

- The Equal Remuneration Act, 1976.
- The Dowry Prohibition Act, 1961.
- The Immoral Traffic (Prevention) Act, 1956.
- The Maternity Benefit Act, 1961.
- The Medical Termination of Pregnancy Act, 1971.
- The Commission of Sati (Prevention) Act, 1987.
- The Prohibition of Child Marriage Act, 2006.
- The Pre-Conception & Pre-Natal Diagnostic Techniques (Regulation and Prevention of Misuse) Act, 1994.
- The Sexual Harassment of Women at Work Place (Prevention and Protection) Act, 2013.

Above mentioned and several other laws are there which not only provide specific legal rights to women but also gives them a sense of security and empowerment.

International Commitments of India as to Women Empowerment

India is a part to various International conventions and treaties which are committed to secure equal rights of women.

One of the most important among them is the Convention on Elimination of All Forms of Discrimination Against Women (CEDAW), ratified by India in 1993.

Other important International instruments for women empowerment are: The Mexico Plan of Action (1975), the Nairobi Forward Looking Strategies (1985), the Beijing Declaration as well as the Platform for Action (1995) and the Outcome Document adopted by the UNGA Session on Gender Equality and Development & Peace for the 21st century, titled "Further Actions and Initiatives to Implement the Beijing Declaration and the Platform for Action". All these have been wholeheartedly endorsed by India for appropriate follow up.

These various national and International commitments, laws and policies notwithstanding women's situation on the ground have still not improved satisfactorily. Varied problems related to women are still subsisting; female infanticide is growing, dowry is still prevalent, domestic violence against women is practised; sexual harassment at workplace and other heinous sex crimes against women are on the rise.

Though, economic and social condition of women has improved in a significant way but the change is especially visible only in metro cities or in urban areas; the situation is not much improved in semi-urban areas and villages. This disparity is due to lack of education and job opportunities and negative mindset of the society which does not approve girls' education even in 21st century.[7]

Whatever improvement and empowerment women have received is especially due to their own efforts and struggle, though governmental schemes are also there to help them in their endeavour.

In the year 2001, the Government of India launched a **National Policy for Empowerment of Women**. The specific objectives of the policy are as follows:

- Creation of an environment through positive economic and social policies for full development of women to enable them to realize their full potential.
- Creation of an environment for enjoyments of all human rights and fundamental freedom by women on equal basis with men in all political, economic, social, cultural and civil spheres.
- Providing equal access to participation and decision making of women in social political and economic life of the nation.
- Providing equal access to women to health care, quality education at all levels, career and vocational guidance, employment, equal remuneration, occupational health and safety, social security and public life etc.
- Strengthening legal systems aimed at elimination of all forms of discrimination against women.
- Changing societal attitudes and community practices by active participation and involvement of both men and women.
- Mainstreaming a gender perspective in the development process.
- Elimination of discrimination and all forms of violence against women and the girl child.

- Building and strengthening partnerships with civil society, particularly women's organizations.

The Ministry of Women and Child Development is the nodal agency for all matters pertaining to welfare, development and empowerment of women. It has evolved schemes and programmes for their benefit. These schemes are spread across a very wide spectrum such as women's need for shelter, security, safety, legal aid, justice, information, maternal health, food, nutrition etc., as well as their need for economic sustenance through skill development, education and access to credit and marketing (Banerjee, 2010).[8]

Various schemes of the Ministry are like *Svashakti, Swayamsiddha,* STEP and *Svabalambana* enable economic empowerment. Working Women Hostels and Creches provide support services. *Svadhara* and Short Stay Homes provide protection and rehabilitation to women in difficult circumstances. The Ministry also supports autonomous bodies like National Commission, Central Social Welfare Board and Rashtriya Mahila Kosh, which work for the welfare and development of women. Economic sustenance of women through skill development, education and access to credit and marketing is also one of the areas where the Ministry has special focus.

Conclusion and Suggestions

In conclusion, it can be said that women in India, through their own unrelenting efforts and with the help of Constitutional and other legal provisions and also with the aid of Government's various welfare schemes, are trying to find their own place under the sun. And it is a heartening sign that their participation in employment—government as well as private, in socio-political activities of the nation and also their presence at the highest decision making bodies is improving day by day.

However, we are still far behind in achieving the equality and justice which the Preamble of our Constitution talks about. The real problem lies in the patriarchal and male-dominated system of our society which considers women as subordinate to men and creates different types of methods to subjugate them.

The need of the hour is to educate and sensitize male members of the society regarding women issues and try to inculcate a feeling of togetherness and equality among them so that they would stop their discriminatory practices towards the fairer sex.

For this to happen apart from Government, the efforts are needed from various NGOs and from enlightened citizens of the country. And first of all efforts should begin from our homes where we must empower female members of our family by providing them equal opportunities of education, health, nutrition and decision making without any discrimination.

Notes

1. Joshi, R., & Joanna L. (1985). "Gender and Colonialism: Women's Organization under the Raj", *Women's Studies International Forum,* 8#5, pp. 521-29.
2. Prema, A. (2012). "Women Status in India." *Indian Streams Research Journal,* 2.1: 1-4.
3. Sharma, T. (1987). *Women in Ancient India from 320 A.D. to C. 1200 A.D.,* New Delhi: ESS Publishers.
4. Basu, A. (1991). "Women's History in India: An Historiographical Survey". In: Karen Offen, Ruth Roach Pierson, & Jane Rendall, (eds.) *Writing Women's History: International Perspectives,* p. 181. MacMillan.
5. Pande, R. (1999). "Women's History: India". In: Boyd, Kelly, (ed.) *Encyclopedia of Historians and Historical Writing,* Vol. 2, Taylor & Francis, pp. 1318-1321.
6. Ramusack, B. (1999). "Women in South Asia". In: Barbara Ramusack & Sharon Sievers, (eds.) *Women in Asia: Restoring Women to History,* Indiana University Press.
7. Choudhary, R. (2013). "Women in Indian Society: A Historical Perspective." *Madhya Pradesh Journal of Social Sciences,* 18#1: 41-53.
8. Banerjee, S.M. (2010). "Debates on Domesticity and the Position of Women in Late Colonial India", *History Compass* 8#6: 455-473.

2

The Roots of Social Identity of Women

Gender Socialization

Pratima Kumari and *Garima Singh*

Introduction

Socialization is the process, through which the child becomes an individual respecting his or her environment's laws, norms and customs. The approach we adopt, what we are in real and how we behave and think is the eventual artifact of socialization. The moment we land on planet earth, we are shaped into the form which society wants us to be. It is through socialization that we also learn our gender roles, i.e. what is appropriate and improper for both genders. Since no human trait is so emphasized as gender, gender socialization by and large leads to the formation of our social identities. Gender socialization begins at the moment after birth when the doctor is questioned whether it is a boy or a girl. The various agencies of socialization help us learn our gender roles, which in future decides our identity in society. The main agencies of socialization existing in our society are the family, peer groups, schools and media. Each of the agencies possibly reinforce the gender stereotypes along with the roots of socialization. Gender differences and identities result from socialization process, especially during our childhood and adolescence. For instance, before we are 3 years old, there are fascinating differences between how boys and girls interact. Boys attempt to dominate, to control, to find out "Am I better than you?" They do this by little contests or by being aggressive, if necessary. They establish their status and then continue to try to use power to improve their position in the "pecking order" (De Angelis, 1989).

Gender Socialization

From infant to adulthood, people receive informal, but potent impressions of the role they are expected to play in society. Gender socialization is a more focused form of socialization, it is how children of different sexes are socialized into their gender roles (Giddens, 1993) and taught what it means to be male or female (Morris, 1988).

The classical example of gender socialization is the experiment that has a baby introduced as a male to half of the subjects and as a female to the other half. The results were interesting and quite disturbing at the same time. When the participants thought they were playing with a baby boy, "he" was offered toys, such as a hammer or rattle, while if the participants thought they were playing with a baby girl, "she" was offered a doll. The participants also touched the baby differently. It was found that baby boys are often bounced, thus stimulating the whole body, whereas girls are touched gently and less vigorously (Gleitman, Friedlund & Reisberg, 2000). Another study found out that words such as "sturdy", "handsome" and "tough" are used to describe boy infants and "dainty", "sweet" and "charming" for girl infants, although there was no differences in the sizes of the infants (Giddens, 1993). These findings show that other people contribute a lot as we see ourselves only on the basis of gender. We observe that boys are socialized to be tough, while girls are supposed to be sweet and charming. These simple stereotypes continue to be enhanced in the future by the agencies of socialization.

The socialization of children in the family unit has been examined in various ways. The general focus of research is on four perspectives, each providing a unique understanding of socialization: the parent effect perspective, the child effects perspective, the reciprocal socialization perspective, and the systemic-ecological perspective. The parent effect perspective addresses how the different styles, behaviours, and dispositions of parents socialize traits and behaviour in children. This perspective is the most common area of inquiry in literature on gender socialization. The child effects perspective reverses the order of operations in family socialization, focusing on how children socialize parents. A common area of inquiry in the child effects perspective examines how the presence of a child forces mothers/fathers to enter the workplace to support the added economic stress a child brings, hence influencing parents to develop additional, new identities. The reciprocal effects perspective examines how both children and parents socialize one another reflexively; the impact of gender and family socialization are mutually tied to both entities. The systemic-ecological perspective considers that gender and family socialization is neither a parent-to-child nor child-to-parent process, but that all family socialization is embedded in an environment or context that can have great impact. This perspective treats family socialization as a social system in which multiple sources of socialization simultaneously impact both parents and children.

Roots of Identity of Women

There are a number of roots identified by social scientists working in the field. Some of the pertinent are discussed below:

Agents of Socialization

Society cultivates masculinity and femininity in children by encouraging them to act in appropriate ways as per their gender and by preventing them not to indulge in deeds inappropriate of gender. In the 1960s, social learning theorists such as Walter Mischel and Albert Bandura emphasized the role of both direct reinforcement and modeling in shaping children's gender role behaviour and attitudes. Also, Freud observed that the first thing we instantly determine when we meet someone new, is gender. It is this "need to know" that connects with "knowing how to act" with this person. According to psychologists Sandra Bem (1993), one cognitive process that seems nearly inevitable in humans is to divide people into groups. We can partition these groups on the basis of race, age, religion, and so forth. However, the major way in which we usually split humanity is on the basis of gender. This process of categorizing others in terms of gender is both habitual and automatic. Its nearly impossible to suppress the tendency to split the world in half, using gender as the great divider. In real life, however, the characteristics of women and men tend to overlap. But, unfortunately gender polarization often creates an artificial gap between women and men.

The socialization root imbibes in us how we behave, and what kind of attitude we develop. Women value being sensitive and maintaining good relationships, i.e. attachment over achievement; men value gaining status by following "the rules," i.e. achievement over attachment. Since our society values competition and individuals being successful on their own, women's orientation towards caring for others and/or cooperatively building the community is considered (by the male dominated society) to be of lesser importance. These value differences are reflected in the gender roles established by our culture.

The traditional gender roles help to sustain gender stereotypes, such as that males are supposed to be adventurous, assertive-aggressive, independent and task-oriented, whereas females are seen as more sensitive, gentle, dependent, emotional and people-oriented. In the same way, males are expected to major in sciences or economics in college, while women should study arts, languages and humanities. Finally, in the workforce these stereotypes persist, more men become doctors, construction workers, mechanics, pilots, bankers and engineers and more women become secretaries, teachers, nurses, flight attendants, bank tellers and housewives. This can be seen from the statistics, how some labour force areas still are male and female oriented. (Brehm, Kassin & Fein, 1999). Traditionally, men are supposed to earn a living to support their families. They are to be aggressive and in charge. Women belong at home cooking, cleaning, and caring for children. They are to be submissive and weak. Gender stereotypes such as these pervade society today (Hetherington & Parke, 1999). Though they are quite obvious among adults, gender stereotypes do not seem like an issue that adolescents would have to face. This is most definitely not the case.

Gender socialization is often examined by sociologists to determine how and why males and females act differently. From the moment that a baby enters the world it is besieged with symbols and language that form its conception of gender roles and gender stereotypes. Language used by families to describe boys is often centred on physical characteristics and such themes as strength and agility, while language appropriated to girls by families might address affection, expressivity, daintiness, or fragility. These differences in treatment of babies by the family serve to shape behaviour patterns and define boundaries. Eventually, these boundaries are internalized to form identity standards—the references in which interactions, settings, and contexts are used to compare the self to others.

One of the central peculiarities in understanding how gender identities are learned by family socialization and preserved throughout life revolves around the concept of homophile. Homophile describes the tendency for network connections to be same-sex rather than cross sex; it begins as soon as children are able to choose their playmates. This homophile is linked to social process and emerges as children learn from their families and through experience that sex differences are permanent personal characteristics. Boys and girls learn and develop in gendered subcultures which generally influence social networks and future interactions.

Research examines how boys and girls are socialized differently to attach themselves to others. For example, when a father (or father and mother) teaches a son to be aggressive and encourages playing sports and doing activities that involve negotiating interchanges with others, the son will likely learn that appropriate behaviour is to interact with a wide range of people in heterogeneous groups. When a mother (or mother and father) encourages a daughter to interact intimately with others and encourage more one on one playing, the daughter will likely internalize messages and cues that promote likewise behaviour later in life. These identities that are internalized early during child socialization (both from the family and from other sources) serve to create a highly differentiated world of acceptable behaviour.

Psychological Grounds of Socialization

Psychoanalytic theory handles gender spindled on two of Sigmund Freud's most important findings: the concept of internal conflict and the indication that we have an unconscious part of ourselves which we are unaware of. These concepts are significant in understanding the differences in how males and females potentially learn gender differently from the family. Freud was one of the first figures to speculate gender as separated from biology—that gender is not fate and innate but rather acquired. The idea that males learn what it means to be masculine by acting in ways that are "not feminine" is a powerful element to the general understanding of gender. Based on psychoanalytic theories of gender, boys tend to have more difficulty achieving gender identities because of their close relationships with their mothers. While both boys and girls are socialized early by their mothers (or primary feminine figure perhaps), girls are provided with cues that they do not abandon as they age while boys must struggle to define their gender as what "is not" like their mother. This is especially true as males are more involved in such searching for cues to determine acceptable behaviour than are females.

While some other researches of West and Zimmerman maintain that gender is created and maintained while actors assume and play out roles in society. Thereby, the fact that many roles and tasks in society tend to be gendered is highlighted. When actors accomplish the anticipations and scripts for these "gendered" tasks they are actually "doing gender". Gender thus is something created and maintained in practice; doing a task associated with a specific gender creates and conserves meanings that define who one is and what it means to be a man or woman, or masculine or feminine. In the "doing gender" perspective, gender is a routine, methodical, and recurrent execution.

The "doing gender" perspective helps us understand the social constructionist aspect to gender and how gender identities are not static but rather fluid entities that are frequently formed in social interactions. Gender may be fundamental, institutionalized, and enduring, but because actors "do gender" as a process in social settings gender meanings and identities are always capable of and ripe for change. The more one "does gender" among others in interactions, the more likely one's gender identity will become more committed, and thus salient within the self.

Formation of Social Identity

Social identities represent an individual's group memberships, and concern an individual's participation in collective groupings. While many social categories refer to identities that are assumed in adulthood, the family is often the primary group that nudges individuals toward the groups in which one eventually becomes attached. Some group memberships are based on gender, and many groups are defined by gendered behavioural norms and expectations.

One's gender identity is socialized in one's early life, and it is in the primary stages of development where individuals learn how being a boy or girl means more than simply assuming a role; it also means sharing similar viewpoints and behavioural expectations with a larger group of similar gendered individuals.

It is easy to see why gender can be conceived as a social identity when considering that individuals often refer to others of same or different gender as part of one's in-group or out-group. For example, a woman who proclaims, "We are women, hear us roar!" is referencing gender as a social category, i.e., as a group in which she belongs, not as a role or idiosyncratic personal characteristic. Notions of gender being a group are commonly found in feminist literature, and many social organizations centre on gender differences for inclusion (e.g., the National Organization for Women). This type of gender socialization certainly occurs in the family, but it is particularly evident in such socializing agents as schools. Research has shown that boys tend to play in large groups (i.e., by playing sports that have multiple member teams, etc.) while girls tend to form smaller, more intimate relationships. This phenomenon is potentially prevalent more in school settings than in the family as there are more opportunities for tactics of inclusion and exclusion for children at school (i.e., there is simply a larger congregation of individuals at school than there is at home). The social identities that boys form are likely to be different than the social identities formed by girls. Since social (or group-based) identities are defined by their uniformity of perception and action among group members, it might be posited that boys learn to incorporate social identities earlier than do girls. If this is so, it is aligned with the idea that boys are socialized to be leaders and to be competitive while girls are socialized to be caretakers and supportive, and also with the fact that men tend to have more powerful positions within social networks than do women.

Conclusion

Social identities are not universally developed by all individuals. They rather are similar to person identities and role identities in that gender socialization (whether from the family or otherwise) greatly determines how identities are formed and maintained. The socialization that children receive by parents or significant authority figures (uncles, grandparents, etc.) within the family align children into separate tracts that are dependent on gender. The social identities, thus, are either constantly, usually, or occasionally activated, these identities are greatly predicated on gendered behavioural expectations that are socialized during the early stages of development.

References

Brody, L.R. (1997). "Gender and Emotion: Beyond Stereotypes", *Journal of Social Issues*, 53, 369-394.

Burke, P.J. (2002). "Marital Socialization, Gender, and Identity Change." Paper presented at The Pacific Sociological Association, Vancouver, BC, Canada.

Carter, M.J. (2013). "Advancing Identity Theory: Examining the Relationship between Activated Identities and Behaviour in Different Social Contexts", *Social Psychology Quarterly*, 76, 203-230.

Carter, M.J. (2013). "Gender Socialization and Identity Theory", *Social Sciences*, 3(2), 242-263.

Carter, R.S. (2000). "Parental Involvement with Adolescents' Education: Do Daughters or Sons get More Help?" *Adolescence*, 137, 29-44.

Cobb, N.J., Stevens-Long, J., & Goldstein, S. (1982). "The Influence of Televised Models on Toy Preference in Children", *Sex Roles*, 8, 1075-1080.

Condon, R.G. & Stern, P.R. (1993). "Gender-role Preference, Gender Identity, and Gender Socialization among Contemporary Inuit Youth", *Ethos*, 21(4), 384-416.

Condry, J.C. & Condry, S. (1976). "Sex Differences: A Study in the Eye of the Beholder". *Child Development*, 47, 812-819.

Crespi, I. (2003). "Gender Socialization within the Family: A Study on Adolescents and their Parents in Great Britain", Department of Sociology, Catholic University of Milan.

Davies, B. & Banks, C. (1992). "The Gender Trap: A Feminist Post-structuralist Analysis of Primary School Children's Talk about Gender", *Journal of Curriculum Studies*, 24, 1-25.

Donna, E. & Hallinan, M.T. (1978). "Sex Differences in Children's Friendships", *American Sociological Review*, 43, 237–250.

Fox, G.L. & Velma, M.M. (2000). "Gender and Families: Feminist Perspectives and Family Research", *Journal of Marriage and the Family*, 62, 1160-1172.

Lever, J. (1978). "Sex Differences in the Complexity of Children's Play and Games", *American Sociological Review*, 43, 471-483.

Moore, G. (1990). "Structural Determinants of Men's and Women's Personal Networks", *American Sociological Review*, 55, 726-735.

Peirce, K. (1990). "A Feminist Theoretical Perspective on the Socialization of Teenage Girls through Seventeen Magazine", *Sex Roles*, 23, 491-500.

Reid, A. & Deaux, K. (1996). "Relationship Between Social and Personal Identities: Segregation or Integration?" *Journal of Personality and Social Psychology*, 71, 1084-1091.

Ridgeway, C.L., & Lynn, S.L. (1999). "The Gender System and Interaction", *Annual Review of Sociology*, 25, 191-216.

Stryker, S. & Burke, P.J. (2000). "The Past, Present, and Future of an Identity Theory", *Social Psychology Quarterly*, 63, 284-297.

Wendy, W. & Karten, S.J. (1986). "Sex Differences in Interaction Style as a Product of Perceived Sex Differences in Competence", *Journal of Personality and Social Psychology*, 50, 341-347.

3

Women's Right in Islamic Perspective

Shoaib Hasan

In many societies, a woman is still regarded as a second-class citizen and deprived of various basic rights enjoyed by the male population. Deeply resenting this discrimination, they have championed a fight to obtain for themselves an equal status which unfortunately to date eludes them in the more modern Western states. Whereas the pendulum has swung to the extremes and has opened the way to licentiousness in the modern society, the West has often regarded Islamic women as being backward in a male-dominated world. On the contrary, Islam was the first religion formally to grant the women a status never known before. The *Holy Quran*, the sacred scripture of Islam, contains hundreds of teachings, which apply both to men and women alike. The moral, spiritual and economic equality of men and women as propagated by Islam is unquestionable. The specific verses of the *Holy Quran*, which address themselves to men or women, deal with either their physical differences or the role they each have to play in safeguarding the moral fiber of the society Islam envisages.

In the divine scheme of regulation of the relationship between men and women, Islam has assigned a position of dignity and honour to woman. Such beneficent regulation is essential for peace, comfort, happiness, continuation of the species and progress. The *Holy Quran* emphasizes that God in His perfect wisdom has created all species in pairs, and so men and women have been created of the same species; as is said:

> "He created you from a single being; then of the same kind made its mate." (39:7)

> "He has made for you mates of your own kind." (42:12)
>
> "O mankind, be mindful of your duty to your Lord, Who created you from a single soul and from it created its mate and from the two created and spread many men and women." (4:2)
>
> "He it is Who has created you from a single soul and made therefrom its mate, so that the male might incline towards the female and find comfort in her." (7:190)
>
> "Of His Signs it is that He has created mates for you of your own kind that you may find peace of mind through them, and He has put love and tenderness between you. In that surely are Signs for a people who reflect." (30:22)

Islam teaches that the faculties and capacities bestowed by God upon man are a divine bounty and must be beneficently employed:

> "*Allah* brought you forth from the wombs of your mothers, when you knew nothing, and gave you ears and eyes and hearts that you may employ them beneficently." (16:79)

This means that they must be exercised at their proper time and on their appropriate occasion, in which case they would be fostered and multiplied. But their neglect or misuse would attract divine wrath.

Some religious disciplines mistakenly esteem celibacy more exalted spiritually than conjugal life. Islam disapproves of celibacy and condemns it. The *Holy Quran* says:

> "They devised monasticism as a means of seeking *Allah*'s pleasure. We did not prescribe it for them, and they did not observe it duly." (57:28)

The whole concept of monasticism originated in the notion that woman was an inferior type of creation and association with her was degrading and demoralizing. The Church Fathers laid the responsibility of man's fall upon woman, and represented her as being without a soul and an instrument of the devil.

Foundations of Islamic Law

The authoritative centre of Islamic law that resides in the *Quran* and *Shari'a* has been defined as "a normative conceptual ideal of the just and good life that is embedded and at items hidden in the text" (Abou El Fadl, 2001: 13). These texts are the *Quran* and the *Hadith*. The task of the legal scholar is to engage the text and, in so doing, to unearth this ideal from the text and make it plain so that Muslims may follow it in their daily lives.

There are four elements upon which Islamic law is based. The first two are the textual sources of the law, i.e., the *Quran* and *Hadith*. The other two are non-textual sources, and these refer to the process through which the law is derived. These processes are called analogous reasoning (*qiyas*) and scholarly consensus (*ijma*).

The *Quran* is the word of God revealed. It was revealed to the Prophet Muhammad (peace be upon Him) over a period of 22 years. Revelation occurred in various stages, at various times and often in response to the realities of the community of believers that gathered around the Prophet.

The *Hadith* refers to a collection of narratives that recorded the sayings, actions and silences of the Prophet. They formed the second source of textual guidance in the derivation of Islamic law.

Because of complexity of women's right in Islam, we tried to highlight some important issues or rights who have been raised in local and regional women's conference, but the answer have not always been satisfactory.

Tawhid

Tawhid or belief in the single God; is the core principal of Islamic jurisprudence. From it flow many secondary principles, including the one that asserts that God is the Supreme Being and that all human beings are creatures of God. Thus, the *Tawhid* principle provides the basis for the fundamental metaphysical sameness of all humans as creatures of God.

The *Quran* then comments on further metaphysical similarities and empirical differences among humans. It states that human beings were all created from the same *nafs* (soul), thus, reemphasizing their metaphysical sameness. It also states that God created humans from a male and female and made them into nations and tribes, so that they would get to know (appreciate, befriend) each other. The *Quran* adds that the most honoured humans in the sights of God are those who are the most pious. Further, the *Quran* states that God created humans, male and female, from the same *nafs* so that they may find tranquility, mercy and affection with each other. The *Quran* also states that male and female believers are each other's *walis* (protectors, guardians). These themes permeate the *Quran* and make it very clear that there is no metaphysical, ontological, religious or ethical primacy for the male over the female. The *Quran* also make it crystal clear that divine will contemplates a relationship of harmony, consultation, and cooperation, as opposed to conflict and domination, between the two genders.

Educational Rights of Women

Quran states that—

> The first guidance revealed by *Allah* to all of human kind "It was *Iqra*", "It was to read". Prophet (PBUH) said, "It is obligatory on every Muslim to acquire knowledge". The Prophet (PBUH) specially told the parents to educate their children specially their daughters. It is duty of husband to give education to his wife especially religious education.

Marriage

Islam guarantees for the women, among other things, the right to an education similar to that of the male, the right to financial independence, and even the right of *ijlihad*. Islam also views marriage as an institution in which human beings find tranquility and affection with each other. The ultimate purpose of marriage in Islam is to win the pleasure of *Allah*, through chastity, fulfilment, contentment and continuation of the species. For instance, among the characteristics of true believers, the safeguarding of chastity through marriage is stressed along with strict and humble observance of Prayer, the shunning of all that is vain, the payment of the *Zakat* and watchfulness of trusts and covenants:

> "These are the true heirs who will inherit Paradise, wherein they shall abide." (23:11-12)

Then there is the direction:

> "Arrange the marriages of widows from among you, and of the righteous from among those under your control, male and female. If they be poor, *Allah* will grant them means out of His bounty."(24:33-34)

The Holy Prophet has said:

> "Conjugal life is our way, he who turns aside from our way is not of us."

According to Islam, the relationship between husband and wife should be characterized by grace. The *Holy Quran* directs:

> "Consort with them graciously. If you dislike them, it may be that you dislike something in which *Allah* has placed much good."(4:20)

The character of the conjugal relationship may be judged from the direction of the Holy Prophet:

> "When you come together, supplicate: 'O *Allah,* safeguard us against *Satan,* and keep *Satan* away from such issue as Thou might bestow upon us'."

As has been mentioned, the *Holy Quran* describes husband and wife as garments for each other (2:188); that is to say, a means of security, dignity and ornament. The whole subject of conjugal relationship is treated in Islam at the elevated level of moral and spiritual consciousness, which excludes all ideas of mere carnal indulgence. This is well illustrated by the following set of directions and exhortations:

> "They ask thee, O Prophet, as to consorting with their wives during their monthly courses. Tell them: it is harmful, so keep away from them during their monthly courses and do not consort with them until they are clean.

> But when they have washed themselves clean, consort with them as *Allah* has commanded you. Indeed, *Allah* loves those who turn to Him constantly, and *Allah* loves those who are clean and pure. Your wives are a tilth for you, so approach your tilth as you may be minded and lay up a store of good for yourselves. Be ever mindful of your duty to *Allah*, and be sure you will meet Him. Give glad tidings to those who believe." (2:223-224)

Any attitude that is likely to affect adversely the capacity and chances of childbearing of the wife is thus disapproved. Purity and promotion of righteousness (*Taqwa*) must always be kept in mind. One of the prayers of the righteous taught by the *Holy Quran* is:

"Lord, grant us of our spouses and our offspring the delight of our eyes and make us a model for the righteous." (25:75)

Duties and Obligations of Husband and Wife

In the Islamic system, marriage is a covenant of a civil nature involving a whole set of mutual obligations. For its validity, it requires the public announcement of the free consent of the parties, the consent of the guardian of the bride, whose duty it is to ensure and safeguard the rights of the bride, and a settlement by the husband on the wife proportionate to his means which is called dower, and is not to be confused with the dowry that may be bestowed upon the bride by her parents or guardian.

Prohibitions to marriage are clearly set out, and this is followed by:

> "Lawful for you are those outside these categories, that you seek them in marriage, by means of your properties, safeguarding yourselves against fornication. For the benefit that you receive from them pay them their dowers as fixed, and there will be no sin upon you in respect of anything that you may agree upon mutually after the fixing of the dower. Surely, *Allah* is All Knowing, Wise." (4:25).

Husbands and wives have reciprocal obligations towards each other, but as man is the breadwinner and has the responsibility of providing for wife and family, in case of a difference in the matter of running the household he has the final word, lest things should get out of hand and the family should be faced with ruin:

> "Wives have rights corresponding to those which husbands have, in equitable reciprocity, though, in certain situations, men would have the final word and thus enjoy a preference. *Allah* is Mighty, Wise." (2:229).

On account of the physical weakness and delicacy of women and their vulnerability, men are appointed guardians over women:

> "Men are appointed guardians over women, because of that in respect of which *Allah* has made some of them excel others, and because the men spend of their wealth. So virtuous women are obedient and safeguard, with *Allah*'s help, matters the knowledge of which is shared by them with their husbands." (4:35)

Divorce

Should all efforts at reconciliation prove unavailing, dissolution of the marriage may alone furnish a way of relief. It should, however, be noted that Islam does not look upon divorce with favour. The Holy Prophet has said: Of that which is permitted, the most obnoxious, in the estimation of *Allah,* is divorce.

Divorce may be initiated by the husband or by the wife; in the latter case the matter must proceed judicially, so that the rights of the wife may be fully safeguarded. If differences arise and, failing reconciliation, the husband vows abstinence from his wife, the situation must be resolved within four months:

> "For those who vow abstinence from their wives, the maximum period for making up their minds is four months; then if they revert towards conciliation, surely *Allah* is Most Forgiving, Ever Merciful; and if they decide upon divorce, *Allah* is All-Hearing, All-Knowing." (2:227-228).

There is a whole set of regulations concerning divorce. These are designed to ensure, *inter alia,* that divorce should not be resorted to light-heartedly, or in a fit of passion or resentment. It should be a deliberate act resolved upon after a careful consideration of the consequences both for the parties and the children, if there are any, of the marriage. With this end in view the procedure is somewhat drawn out, so that the parties may have opportunities for cool reflection and for reconciliation, before the divorce becomes irrevocable:

> "Revocable divorce can only be pronounced twice; where after there should be reconciliation in approved form, or final separation with beneficence. It is not lawful for you to take away anything of that which you have given your wives; unless it should be a case in which the wife insists upon separation without any default on the part of the husband and they are afraid that they would not be able to observe the limits prescribed by *Allah,* if they were to continue their association. In such case there will be no sin on either of them in respect of that which the wife may surrender by way of compromise. These are the limits prescribed by *Allah,* so transgress them not; whoso transgresses the limits prescribed by *Allah,* it is they that are the wrong-doers." (2:230).

A further check on hasty divorce is:

> "Should the husband divorce the wife a third time, the divorce would become irrevocable, and she would not be lawful for him thereafter, except in case she should marry another husband and he too should happen to divorce her, or should die. In such contingency, it would be no sin for them to return to each other, provided they are sure that they would now be able to observe the limits prescribed by *Allah*. These are the limits prescribed by *Allah* which He makes clear to the people who possess knowledge." (2:231).
>
> "In the case of a revocable divorce, when the end of the appointed period of waiting approaches, there should be reconciliation in approved form, or final separation in approved form; but do not hold back such women to

impose hardship upon them. Whoso does that, surely wrongs his own self. Do not bring the commandments of *Allah* into contempt, and keep in mind the favour that *Allah* has bestowed upon you and that which He has sent down to you of the Book and Wisdom, whereby He exhorts you. Be mindful of your duty to *Allah* and be sure that *Allah* knows all things well." (2:232).

"When you divorce your wives and they reach the end of their waiting period, and the divorce becomes irrevocable, do not hinder them from marrying their chosen husbands, if they agree between themselves in an approved manner. This is an admonition for everyone of you who believes in *Allah* and the Last Day. It is most blessed for you and purest. *Allah* knows and you know not." (2:233).

"Divorced women shall wait, concerning themselves, for the space of three courses. It is not lawful for them to conceal what *Allah* may have created in their wombs, if they believe in *Allah* and the Last Day. If their husbands should desire reconciliation during this period, they would have the stronger right to the continuation of the marriage than that it should be irrevocably dissolved." (2:229).

Should the husband and wife consort together after the pronouncement of a revocable divorce, the pronouncement would be voided altogether. "Women who survive their husbands shall wait concerning themselves for four months and ten days, and when they arrive at the end of that period there shall be no blame on you for anything that they do with regard to themselves according to what is fair. *Allah* is aware of what you do." (2:235).

"There shall be no blame on you in hinting at a proposal of marriage to divorced or widowed women, or in contemplating the possibility in your minds. *Allah* knows that you will think of them in that connection; but do not enter into any secret engagement with them, beyond conveying some indication to them of your inclination. Do not, however, resolve on the marriage tie until after the expiry of the period of waiting. Be sure *Allah* knows what is in your minds, so be mindful of Him. Know also that *Allah* is Most Forgiving, Forbearing." (2:235)

"Those of you who die leaving behind surviving widows, the legacy for their widows would be provision for a year without being turned out of the marital home. Should they depart therefrom on their own, after the expiry of the period of waiting, there shall be no blame upon you with regard to any proper thing which they do concerning themselves. *Allah* is Mighty, Wise."(2:241).

"For divorced women also there shall be provision according to what is fair. This is an obligation binding on the righteous." (2:242).

"It will be no sin for you, if need arises, to divorce women whom you have not touched and for whom no definite dower has been fixed. In such case, make provision for them—an affluent one according to his means, and a poor one according to his means—a provision in a becoming manner. This is an obligation binding upon the virtuous." (2:237).

"If you divorce them before you have touched them, but you have fixed a dower for them, then make over to them half of that which you have fixed, unless they should remit it or the guardian for the marriage should remit it, or unless the husband should voluntarily decide to pay a sum in excess of the half. That she should remit or you should pay a larger sum, as the case may be, would be closer to righteousness. Do not neglect any chance of behaving benevolently towards each other. Surely, *Allah* sees what you do." (2:238).

"In cases of divorce, mothers shall give suck to their infants for two whole years, where it is desired to complete the suckling, and the father of the child shall be responsible for the maintenance of the mother during that period according to usage. No one shall be burdened beyond his capacity. No mother shall be made to suffer on account of her child, and no father shall be made to suffer on account of his child; and the same is the obligation of the heir. If the parents should agree by mutual consultation and consent upon weaning the child, there shall be no blame on them. Should you desire to engage a wet-nurse for your children, there shall be no blame on you, provided you hand over what you have agreed to pay, in a fair manner. Be ever mindful of your duty to *Allah*, and be sure that *Allah* sees what you do." (2:234).

Social Rights

With the advent of Islam, the darkness of that era vanished and *Allah* enjoined kindness, love and compassion towards girls. Islam prohibited any killings of female children. *Allah* says in Surrah Al-An'am verse 151 and in Surrah Bani-Israil verse 31: Kill not your children for fear of poverty. It is *Allah* Who provide for them and for you. Surely, the killing of them is a great sin.

There was a programme on BBC named "Let her die". It was reported in the programme that there are more than 3000 foetuses which are being aborted in India everyday after the parents come to know that expected baby is a girl. This means every year more than million girls are being killed in the wombs of their mothers even only in India. It is advertised on the boards that spend Rs. 500 and save Rs. 5,00,000 Means do the ultrasound and if the child is female then abort her and save Rs. 5,00,000 which parents have to spend in the form of dowry for marriage.

Allah does not only prohibit the killing of female children, *Allah* even rebuked and badly criticized the thought of a person who is becoming sad at the news of the birth of a female child. *Allah* says in Surrah Al-Nahl verses 58-59.

And when to one of them is conveyed the tidings (news) of the birth of a female, his face become darkens, while he suppresses his inward grief. He hides himself from the people because of the bad news he has had: 'Shall he keep it in spite of disgrace or bury it in the dust?' Verily, evil is that which they think.

Economical Rights of Women

Of the great faiths, Islam has been foremost in assigning to woman a position of economic independence. It is well known that in the United Kingdom till as late as 1882, when the first Married Women's Property Act was passed by Parliament, a married woman could hold no property of her own, independently of her husband. Any property that a feme sole (unmarried woman) held in her own right vested automatically in her husband on her marriage. A hundred years later traces still linger in certain aspects of British Law which illustrate a married woman's position of dependence upon her husband.

In Islam, the independent economic position of woman has been established since the very beginning. Mention has been made of the obligation of the husband to make a settlement on the wife, in proportion to his means, at the time of marriage. This settlement is called dower (*mehr*). If at the time of the death of the husband the wife's dower should be still unpaid, it ranks as a debt to be discharged out of his estate, in priority to all his other debts. In addition, the widow is entitled to her share in the husband's estate, which is determined by law. Any property that a woman might acquire by her own effort, or might inherit as an heir or receive as a legacy or gift, belongs to her independently of her husband. She may ask her husband to manage it, but if she chooses to manage or administer it herself, he cannot interfere in her management or administration of it. A married woman who possesses means of her own may, and in most cases does, contribute a portion or the whole of her independent means towards the upkeep of the household, but is under no obligation to do so. The upkeep of the household is the entire responsibility of the husband; even when the wife is in her own right better off than her husband. This is well illustrated by the following incident. The Holy Prophet, peace be on him, on one occasion admonished women to spend in charity out of their own means also. Thereafter two women, both bearing the name of Zainab, one of them the wife of the well-known companion Abdullah bin Masood, came to him and told him that their respective husbands were men of straitened means, but that they in their own rights were comparatively better off. Would it be an act of spiritual merit if they were to assist their husbands out of their own means? The Holy Prophet assured them their spending on their husbands would be doubly meritorious, as it would rank both as charity and as graciousness towards kindred.

The *Holy Quran* admonishes:

> "Covet not that whereby *Allah* has made some of you excel others. Men shall have a portion of that which they earn and women shall have a portion of that which they earn. Ask *Allah* alone of His bounty. Surely *Allah* has perfect knowledge of all things." (4:33).
>
> "For everyone leaving an inheritance We have appointed

> heirs, parents and near-relations, and also husbands and wives to whom you are bound by solemn covenants. So give all of them their appointed shares. Surely, *Allah* watches over all things." (4:34).

The Islamic system of succession and inheritance, set out in 4:12-13 and 177, aims at a wide distribution of property. If a person should die leaving his or her surviving parents, wife or husband, sons and daughters, they all share in the inheritance; the general rule being that the share of a male is double that of a female in the same degree of relationship. In this there is no discrimination against female heirs in view of the obligation of the male to provide for his family, while the female has no such obligation. In practice, the rule works out favourably for female heirs.

A Muslim may not dispose of more than one-third of his assets by testamentary directions. Legacies, whether for charity or in favour of non-heirs, must not exceed one-third of net assets; nor may the share of an heir be augmented or diminished by testamentary direction. There is no room for discrimination between the heirs under the Islamic system of inheritance, like, for instance, primogeniture, or exclusion of females. A direction designed to secure the preservation of testimony relating to civil transactions, which requires that they must be reduced to writing, is sometime mistakenly seized upon as evidence of discrimination against females. The direction is as follows:

> "Procure two witnesses from among your men; and if two men be not available, then one man and two women, of such as you like as witnesses, so that if either of the two women should be in danger of forgetting, the other may refresh her memory." (2:283).

There is here not the slightest trace of discrimination. The normal rule is that women should be safeguarded against the contingency of having to appear as witnesses in judicial proceedings. Therefore, normally a woman should not be called upon to attest a document recording a transaction. This rule may be relaxed in an emergency. But then another difficulty would arise. In the case of male witnesses their memory of a transaction that they attest as witnesses would be refreshed when they met socially and the transaction was recalled for one reason or another. In the case of a document recording a transaction, which is attested by one male and one female witness, the female witness, under the Islamic social system, as will presently be appreciated, would not normally have frequent occasion to meet the male witness and talk to him, so that there would be little chance of her memory of the transaction being refreshed. To overcome this lack of opportunity of refreshing the memory, it is wisely provided that where only one male witness is available two female witnesses may be called upon so that, in the very words of the text, one may refresh the memory of the other. This provision is concerned only with the preservation of evidence, and does not deal with the weight to be attached to the testimony of a male or female witness. An illustration may help to clear up any doubt on the matter. Assume that a transaction recorded in a document attested by one male and two female witnesses becomes the subject of a dispute which comes up for judicial determination. It is then discovered that one of the two female witnesses has in the meantime died. The male witness and the surviving female witness are examined in court and the judge finds that their respective accounts of the terms of the transaction are not entirely in harmony; but he feels very strongly that taking every relevant factor into consideration the testimony of the female witness is more reliable than that of the male witness. In such a case, it would be his plain duty to rely on the testimony of the female witness in preference to that of the male witness. There could be no question of discrimination in favour of or against a woman.

Political Rights of Women

In Surrah Taubah verse 71.

> **And the believers, men and women, are friends of one another. They instruct good and forbid evil and observe Prayer and pay the *Zakat* and obey *Allah* and His Messenger. It is these on whom *Allah* will have mercy. Surely, *Allah* is Mighty, Wise.**

This means believing men and believing women are supporters of one another not only socially but also politically. Women have also obligation to spread the message of *Allah* and

His Prophet (PBUH). They have also obligation to struggle for making Islamic societies and Islamic governments. Woman can also take part in law making. There are few societies in the world where the ordinary citizen can confront with the ruler face to face and challenge his policies. But in pure and true Islamic societies, rulers of the time were always open and accessible. Women even took part in the battlefield. They provide first aids to the soldiers, give water to them. In the battle of Uhud, Hazrat Nafeesa was amongst another sahaba who was around the Prophet (PBUH) and received many wounds and Prophet (PBUH) made *dua* for her.

Conclusion

In short we can say that Islam gave women all rights before 15 centuries which anyone can expect in today's highly modern world. Believing men and believing women are supporters of one another not only socially but also politically. Women have also obligation to spread the message of *Allah* and His Prophet (PBUH). They have also right to vote.

Islam gave economic rights to women 1400 years ago, 1300 years before the Western world. In Islam, any adult women whether married or un-married, she was allowed to own or dis-own her property without the permission of anyone else. If women works by following the Islamic *Sharia* then whatever she earns, she need not to spend on her family. She can keep all of her earning for herself. In Islam during marriage, women are also on the receiving end.

Prophet (PBUH) said, "It is obligatory on every Muslim to acquire knowledge". The Prophet (PBUH) specially told the parents to educate their children specially their daughters. We have examples of many women 1400 years ago who were highly educated, learned and scholars in both religious and worldly knowledge.

With the advent of Islam, the darkness of that era vanished and *Allah* enjoined kindness, love and compassion towards girls. Prophet (PBUH) also said, "Anyone who up-brings two daughters with love and affection, and also did not favour his sons over daughters, he shall enter into *Jannat*".

Therefore, Islam is not only complete code of life for men it is also complete code of life for women. Islam actually liberates the women, given them rights in the 6th century that we have only gained in this century in this country: the right to own property and wealth and to maintain her original name after marriage; the right to vote; and the right to divorce.

References

Abou El Fadl, Khaled (2001). *Speaking in God's Name: Islamic Law, Authority and Women*. Oxford: One World.

Al-Hibri, A.Y. (2001-2002). "Muslim Women's Rights in the Global Village: Challenges and Opportunities." *Journal of Law and Religion*, Vol. XV, Nos. 1 & 2.

Ali, K. (2006). *Sexual Ethics and Islam: Feminist Reflections on Qur'an, Hadith, and Jurisprudence*. Oxford: One World.

Awn, P.J. (1994). "Indian Islam: The Shah Bano Affair." In: John Stratton Hawley, (ed.) *Fundamentalism and Gender*. New York: Oxford University Press.

Badran, M. (2005). "Between Secular and Islamic Feminisms: Reflections on the Middle East and Beyond", *Journal of Middle East Women's Studies* 1, no. 1 (Winter 2005): 6–29.

Badran, M. (1995). *Feminists, Islam, and Nation: Gender and the Making of Modern Egypt*. Princeton: Princeton University Press.

Badran, M. (1999). "Toward Islamic Feminisms: A Look at the Middle East", 159–88. In: *Hermeneutics of Honor: Negotiating Female "Public" Space in Islamic/ate Societies*, (ed.) Asma Afsaruddin. Cambridge, MA: Harvard University, Centre for Middle Eastern Studies.

Badran, M. & Miriam C. (eds.) (2004). *Opening the Gates: An Anthology of Arab Feminist Writing*, (2nd ed.) Bloomington: Indiana University Press.

Cunningham, K.J. (2005). "Women, Political Violence, and Democratization." In: William Crotty, (ed.) *Democratic Development and Political Terrorism: The Global Perspective*. Boston: North-eastern University Press.

Cwikel, J., Rachel L.W., & Alean Al-Krenawi. "The Physical and Psychosocial Health of Bedouin Arab Women of the Negev Area of Israel: The Impact of High Fertility and Pervasive Domestic Violence", *Violence Against Women* 9, no. 2 (February 2003): 240–58.

Darrow, W.R. (1987). "Marxism and Religion: Islam." In: Charles Wei-hsun Fu and Gerhard E. Spiegler, (eds.), *Movements and Issues in World Religions: A Sourcebook and Analysis of Developments Since 1945*. Westport, CN: Greenwood Press.

Doumato, E.A. & Marsha, P.P. (eds.) (2003). *Women and Globalization in the Arab Middle East: Gender, Economy, and Society*. Boulder: Lynne Rienner.

Gülük-S., G. & Semsa Özar (2001). "Gender-Based Occupational Segregation in the Turkish Banking Sector." In: Mine Cinar, (ed.), *The Economics of Women and Work in the Middle East and North Africa.* Amsterdam: JAI Press.

Haddad, Y.Y. & John L.E., (eds.) (1998). *Islam, Gender, and Social Change.* New York: Oxford University Press.

Khan, S. (2000). *Muslim Women Crafting a North American Identity.* Gainesville, FL: University Press of Florida.

Mutahhari, M. (1981). *The Rights of Women in Islam.* (1st ed.) Tehran, Iran: World Organization for Islamic Services.

Najmabadi, A. (1998). "Feminism in an Islamic Republic: Years of Hardship, Years of Growth." In: Yvonne Yazbeck Haddad and John L. Esposito Islam, eds., *Gender, and Social Change.* New York: Oxford University Press.

Najmabadi, A. (1991). "Hazards of Modernity and Morality: Women, State, and Ideology in Contemporary Iran", In: Kandiyoti, ed., *Women, Islam and State,* pp. 48-77. Springer.

Schacht, J. (1982). *An Introduction to Islamic Law.* Oxford [Oxfordshire]; New York: Clarendon Press.

Sonbol, A. El-A., (ed.) (1996). *Women, Family, and Divorce Laws.* Syracuse, NY: Syracuse University Press, 1996.

Stivens, M. (2003). "(Re)framing Women's Rights Claims in Malaysia." In: Virginia Hooker and Noraini Othman (eds.), *Malaysia, Islam, Society, and Politics: Essays in Honour of Clive S. Kessler.* Singapore: Institute of South-east Asian Studies.

Women's Rights in Muslim Communities: A Resource Guide for Human Rights Educators, June 2009, p. 13.

Section B

Barriers of Social Justice in Women

4

Problems of Social Justice in India

Sunil Kumar

It is a fact that the problem of social justice are not related to a particular religion, caste or a community, but belong to the whole of Indian society. In fact, they are the national problems. No doubt, they do exist in other countries, too; but we wish to explain them in the context of India alone.

The problems of social justice are usually related to its enemies, for they create them, aggravate them in order to serve their selfish motives. The agencies and the friends of social justice come together for seeking their right solution; but due to anti-forces and other obstructive elements, the problems continue to affect the brightsome field survey, we will have a long list; they are, however, innumerable and challenging and so acute that to face and solve them, is really a stupendous task. Some of the main, impending complicated problems may be discussed as follows :

Labourhood

A bit different from bonded labourers, the bonded labour (*Mazduri*) also exists in our society. Some contractors, or agents or big suppliers, on the pretext of improving their conditions, give some advance to agricultural or brick-making workers, mostly seasonally employed and bring them to the field and factories; they are mortgaged to the landlords and contractors for a certain period on very meager wages. They are kept there for long time and forced to work hard; and these labourers, too, are bound by certain condition of exploitive and oppressive nature forcibly since they are there in their captivity; they are not allowed to move outside of the fields or factories where they work lest they run away. In fact, they are heavily indebted with advances so that they never happen to be free from debts and advances. Even interest rates of debts charged are so high that the original capital amount goes on increasing, thus becoming double or even triple. In lieu of such interest rates, the labourers, their wives and children, work day and night, but without any relief from dusty work and the burden of heavy debts. Thus, these people and their children do not hold any better future except being coerced and oppressed by their owners, or masters, or beastly nature. It is not only a problem of social justice, but also a challenge for which freedom movements for the bonded labourers are active in various ways in Indian society.

Beggar Pratha

Closely akin to *Bandhua Pratha* and *Bandhua Mazduri*, is Beggar *Pratha* (Forced labour), which also stands as an acute problem of social justice. This, too, exists in remote villages, where no light of education, communication and other means of modern science, has reached. In beggar *pratha*, no wages are given, neither clothes, nor even food to the persons engaged in beggar, i.e. strictly forced labour without any reward or appreciation. In the beggar *pratha*, the big landlords, feudal lords, Jats and Rajputs, ask the shudras, untouchables, the poverty-ridden persons, or other lowest caste individuals, both their children and womenfolk, to come to their big houses (*Kothis* or *Havelis*) in order to clean them, to take care of their fields or to look after their animals from time to time. Whenever required, they are called and sent for doing even the meanest work. Such work or duties are not regular, yet these are got done by persuasion, at times, by coercion and force. They have to do all such things for they have to live in their villages without raising any voice against the *zamindars*. However, certain movements have studied their problems, and are busy in organizing those, who are suffering from beggar *pratha*. The government and its agencies, too, have come forward to help them by legally abrogating all kinds of beggar, bonded labour or bonded *mazduri*.

Sudkhori

It is the oldest system, and still exists in both cities and villages. *Sudkhori* means money-lending to the poor labourers and small farmers, also to the low-paid employees and daily wage earners on high rates of interest by the rich, called *Sahukars* or *Mahajans*. They lend money to them and in lieu of it, mortgage their ornaments, houses or agricultural lands. The poor fellows usually remain under heavy debts. And do not find themselves in a position even to pay the interest on the capital amount. As a consequence, interest on interest increases month after month. The poor labourers, or farmers, only repay the interests, and ultimately, they feel unable to redeem their properties, which in due course of time, are confiscated by the mortgagers. They, thus, remain as poor, lowly and weak as they were in previous times. Who are the main victims of *Soodkhori pratha*? Only the weaker sections of society who do not have adequate income, or at times, when natural calamities, diseases or accidents surround them, they necessarily happen to be the most helpless victims. Though Government has enacted the "Money-Lending Act" to regulate the money-lending, but that has not worked satisfactorily so far; and the sudkhori still exists as a challenge to social justice.

Unemployment

It is, in fact, a problem almost of all countries; but in India, it has assumed an alarming form. Not only the illiterate, uneducated men and women are unemployed; but also graduates, post-graduates, engineers, doctors, technicians and a host of others are the victims of unemployment. Since they face material hardships, they accept jobs on conditions that are undesirable. They do not find jobs in accordance with their liking, ability and capacity, but become the victim at the hands of industrialists, capitalists and landlords. Some of the youth, both male and female, are totally unemployed, and when they do not get proper or adequate employment and no hope is left for them, they join illegal groups of smugglers, thieves or is left for them, they join illegal groups of smugglers, thieves or dacoits; or else, for their livelihood, pursue unconstitutional means just to live on. The unemployed youth, even elders, engage themselves in loot, theft, smuggling, dacoity, violence, murder and the like for their subsistence. This way first they became the victims of unemployment, and then, the enemies of social justice. Some of them even join the terrorist groups and revolutionary movements in order to get money thereby to serve their family members, who, too, are enemployed due to old age or otherwise. So unemployment not only is a problem, but also a challenge to be met with all seriousness.

Population Explosion

Apart from acute unemployment problem it is needless to emphasize that the success of social justice movement, or otherwise of any economic policy in India would depend upon whether the country has and is following a compatible population policy or not. Rapidly increasing population in our country has been adding the woes of poverty, illiteracy, unemployment, disease etc. As a result, we find malnutrition, women's oppression and child labour everywhere in our society. The more the population explosion, the less the educational opportunities, environmental cleanliness, opportunities for employment. Apparently, people do not find proper places to live in; they gather themselves in huts and mud-houses; drink polluted water; and do not have lights and roads, dwell near heaps of garbage and stinking ponds. All sorts of illegal activities such as theft, intoxication, violence, opium taking, rape or murder are encouraged. They create not only the law and order problem; but also cause things of undesirable nature. It is extremely disturbing to note that the country's most urgent problem, namely, population crisis, which is as the root of almost all problems is being totally ignored by the political parties or even the supporters of social justice. In fact, for any welfare measure, social justice or any other movement with similar aim, to be adequate, sustainable or implemented, population control has to be a necessary pre-requisite.

Child Labour

Like the problem of bounded labourer and bonded muzduri, child labour also comes in the forefront. This problem is the result of population explosion and lack of social security. When the adult persons of a family are unable to earn much to feed all the members adequately, they engage their children in their own professions or calling, and also send them to other jobs, without giving any heed to their tender age and education. They only think that the children, of the family. For these are the days of high prices of commodities, costly clothes and other household articles. Such child labourers lead a very wretched life, because in places like hotels, dhabas, repair shops and tea-stalls, they work from early morning to the late evening. They get tattered clothes to wear; and little time to bathe and clean themselves. They get very meager wages and hardly any time to sleep. All these things stand as a challenge to social justice.

Children all over India continue to be a major victim of human rights violation, whether it is sexual exploitation of minors, bonded labour or child labour, almost in every community of our country. The children are beaten or sexually abused by adult, ravaged beyond their years by hard living and drug abuse on the streets.

Victims of Injustice

This lot of children has to face the trauma of poverty and disease, and out of it, a large number of female children turn to be prostitutes or male children to be killers of landlords, when they are engaged as domestic servants. Both young boys and girls are forced into a lonely life as domestic workers, and deprived of education and health, they are treated as less than human beings and worse than beasts. The children pose a great problem for social justice, and therefore, they need help and protection.

Child Marriage of Girls in spite of its against Law

Besides child labour, child marriage, too, is a problem of social justice. This system exists not only among the illiterate, but also among the educated families. At the time of their marriage, very young boys and girls, when joined together in marriage ceremonies, feel happy, because they get sweets, new dresses or enjoy entertainments; but it hampers their chances for education, proper bodily and mental growth. Later on, some of them, anyhow, become educated and get government jobs, or become big officers, and then, they feel ashamed of having uneducated, ill-mannered or ugly wives. Afterwards, they leave them in villages or get separation through panchayats of their castes. So the child marriages begin with unjust matrimonial relationships and also end in unhappy separation of the adults. Such marriages create certain problems not only for the couple and their family members, but also for the moral order of society. All this stands against the spirit of social harmony and justice.

Dowry System

There is no harm in giving certain things such as household articles, or some cash, according to one's capacity, to the daughter and son-in-law at the time of marriage; but today dowry has assumed a dangerous proportion that obstructs the prospects of social justice in the context of womenfolk. On the one hand, to provide education to girls, to make them professionally trained, and then, to seek jobs for them, has become a costly affair, and on the other, to spend a huge amount, along with several costly articles, is much more painful not only to the girls, but also to the parents. The greed for dowry results in torture and murder of the girls in their in-laws house; in some cases, they are burnt alive in connivance with their well-educated, even rich, husbands. In the name of dowry, heinous crimes are committed against womenfolk. This is beyond the understanding of the common people; but what happens, is unjust and inhuman.

Women's Oppression

In a social set up of this kind, it is almost pre-destined that a diffident and insecure womenfolk will be vulnerable to gross social and sexual abuse both by the family and outside forces, especially if they belong to the weaker sections or the lower-caste society in rural areas. On one or the other pretext, they are harassed and oppressed in our male-dominated society. Working women, educated and well-dressed young girls are often select targets of male hackling and abuse, because they pose a challenge to the traditional power structure. In an atmosphere such as this, molestation and violent abuse of women, even torture or rape of women, including the minor and grown-up girls, are the events that express man's mode of superiority complex through immoral means. What is accomplished by mass rapes during communal riots and caste- wars is clearly the subjugation of women's clan and community as well. '*Sati*' custom and branding old propertied widows as 'witches' by their greedy kin, and subsequently, burning of young widows with their dead husbands as '*Satis*' or 'witches' being stoned to death, are the glaring examples of women's oppression.

Child labour, as earlier referred to, not only takes place only in case of boys, but minor girls are also victimized in this profession. In poor families, each girl that can, has to work, no matter what risks it may expose them to. A large majority of girl child labour is involved in non-monetary work, domestic as well as undomestic. As far as wage labour is concerned, in the rural areas girls usually work alone with the family in fields or a construction sites, and in urban areas girls usually work alone with the family in fields or at construction sites, and in urban areas they are mostly employed as domestics or rag pickers. This causes (in large number) girls to run away from schools and earn money for their families. So women's oppression and girl child labour both pose a challenge to social justice in our male-dominated society.

Prostitution

This is another way of women's oppression, a blatant injustice towards womenfolk, found almost in all societies of the world in one way or the other. Prostitution is the most hated problem of social justice. The brothels in metropolitan cities are full of child prostitutes sold or driven into the profession by the vested interests, also by their families or lured by pimps. This profession has registered an alarming increase in recent years, for the reasons that girls do not get proper education, are regarded as unwanted in most of the poor or tribal families, are forced to earn money for their families, and are also misguided by certain anti-social elements. Not only the un-educated and poor, but also the well-educated and rich persons encourage this profession just to enjoy and satisfy their sex appetites. The well-paid agents cleverly arrange the sale of girls after kidnapping them anyhow from various places. It is an acute problem and involves the risks of aids and other dreaded diseases for both the prostitutes and the so-called enjoyers.

Carrying Nightsoil

Though the sweepers in India, derogately called *'bhangis'*, have numerous problems such as illiteracy, ignorance, poverty, unemployment, population increase, intoxication, child marriage and child labour in their community, yet the most hated work done, both by male and female, is to collect and carry the nightsoil on their heads to throw outside the populated places. The nightsoil necessarily spreads stinking smell and if a thin lot, it leaks from wooden tokaries to drop on the bodies of the bhangis, who do this work usually in the mornings. Though this practice has been widely condemned by all yet it exists mostly in cities. As a consequence, such males or females are looked upon with hatred and contempt; their children hardly get chances to be educated in schools; and they mostly live in slums outside the cities or villages. They are still the victims of discrimination and untouchability. They are, in fact, an ostracized lot of the Indian society, facing or fighting against innumerable problems.

Begging

This is also a challenge to social justice, a widely spread social phenomenon in India. In a country, like India, where all the citizens have been endowed with equal right and opportunities, the involvement of crores of men and women, boys and girls, old and young, disabled and healthy, into earning through begging, is an insult to all of us. It has become a profession; and certain well-planned groups pickup minor girls or boys, make them handicapped, disabled, as human beings who need help, and thus, drive them into begging profession. We can usually see such beggars in public places like bus stations, railway stations, temples or tourist places and public gardens. The minors are paid meager amount and the rest is usurped by the ring-leaders of begging groups. However, certain persons, in fact, because of being naturally helpless, unemployed or abandoned by their families, do beg in order to earn their livelihood. Though begging has been banned by the government, yet it still continues everywhere in Indian society posing a challenge to the process of social justice.

Communalism, T.V., Print

Picking up quarrels on certain issues by the rival communities or castes, making them hot just out of their dogmatic beliefs or fanatic attitudes, then engaging in mutual looting, torture, arson, rape, devastation and murder, are some of the ugly forms of communalism. Whenever communal and casteist feelings grow, the number of crimes, especially against womenfolk and the weaker sections of society, goes up. All this forcibly deprives a large number of people, belonging to all castes and communities, of their democratic right of freedom of speech and expression, free movement and the like. The clever leaders or instigators, anyhow, escape; but the innocent men and women, minor girls and boys, become the direct victims of communal attacks and riots. There may be different reasons for escalating the communal feeling; but this has become a persistent problem in our country.

Casteism

In a similar way, casteism, too, poses a challenge to social justice. The caste set-up manifests itself into untouchability, feelings of low and high, oppression of the lower caste people by the higher castes, at times, into caste riots, especially in villages. Due to casteism, crores or people, belonging to the weak and poor and lower castes, live a wretched life; they are treated as less than men and worse than beasts; they do not get adequate opportunities to improve their socio-economic conditions; and still happen to be the victims of bonded labour, forced labour and the like. In fact, they still remain deprived of their legitimate rights and live a life of second-grade citizens in our democratic set-up. Most of the ills of bhangi community are due to casteism and its allied evils. In short, casteism has entered almost in all walks of Indian society, whether politics, business or bureaucracy.

Reservation

Initially, the grant of reservation to the Scheduled Castes and Tribes in government services and educational institutions was basically a step in the direction of social justice. The reservation policy has benefited these sections and they have advanced, become educated and conscious of their position and rights. Not all of them, but some of the men and women of the weaker sections of society have risen in life because of reservations. However, recently the reservation system has emerged to be a bone of contention. Every political party has made it an issue, rather a way to turn it into vote-banks, by demanding reservations for each and everyone. Should it be on the basis of caste or of poverty? Should it be continued for those, who have become elites due to reservation as big officers? Is reservation in promotions just? Who actually need reservations now? These are some of the pertinent questions that have created tensions mutual hatred and contempt among the different communities. 'To whom should reservations be granted' is a difficult question to answer, but it has now become a problematic matter, and needs re-valuation in the larger interest of Indian society. Even among the scheduled castes and tribes the benefits, from reservation, have been circumvented by a few; and the most poor, lowly and the weak, are still far away from these benefits. The backward classes have the reservation; now the Muslims, too, have come forward to demand it. Therefore, how to deal with issues of such reservations has emerged as a challenge in the process and implementation of social justice.

Wandering Groups

There are innumerable wandering castes, tribes or groups in India, which do not have their own houses, agricultural lands or permanents abodes. Babari, Sansi, Kalvelia, Kanjar and Bhubharia are some of the castes or tribes, which do not reside at permanent places; their professions, too, are not regular and permanent; their children do not go to schools, and their womenfolk are also illiterate. On the one hand, the administration does not take much interest in rehabilitating them at permanent place; and on the other, police looks at them suspiciously. As a result, such person, both male and female, are arrested on the pretext of alleged theft, dacoity or illicit liquor production; policemen pick up all their belongings, and thus, render them homeless or helpless otherwise. Bribes are extorted from them in lieu of freeing them from police stations. Luhars are also a wandering tribe, whose socio-economic conditions are pitiable. Though they earn their livelihood by making iron articles independently yet they are regarded as the low king of people. Thus, all of them are deprived of their legitimate rights and their children, too, do not get opportunities for rising in life.

Displaced Groups

Apart from wandering castes and tribes, there are certain groups, which are rendered displaced because of natural calamities like earthquakes, floods epidemic diseases, or due to the construction of big dams. They are deprived of their agricultural lands and other properties. Such people belong to all castes, creeds and communities. No doubt, they are provided alternatives; but that does not help them much since their regular life is disturbed and their children, too, hardly find opportunities for education. Due to terrorism in Kashmir, Punjab or some far eastern states, people migrated to safer places; but their socio-economic conditions, educational facilities did not improve. They have been fighting against all odds such as lack of proper light and sanitation, paucity of education and employment, absence of other civil amenities. They do not get proper housing facilities and continue to live in tents and huts. Even master-plans, too, displace certain persons, who, too, need help. Thus, all the displaced groups, irrespective of the reasons why they were rendered so, pose a challenge to social justice.

Poverty

Another most disturbing problem is that of acute poverty. There are crores of people, who are poverty ridden. It is the root of all suffering. There may be several reasons for poverty; but two-thirds majority of population in India lives below poverty-line, which means that such families hardly get two meals a day. The poor people face other problems of population explosion, acute unemployment, lack of accommodation and illiteracy; and at the same time, they become victims of injustice, exploitation, oppression, forced labour, bonded mazduri, girls-boys child labour and the like. Though the alluring slogans are usually raised by political parties to remove poverty; yet poor families are hardly identified honestly by any agency. In fact, advantages of various plans, sponsored by government to help the poor classes, are usurped by the clever and dishonest leaders or a gents. Mostly, the families belonging to the weaker sections, especially the chamars and bhangis, still live in utter poverty even after 72 years of Independence. Freedom and economic policies of the government have not benefitted them. Though in certain cases, agricultural lands have been allotted to the poor families, yet the big zamindars obstruct them from occupying and ploughing the lands. Poverty is the result of a bad social set-up and immoral habits of the vested interests. Anyhow, the poor millions pose a challenge to social justice.

Legal Process

The provisions of social justice have provided a lot of facilities and right to the weaker sections of society; but these still exist on paper and files; and to get them through legal process or by courts of law, is beyond their reach. First, they do not have enough money to expend on litigation, and second, the legal process is so complicated that they can hardly hope of any immediate relief. The legal fight is also very costly, a tedious job to pursue unto the last; and moreover, the delay in its process, mars the very spirit of justice. As a result, mostly the suffering parties remain deprived of their legitimate claims. The government has provided free legal aid to the poor and needy; but that is inadequate to meet the challenge of anti-forces. Persons, arrested under Acts like TADA, languish in jails for years together without trial. So the intricacy of legal process, its delay and high cost, all form a painful aspect of social justice. Even the legal agencies seem to be indifferent to bring about legal revolution in India, though the legislatures and enacted laws have done commendable work; still much is to be accomplished in the field of social justice.

Violent Revolution

Social justice is certainly a revolution change, and whenever such changes occur things become hot. At the time, when reservation was granted to the backward classes, there were violent clashes, and its opponents, especially the youth, both boys and girls, destroyed, properties worth crores of rupees and some of them also immolated themselves to show their vehement hatred for it. Even otherwise, violent clashes, in the name of revolution, lead to blood-bath or killing of innocent people. So, the question is:

whether bloody revolution is desirable for justice or not? Will not the peaceful or constitutional means suffice to bring about a just socio-political and economic order? In India, some movements or organizations, committed to bring about social and economic justice through the barrel of guns, have come up; their argument is that without bloody revolution, no justice will be available to the poor, lowly and the weak in a dogmatic, superstitious and conservative society. It is also right that in rural areas or remote tribal regions, without violent means, the feudal and brahmanic forces cannot be defeated. However, there are certain movements and organizations, which stand to achieve this aim through peaceful and constitutional means. Thus, to achieve social justice either through violence or by legal process, has become a problem, though at times certain violent clashes between pro and anti-forces can hardly be avoided.

Booth Capturing

With the independence, the constitution has bestowed all the citizens with equal rights. "One man, one vote" is the rule of all elections to the parliament, Assemblies and Panchayats. It is by all means a milestone in the process of social justice, the equality of all citizens being the guiding principle. However, in certain places, especially in remote villages, where the dominant castes are found, they forcibly take the ballot papers, stamp and drop them in ballot boxes in favour of their candidates, before the poor, lowly and the weak voters arrive at the polling booth; or else, the booths are looted, the ballot boxes are thrown into wells, if they think, they have failed in nefarious activities. This is called "booth capturing" a blatant violation of the equal rights to voting and freedom. This deprives a lot of people of their legitimate rights. It is a general practice, not limited to any caste or party. Whoever, being dominant in any capacity, can do so, in both urban and rural areas. At the time of elections, voters are also allured by offering money, liquor or other gifts; but booth capturing is a burning problem in the field of social justice and political equality.

Appeasement Policy

From the national standpoint, the policy of appeasement has

assumed a dangerous form, which is a result of the policy of creating "vote banks" among the minorities and the weaker sections of society. The policy of appeasement is usually pursued by almost all political parties just to win the favour of votes. In it, certain demands and conditions are openly agreed to by a political party in order to maintain its hold on the minorities, weaker sections or backward classes, which blatantly violate and suppress the legitimate claims of other communities and castes. The political parties in power provide certain facilities or economic benefits to some particular communities and castes in order that they continue to hold the power and authority in their hands. This happens only for those, who are dominant groups in society; but for those, who are the weakest ones, nothing is done for them. This way the policy of appeasement results in discrimination, favouritism and injustice, that again results, at times, in casts tension and communal flare-up. Thus, the policy of appeasement, though not bad in polities, yet poses a problem to the larger interest of social justice.

Evidently, in a social set-up, that we have in India, innumerable problems arise; some are periodically added to; and besides the foregoing ones, the issues of illiteracy, ignorance, corruption, terrorism, dogmatism, fanaticism, regionalism, linguism, political chauvinism, insecurity in old age, rehabilitation of abandoned children, widow remarriage, increasing cases of rape, leprosy, violation of law etc. are the challenging obstructions in the way of social justice, political equality and economic emancipation. Though shouting slogans and making attractive speeches in favour of social justice is easy; yet to identify a single acute problem and to make strenuous efforts, or to lead a meaningful movement without ulterior motives, is a very difficult task. In the grab of social justice or economic welfare, some justice or economic welfare, some of the political parties and organizations raise vogue and blind demands just to make things hot. This makes the issues of social justice more complicated, along with anti-forces, which aggravate the situation. Nevertheless, the movement for social justice, its process and struggle, is advancing day by day, desirable results are coming up partly; and its friends, too, are becoming stronger, though much more is needed to make it an effective reality in the larger interest of Indian society.

5

Prejudices Against Women and Its Consequences

Nazish Bano

Introduction

A women is a female human, the term women is usually reserved for an adult, with the term girls being the usual term for a female child or adolescent. The term women is also some-times used to identify the female human, regardless of age, as in phrases such as "women's rights". Women may also refer to a person's gender identity.

In many pre-historic cultures women assumed a particular culture role. In hunter-gatherer society, women are generally the gatherers of plant foods, small animal foods and fish, while men hunted meat from large animals. In more recent history gender roles have changed greatly, originally, starting as a young age, aspirations, occupationally are in specific directions according to gender. Sharpe (1976). Traditionally, middle class women were involved in domestic tasks emphasizing child care. For poorer women especially working class women, economic necessity compelled them to seek employment out-side the home. Many of the occupations that were available to them were lower in pay them those available to men.

As change in the labour market for women came about availability of employment changed from only 'dirty', long hour factory jobs where more educations was demanded, women participants in the U.S. labour force rose from 6 per cent to 23 per cent in (1900). These shifts in the labour force led to changes in the attitudes of women at work, allowing for the revolution which resulted in women becoming career and education oriented. In the 1970s many female academics, including scientists, avoiding having children however, throughout the 1980's institutions tried to equalize conditions for men and women in the workplace. However, the inequalities at home stumped women's opportunities to succeed as far as men. Professional women are still responsible for domestic labour and child care. They have a double burden which has not allow them the time and energy to succeed in their careers.

Furthermore, though there has been an increase in the endorsement of egalitarian gender roles in the home by both women and men, a recent research study showed that women focused on issues of morality, fairness and wellbeing, while men focused on social conventions. Gere and Helwing (2012). Until the early 20th century U.S. women's colleges required their women faculty members to remain single, on the grounds that a women could not carry on two full time professions at once. According to Schiebinger (1999), being a scientist and a wife and a mother is a burden in society that expects women more often than men to put family ahead of carrier, equality of opportunity for both gender and equal rights irrespective of gender movements started.

Though a combination of economic changes and the efforts of the feminists movements, in recent decades women in many societies now have access to career beyond the traditional home maker. Although a greater number of women are seeking higher education, salaries are often less than those of men. Unequal status, frustration distinctiveness etc. are the social sources of prejudice. Prejudiced behaviours occurs against weaker section of the society (i.e. women). The unequal social, economic, political, religious, educational status are the root of the socialization of anti social behaviours against weaker section of the society. Unequal status breeds prejudice, it was a common thing in past that slaves are viewed by their masters as lazy, irresponsible, lacking ambition as having just those traits that justify the existing social structure : slavery what the historical forces were that created the unequal status is a question for historians. But once inequalities exists, prejudice can be used to justify the economic and social superiority of those who have wealth and power. Discrimination also breeds prejudice, and prejudice rationalize unequal status. Halen Mayer Hacker (1951) observed, how stereotypes of blacks and women helped rationalize the inferior status of each. Both groups were viewed as being inferior in intelligence, as being emotional and primitive, and as contented with their subordinate role, blacks were inferior, women were weaker, blacks were all right in their place, women place was in the home. In India also the condition of Dalits and women are same as blacks. These types of anti-socialization process creates anti social activities against weaker section of the society, as sexual violence is a serious problem in India, many women report physical and sexual violence and many more will continue to suffer violence, by hands of husbands, other family members and outsiders. The National Crime Record Bureau report shows that there were 2,229 cases of crime against women in 2001 and 4,536 cases of sexual harassment in (2012) against women. Anjela (2015), observed that in India, women in conflict zone are specially unsafe and susceptible to different kinds of sexual exploitation. In Jharkhand in many naxal hit villages the young girls are kidnapped, they are victims of violence and later on they join these groups. They are actually treated by the male members as the material, to satisfy their sexual instincts. When the "operation green hunt ", took place in Jharkhand, many school girls and women in villages were sexually assaulted by the armed force sent to villages for the operation. Jharkhand is a burning case of sexual violence related crimes and its consequences.

Pain and frustration can evoke hostility, when the cause of frustration is too intimidating or too vogue, the person redirect his hostility. This phenomenon of displaced aggression may have contributed to the lynching of blacks in the U.S. South. Between 1882 and 1930 there was a tendency for more lynching to occur in years when the cotton price was low and economic frustration was high. Havland and Sears (1940), Mitz (1946) similarly, Bettelheim and Janowitz (1950), A.A. Campbell (1947) observed in a survey that those whose job satisfaction is low, have been more intolerant than less frustrated people who are satisfied with their jobs. Frustration intensify hostilities against those already disliked (Wealthrley, 1961). Personality needs and status of the person are also the influencing factors of prejudiced and discriminations for the weaker section if the society. Grube Kleinhuscelink, and Kathleen Keaney (1982), studied that men with low self-acceptance dislike strong, non-traditional women but men with high self acceptance tended to be more attracted to non-traditional women.

Lack of education of weaker section of the society plays major role of prejudiced behaviours towards them. There are cognitive sources of prejudiced behaviours also categorization, i.e. to categorize by clustering objects into groups. Once we have organized people into categories or built schemas, we can more easily think and remember information about them. To the extent that persons in a group are similar (either women or weaker section of the society), Knowing there group enables us to predict better their individual's behaviour, there are categorizations benefit. However, the benefits exact a cost, Kraut & Poe (1980). We have already considered one social cost; the in-group bias, merely dividing people into groups can tiger discriminations. Ethnicity and sex are in our current world, powerful ways of categorization does provide a foundation for prejudice. Distinctive people draw more attention, Taylor *et al.* (1979). However, it is possible for people to perceive others, reacting to their distinctiveness when actually they are not. Distinctive cases are most easily remembered, they tend to dominate our images of various groups. We are prone to over generalize from vivid cases is in disputed The questions have become, when are we most likely to do so ? Quattrone and Jones (1980), report that the tendency to form stereotypes from the behaviour of a single person is specially strong when one's prior expectations are weak and when the person is a member of an unfamiliar group. Stereotypes assumes a correlation between people's group membership and their characteristics, i.e. women are weak, less intelligent, emotional etc. Stereotypes directs our interpretations, whenever a member of a group behaves as expected the fact is duly noted that the prior belief is confirmed, when a member of the group behaves inconsistantly with the observers expectations, the behaviour may be explained away as due to special circumstances (Crocker, Hannah and Weber (1982), or it may be misinterpreted, leaving the prior belief intact. Pre-judgements directs our interpretation and our members (Rose & Hamilton, 1979). Here a stereotype males behave more aggressive, is confirmed, with evidence ranging from anthropology to social psychology. Mead (1935) did find societies where both men and women were characteristically hostile and aggressive or gentle and warm. But all societies have some division of labour between men and women, and inevitably hunting and fighting are primarily the men's role (Murdock, 1935). In united states most violent crime is committed by men, in school and other real life situations, girls are the prominant investigators has consistently found less aggressive at all times regardless of how aggression is measured (Eron, 1980). Boys are also more likely than girls to engage in mock fighter

(Maccoby & Jacklin, 1974). It makes one wonder hypotheses : If women were the world's political leaders would there be fewer war? Broverman and associates *et al.* (1970) and Broverman (1972) surveyed college students and adults, they found men and women in striking agreement, males were seen as generally more competent (aggressive, independent, dominant, decisive, ambitious) and female as warmer and more expressive (aware of others, feelings, tactful, gentle, exhibiting tender feelings).

Stereotypes are simply true or false generalizations about a group of people.

Objectives

To explore and highlighted the psycho-social factors of prejudices against women and its consequences and control.

Methodology

Sample

One hundred male and female married adults and One hundred male and female unmarried youth (students) randomly selected from Deoria district of Uttar Pradesh, with ages ranging from 18 to 40 years, i.e. two hundred male and female participants are selected.

Procedure

A Yes/No type questionnaire is developed with 23 selected statements, which is related to various dimensions, i.e. Co-operation, Dependence, Adjustment, Social status, Inferiority complex, Co-operation for healthy life, Family and tradition, (commitment), Ability, Power, Adjustment difficulty, Capability, Self-respect, and Independence, Liberty, Security, Un-equality, Orientation towards their child, Carelessness, Welfare and Well-being, Economic stability, Present demand, Weakness, Conditional Job and Health-consciousness. The statements are related to either positive or negative attitudes toward the role of male and female for their personal, financial, social, economical, cultural environment.

The participants are instructed to give their acceptance or rejection on the basis of tick mark. The result was computed on the basis of percentage of acceptance or rejection.

Table 5.1: Result and Discussions—Observation Table

Sl. No.	Dimensions	Married				Unmarried			
		Male		Female		Male		Female	
		Acceptance %	Rejection %	Acceptance %	Rejection %	Acceptance %	Rejection %	Acceptance %	Rejection %
1.	Cooperation	100			100		100		100
2.	Dependence	83	17	50	50	100	–	100	–
3.	Adjustment	33	67	50	50	100	–	100	–
4.	Social status	100	–	100	50	50	–	100	–
5.	Inferiority complex	–	100	50	50	100	–	100	–
6.	Healthy life	100	–	50	50	50	50	100	–
7.	Family, commitment	100	–	50	50	–	100	100	–
8.	Ability	100	–	100	–	100	–	–	100
9.	Power	100	–	100	–	100	–	–	100
10.	Adjust Difficulty	–	100	50	50	–	100	–	100
11.	Capability	–	100	100	–	50	50	–	100
12.	Self respect, independent	100	–	50	50	50	50	100	–
13.	Liberty	100	–	100	–	50	50	–	100
14.	Security	–	100	–	100	–	100	–	100
15.	Unequality	100	–	–	100	100	–	–	100
16.	Child orientation	–	100	50	50	100	–	100	–
17.	Carelessness	–	100	–	100	50	50	–	100
18.	Well-being	100	–	100	–	50	50	100	–
19.	Economic stability	100	–	100	–	50	50	100	–
20.	Present demand	100	–	100	–	100	–	100	–
21.	Weakness	100	–	–	100	–	100	–	100
22.	Conditional job	–	100	–	100	50	50	–	100
23.	Health conscious	100	–	50	50	–	100	–	100

Source: Author's empirical data collection.

Table 5.1 shows that married and adult male and female both are accepted that the women do not have support from men, but the unmarried youth either male or female accepted that women have support from men. They also accepted that dependent female have low confidence, mostly males do not help to the women of their familial, economic and social adjustment. They also have the attitudes that the husband have inferiority complex if his wife is on high status. Men and women both should be working, this is the present demand for betterment of the life, working women have not care to her family and traditions both. Every person either male or female should be prove their ability. Females are always under the men, but the working women are easily adjusted, she is able to do work in and out the home, she is self-dependent and self-respectable while the adult married males and females both have not clear attitudes on these points. The adult and married male and female participants accepted that the job is a way of independence, while the young unmarried males and females accepted that job is a source of earning money too. The adult and married male and female participants agree on the point that the working women are responsible for both : family and work, she do support economically to their family, the status of family is either better or not, women should cooperate economically to their family. But the young and unmarried male and female are not agreeable on this point, they said that it is not necessary that the women could enhance their economic status without support of men. Women cannot equal to the men. An woman either she is working or not working, pay more attention to their children, so working women would be responsible or not for their work and family, depends on their personality. It is doubtful that the working women will be responsible for family and work. The working women are not health conscious and suffering from role stress :it is the attitude of young and unmarried both men and women participants.

Focuses on women's unfavourable conditions drawing attention to the issues and processes that have an impact on women's dignity and status. Women as a group are one of the oppressed exploited and disadvantaged people among others like the poor, the lower castes. The scope is limited to women.

There are visible and invisible aspects of gender injustice. Women's illiteracy, exploitation, dowry demands, economic dependency etc. are the visible aspects of the process and ideology which gives origin to this situation i.e. stereotyped roles, lack of education and jobs, gender oppressive practices like male child preference, restricted social mobility are the invisible manifestations of the gender differentiating system which need to be undermined. Role stress is a state of tension created by multiple demands and conflicting directions from two or more individuals in the performance of a role, resulting in anxiety. Role stress, has been defined as the degree of incomparability of expectations communicated to a focal person by his role given. Housewives experienced more negative, and positive personal stress more personal efficacy and a lower degree of anxiety as compared to working women as nurses, Kumari Patiraj Singh and Ashok (2000). A significant negative relationship between occupational stress and mental health was observed among women employed in different professions [Rastogi, Renu, Kashya and Kavita (2001)]. More dissatisfied employees and less job involved employees experienced greater role stress Gupta, Sharmishtha and Kulkarni (2001). To reduce the mental stress, the working women used technique like postponing certain tasks due to storage of time and changing the level of performance more frequently, while non working women relied more on positive thinking Anjula and Hashpinder (2002). Unmarried working women reported high stress at work place due to group political pressure and for married women, it was due poor peer relations, group differences were not significant on there dimensions Osmany and Khan (2003). Common and specific need patterns contributing to stress tolerance, for working and non-working women Adity and Kumari (2005). Role stress, work stress, low self-esteem, lack of self-respect, economic dependency, impact of role model, lack of physical and mental supports expected to her family and society, misuse of reinforcement etc. in women, are the responsible phenomena of deviated socialization process, which form incomplete picture of the women in family as well as society, consequently faulty perception towards women generate prejudices and discriminations. Prejudices and discriminations, domestic violence creates physical and mental health problems in women, the victim gradually shifted in traumatic situations in our society generally the victims are women. Trauma is the result of an overwhelming amount of stress that exceed one's ability to cope or integrate the emotions involved with that experience. Trauma differs between individuals according to their subjective experiences. All psychological trauma originate from stress, a physiological response to an unpleasant stimulus (Crossarth Maticek, *et al.*, 1994). Long term stress increases the risk of poor mental health and mental disorder, which can be attributed to secretion of glucocorticoids for a long period of time. Such prolonged exposure causes many physiological dysfunctions such as the suppression of the immune system and increase in blood pressure (Seyle, 1976) These elements are not only diversely responsible, for women's development but also for our Nation's developments. We cannot be progressive.

Suggestions and Conclusions

Negative generalization about a gender or a group of a people originates so many psycho-social, economical, cultural problems from family to nation. Prejudiced behaviours and thoughts against women are the barrier of the development and progress in our country. Positive interactions and support of men and women can change the environment in positive way. Strategies should be develop for changing anti social norms and enhancing the status of the women, because change in perception of society towards the women is needed for their dignity. Women should be aware about their rights, legal reforms are required. Family is a first place where the socialization process of a child begins and the family members, especially mother and father are the master agents of socialization, so, it is the demand of present situation that parents should provide equal opportunities of nutrition, health, education and related to all development of personality irrespective of male or female child. The government should be committed and involved to open the training and counselling centres.

References

Aditi, N. & Kumari, B. (2005). "Impact of personality pattern and employment status on psychological stress tolerance of women in Kerala", *Indian Psychological Review*, 64 (2), 103-106.

Anjela, S.K. (2015). "Sexual violence against women in Jharkhand", *Journal of Social Development* 7(2), 80-86.

Bettelheim, B. & Jonowitz, M. (1950). *Dynamics of Prejudice: A Psychological Study of Veterans*, New York: Harper.

Broverman, I.K., Broverman, D.M., Clarkson, F.E., Rosenkrantz, P.S. & Vogel, S.R. (1970). "Sex role stereotypes and clinical judgement of mental health", *Journal of Consulting and Clinical Psychology*, 34, 1-7.

Compbelt, A.A. (1947). "Factors associated with attitudes Jews". In: T.M. NewComb & E.L. Hartley (Eds.), *Readings in Social Psychology*, 62, 454-457.

Croker, J., Hannah, D.B. & Weber, R. (1982). "Personal memory and casual attributions", *Journal of Personality and Social Psychology*.

Eron, L.D. (1980). "Prescription for reduction of aggression", *American Psychology*, 87, 215-217.

Gere, J. & Halwing, C.C. (2012). "Young adult's attitudes and reasoning about gender role in the family context", *Psychology of Women Quarterly*, 36, 301-313.

Grube, J.W., Kleinhesselnk, R.R. & Kearney, K.A. (1982). "Male self-acceptance and attraction toward women", *Personality and Social Psychology*, Bulletin 8, 107-112.

Gupta, Sharmishtha & Kulkarni, A.V. (2001). "Job satisfaction, job involvement and organizational role stress", *Indian Psychological Review*, 568, 57 (4), 41-46.

Haker, H.M. (1951). "Women as a minority group", *Social Forces*, 30, 60-69.

Havland, C.I. & Sears, R. (1940). "Minor studies of aggression: correlation of lynchings with economic indices", *Journal of Psychology*, 9, 302-310.

Kraut, R.E. & Poe, D. (1980). "Behavioural roots of person perception: The deception judgements of customs in specter and lay men", *Journal of Personality and Social Psychology*, 39, 784-798.

Kumari, P.S. & Ashok, P. (2000). "Life stress and same personality variables: A comparison of working women and house wives", *Journal of the Indian Academy of Applied Psychology*, 26 (1-2), 25-31.

Maccoby, E.E. & Jacklin, C.N. (1974). *The Psychology of Sex Differences*, Stanford, Calif: Stanford University Press.

Mead, M. (1935). *Sex and Temperament in Three Primitive Societies*, New York: Morrow.

Murdock, G.P. (1935). "Comparative data on the division of labour by sex", *Social Forces*, 15, 551-553.

Osmany, M. & Khan, W. (2003). "Organizational stress in working women", *Indian Psychological Review*, 61, 2-6.

Rastogi, R., Kashyap & Kavita (2001). "A study of occupational stress and mental health among married working women", *Journal of Community Guidance and Research*, 18(2), 189-196.

Rose, T.L. & Hamilton, D.L. (1979). "Stereotypes as schemata", paper presented at the Western Psychology Association Convention.

Schiebinger, Londa (1999). "Has feminism changed, science?" *Science and Private Life*. Cambridge: Harvard University Press.

Sharpe, S. (1976). *Just like a Girl*, London: Penguin.

Taylor, S.E., Crocker, J., Fiske, S.T., Sprinzen, M. & Winkler, J.D. (1979). "The generalizability of salience effects", *Journal of Personality and Social Psychology*, 37, 357-368.

Weatherly, D. (1961). "Anti-semitism and the expression of fantasy aggression". *Journal of Abnormal and Social Psychology*, 62, 454-457.

6

Impact of Injustice on Women Health

Asha and *Anupam Nath Tripathi*

Injustice

Justice in the legal sense refers to women and men objectively receiving what the law designates they should receive. Justice studied from a social science perspective refers to an individual's subjective perceptions of whether s/he is treated fairly or not (Mowday, 1982; Markovsky, 1985; Hegtvedt, 1994).

Injustice is a quality relating to unfairness or undeserved outcomes. Gender discrimination is the consequence of persistent inequality between men and women in all spheres of life. The dimension and degree of discrimination against women manifests itself in different culture, politics, race, region, countries, and economies differently. However, gender discrimination is considered as a tremendous constraint towards the development process and it is found as a causal factor of violence against women. (Jannatul Ferdaush, K.M. Mustafizur Rahman, 2011). Gender equality; therefore, is the current subject of concern among the policy makers of the world because of enhancing economic growth and maintaining continuity of the development process as well (CPD-UNFPA, 2002).

Women are facing injustice since birth in family and society. Discrimination in male and female child is one of root cause of injustice with women. Women have been the victims of exploitations since long time in different fields of their life physically, socially and mentally. Due to gender discrimination women face several types of violence, exploitation in their family and society.

Women are facing various types of injustice, discrimination and exploitation in their family such as: female infanticide and feticide, dowry, domestic violence, honour killing and in social context they also face an injustice at workplace. Like: workplace discrimination, workplace harassment, sexual harassment, acid attack and workplace bullying (Rospenda, Richman and Shannon, 2009; Fitzgerald *et al.*, 1999; Grubb, Roberts, Grosch and Brightwell, 2004).

There are several incidences of sexual as well as moral abuse which are very often highlighted by the media in modern society, and a lot of those also remain unexplored. Women are not safe even if they belong to any educational status, class, caste and creed. Women are victims of crime directed specifically at them as rape and sexual assault, domestic violence, sexual harassment in the workplace and in matrimonial disputes. It can be seen in many forms of injustice with women which has badly affected women's physical and mental health and women are prone to psychological distress.

Psychological Distress

Discrimination has been shown to be a risk factor for psychological distress in several studies (Gonzalez-Castro and Ubillos, 2011; Yip, Gee and Takeuchi, 2008). Psychological distress is often caused by an injustice, either real or perceived, which can lead to depression, anxiety, stress, frustration, irritability, exhaustion and disengagement from fellow workers.

Psychological distress is largely defined as a state of emotional suffering characterized by symptoms of depression (e.g., lost interest, sadness, hopelessness) and anxiety (e.g., restlessness, feeling tense) (Mirowsky and Ross, 2002). These symptoms may be tied in with somatic symptoms (e.g., insomnia, headaches, lack of energy) that are likely to vary across cultures (Kleinman, 1991; Kirmayer, 1989).

Additional criteria have been used in the definition of psychological distress but these criteria do not make consensus. In particular, sufferers of the stress-distress model posit that the defining features of psychological distress are the exposure to a stressful event that threatens the physical or mental health, the inability to cope effectively with this stressor and the emotional turmoil that results from this ineffective coping (Horwitz, 2007; Ridner, 2004). They argue that psychological distress vanishes when the stressor disappears or when an individual comes to cope effectively with this stressor (Ridner, 2004). There is plenty of evidence confirming the effect of stress on distress.

The signs and symptoms of psychological distress:

- Feelings of anxiety, sadness, anger. Wanting to be alone;
- Feeling "out of control" or overwhelmed much of the time;
- Difficulty coping with everyday problems;
- Unable to talk about ways to solve problems or talk about fears;
- Needing the help of others to make decisions;
- Trouble sleeping;
- Not taking care of self;
- Looking sad, frowning, Crying easily, Loss of hope or sense of comfort;
- Laughing at odd times;
- Aches and pain, Feeling that your heart is racing;
- Thoughts of suicide or hastening death; and
- Not wanting to follow the advice of the healthcare team.

It can be said that injustice with women is strongly associated with psychological distress which badly affects women's physical and mental health. Our concern in this chapter is to explain Impact of Injustice on Women Health.

Violence against women has been clearly defined as a form of discrimination in numerous documents. The World Human Rights Conference in Vienna, first recognized gender- based violence as a human rights violation in 1993. In the same year, United Nations declaration, 1993, defined violence against women as "any act of gender-based violence that results in, or is likely to result in, physical, sexual or psychological harm or suffering to a woman, including threats of such acts, coercion or arbitrary deprivations of liberty, whether occurring in public or private life". (Cited by Gomez, 1996).

Impact of Injustice on Physical Health

Physical sexual and psychological violence occurring within the general community, including rape, sexual abuse, sexual harassment and intimidation at work, in educational institutions and elsewhere, trafficking in women and forced prostitution. Physical, sexual and psychological violence perpetrated or condoned by the state, wherever it occurs. This definition added "violence perpetrated or condoned by the State", to the definition by United Nations in 1993.

Klein and Renate (2004) have reported that the consequences of gender-based violence include severe short- and long-term damage to women's health and significant risks for the health of their children. The most immediate physical health consequences are the consequences of injuries such as acute and chronic pain, cuts, burns, bruises, broken teeth, broken bones, damages to eyes and ears. For women the risk of injury from physical assault seems to increase when the assailant is an intimate (Klein, & Renate, 2004). According to Campbell (2002) chronic stress-related problems include functional gastrointestinal disorder, appetite loss and viral infections such as cold and flu. Violence during pregnancy poses a threat to health and at its extreme can result in death of the mother and her unborn child (Bacchus, Loraine, Mezey, Gillian, Bewley and Susan, 2004). Gynaecologic problems are the most consistent physical health difference between battered and non-battered women (Rob, Koenig and Saifuddin, 2006).

Gender-based violence is associated with a range of serious health problems, including infection, chronic pain, sexual dysfunction, and obstetric complications (Outlook, September, 2001). Klein and Renate (2004) have investigated that sexual violence has profound impact on the mental, physical and reproductive health of the victim. The acts of sexual violence have severe consequences for women's reproductive system causing non-specific pelvic, genital and breast pain, severe menstrual problems, urinary tract infections, sexually transmitted diseases including HIV/AIDS (Klein & Renate, 2004).

Evidence from health facilities suggests that abused women's reproductive health is compromised through much higher rates of gynaecological problems, HIV and sexually transmitted infections (STIs), miscarriages, abortions, low birth weight, and unwanted pregnancy (Kishor, Sunita and Johnson, Kiersten, 2006) Sexual violence also results in unplanned pregnancy.

Impact of Injustice on Mental Health

Domestic violence is strongly associated psychological distress like—depression, anxiety, somatisation, attempted suicide, and chemical abuse (Jaffe, Wolfe, Wilson and Zak, 1986; Kemp, Rawlings and Green, 1991).

The physical side of abuse is easily seen, but the psychological wounds are hardly seen and these affect every single aspects of the life of the victim. The psychological impact of domestic violence affects women more than the physical injuries. Physical and sexual violence negatively impacts women's mental health. Women living with violent men are more prone to suffer serious mental and health problems as a consequence of the repeated violence and fear they experience. Stark and Flitcraft (1996) have identified this as "Battered Woman Syndrome", characterized by recurrent assaultive injuries, stress-related injuries, isolation, substance abuse and mental illness (Abbott & Williamson, 1999). Walker (1979) has reported that battered female victims identified depression, feelings of low self-esteem, helplessness, and generally severe stress reactions coupled with somatic complaints.

Mental health consequences include depression, Post-traumatic Stress Disorder (PTSD), anxiety, sleeping disorder, eating problems, suicidal tendencies, and increased use of alcohol and other drugs (Klein and Renate, 2004).

According to Panagioti and Maria (2009) PTSD is commonly conceptualized as an anxiety disorder occurring subsequent to a traumatic event which is perceived as highly threatening. There is some evidence that PTSD is directly associated with more suicidal attempts and this mediates the link between partner violence and suicidal attempts (Panagioti & Maria, 2009).

A number of researchers have documented that the "association between violence from one's spouse, low self-esteem, and suicidal tendencies is very strong, especially when compared to the women's pre-battering life phase" (Fischbach, L. Rutha and Herbert, Barbara, 1997).

In the context of workplace injustice, Payne & Doyal, (2010) have found ageism and sexism can operate concomitantly to negatively influence the health of older working women. Some studies indicated that even though the experience of workplace injustice is often not life-threatening, the experience threatens the inner world of the target by shattering basic cognitive schema about fairness and justice and negatively influences one's social and personal identity leading to PTSD.

Conclusion

In sum up on the basis of review of literature it can be said that all types of violence and discrimination in family, society and workplace with women, are an injustice. And this leads to psychological distress in women. Psychological distress affects women's physical and mental health due to which women face several problems in their life. It is time to rethinking about women rights and their well-being. How women stand in society with confidence and feel secure in family and society even being alone. They live their lives with respect and enjoy every movement of life. Here some suggestions are given:

- To educate boys from childhood that violence against women is not only an offense but also society hates and boycotts such people.
- To educate communities that women are not chattel or movable property but individuals who need to be valued and not abused.
- To empower women and making them understand that the violence they experience is unacceptable.
- To skill to cope with stress and anger management issues.
- To provide Counselling to survivors, and incorporate a variety of therapeutic approaches: Cognitive-behavioural, individual counselling, and group counselling, (Howard, Riger, Campbell and Wasco, 2003). Counselling treatments designed for survivors hold promise for reducing depression and anxiety, and enhancing well-being.
- All these suggestions may be beneficial for society and violence survivors and their well-being.

References

Abbott & Williamson (1999). "Women, Health and Domestic Violence", *Journal of Gender Studies*, 8(1):83-102.

Bacchus, L., Mezey & G.B. Susan (2004). "Domestic Violence: Prevalence in Pregnant Women and Associations with Physical and Psychological Health", *European Journal of Obstetrics & Gynecology and Reproductive Biology*, 113: 6-11.

Campbell, J.C. (2002). "Health Consequences of Intimate Partner Violence", *The Lancet*, 359(13): 1331-1336.

CPD-UNFPA Paper 19 (October 2002). Gender-Related Development Index, For 64 Districts of Bangladesh.

Fischbach, L.R. & Herbert, B. (1997). "Domestic Violence and Mental Health: Correlates and Conundrums within and across Cultures", *Social Science Medicine*, 45(8):1161-1176.

Fitzgerald, L.F., Magley, V.J., Drasgow, F., & Waldo, C.R. (1999). "Measuring Sexual Harassment in the Military: The Sexual Experiences Questionnaire (SEQ-DoD)", *Military Psychology*, 11, 243-263.

García-M., & Stock, H. (2009). "Protection of Sexual and Reproductive Health Rights: Addressing Violence Against Women", *International Journal of Gynecology and Obstetrics*, 106:144-147.

González-C., J.L. & Ubillos, S. (2011). "Determinants of Psychological Distress among Migrants from Ecuador and Romania in a Spanish City", *International Journal of Social Psychiatry, 57*, 30-44.

Grubb, P.L., Roberts, R.K., Grosch, J.W., & Brightwell, W.S. (2004). "Workplace Bullying: What Organizations are Saying", *Empl. Rts. & Employ. Pol'y J.*, 8, 407-523.

Hegtvedt, K.J. (1994). In Foschi, M. and Lower, E. (eds.) *Group Processes: Sociological Analyses*, 177-204, Chicogo: Nelson-Hall.

Horwitz, A.V. (2007). "Distinguishing Distress from Disorder as Psychological Outcomes of Stressful Social Arrangements." *Health*, 11: 273-289.

Jaffe, P., Wolfe, D.A., Wilson, S. G Zak, L. (1986). "Emotional and Physical Health Problems of Battered Women", *Canadian Journal of Psychiatry*, 31, 625-629.

Jannatul F., K.M. & Mustafizur R. (2011), *Gender Inequality in Bangladesh, Unnayan Onneshan: The Innovators.*

Kemp, A., Rawlings, E.I. & Green, B.L. (1991). "Post-Traumatic Stress Disorder (PTSD) in Battered Women: A Shelter Sample", *J. Traum. Stress*, 4, 137–148.

Kirmayer, L.J. (1989). "Cultural Variations in the Response to Psychiatric Disorders and Psychological Distress." *Social Science and Medicine*, 29, 327-339.

Kishor, S. & Johnson, K. (2006). "Reproductive Health and Domestic Violence: Are Poorest Women Uniquely Disadvantaged?" *Demography*, 43(2), 293-307.

Klein, R. (2004). "Sickening Relationship: Gender-based Violence, Women's Health, and the Role of Informal Third Parties", *Journal of Social and Personal Relationships*, 21(1), 146-165.

Kleinman, A. (1991). *Rethinking Psychiatry. From Cultural Category to Personal Experience*. New York: The Free Press.

Krantz, G. & Garcia-Moreno, Claudia (1979). "Violence against Women", *Journal of Epidemiology and Community Health*, 59(10), 818-821.

Kumar, S., Jeyaseelan, L., Suresh, S., & Ahuja, R.C. (2005). "Domestic Violence and its Mental Health Correlate in Indian Women", *The British Journal of Psychiatry*, 187, 62-67.

Markovsky, B. (1985). "Toward a Multilevel Theory of Justice", *American Sociological Review*, 50, 822-839.

Mirowsky, J. & Ross, C.E. (2002). "Selecting Outcomes for the Sociology of Mental Health: Issues of Measurement and Dimensionality", *Journal of Health and Social Behavior*, 43, 152-170.

Mowday, R.T., Porter, L.W. & Steers, R.M. (1982). *Employee-Organization Linkages: The Psychology of Commitment, Absenteeism and Turnover*, New York: Academic Press.

Outlook, September (2001). Violence against Women: Effects on Reproductive Health.

Panagioti, M., Gooding, P. & Nicholas T. (2009). "Post-Traumatic Stress Disorder and Suicidal Behaviour: A Narrative Review", *Clinical Psychology Review*, 29, 471-482.

Payne, S. & Doyal, L. (2010). "Older Women, Work and Health", *Occupational Medicine*, 60(3), 172.

Ridner, S.H. (2004). "Psychological Distress: Concept Analysis." *Journal of Advanced Nursing*, 45, 536-545.

Rob, Stephenson, Koenig, Michael A., & Ahmed, Saifuddin (2006). "Domestic Violence and Symptoms of Gynaecologic Morbidity among Women in North India", *International Family Planning Perspectives*, 32(4), 201-208.

Rospenda, K.M., Richman, J.A., & Shannon, C.A. (2009). "Prevalence and Mental Health Correlates of Harassment and Discrimination in the Workplace", *Journal of Interpersonal Violence*, 24(5), 819.

Sheela S.M. (2000). Institute of Social Studies Trust (ISST), www.google.co.in

Stark, E. & Anne, F. (1996). "Women at Risk", *Domestic Violence and Women's Health*, Thousand Oaks, CA, London, New Delhi: Sage Publications, p. 264.

U.S. EEOC (2011) http://en.wikipedia.org

United Nations General Assembly (1993). Declaration on the Elimination of Violence Against Women. Proceedings of the 85th Plenary Meeting, Geneva, December 20, 1993. United Nations, Geneva.

Walker, L. (1979). *The Battered Woman,* New York: Harper & Row.

Yip, T., Gee, G.C. & Takeuchi, D.T. (2008). Racial Discrimination and Psychological Distress: The Impact of Ethnic Identity and Age among Immigrant and United States-born Asian Adults", *Developmental Psychology*, 44, 787-800.

7

Psychological Dynamics of Domestic Violence

Consequences, Issues and Responses

Sushma Pandey

Violence is a social psychological phenomenon, which is witnessed at epidemic threshold around the globe and it has challenged the very existence of human race in general and female population in particular. Aggression or violence is an extensively studied area in psychological researches however, issues related to intimate violence (domestic violence) has received major focus of research interest among academicians over the last decade. This article analyzes the psychological dynamics of domestic violence, epidemiology, causative factors and consequences on health and well-being of victimized women. Finally, some recommendations have been made to control the incidence and prevalence of domestic violence.

During the last few decades, women violence related issues inflamed women organizations of both Governmental and Non-Governmental cells as well as feminist organizations. On 8th March, 1984, an autonomous women's group across the country celebrated International Women's Day and focused on the theme of violence against women and major emphasis was given on domestic violence in the forms of bride burning/dowry deaths, infanticide, foeticide, sexual harassment, and wife battering etc. Consequently, various laws were framed and enforced to prevent this evil. Despite this, the rate of perpetrators and abused victims is dramatically increasing day by day and endangering the survival of a large segment of women population.

Figure 7.1 displays incidence of total crime against women since 2010-2013.

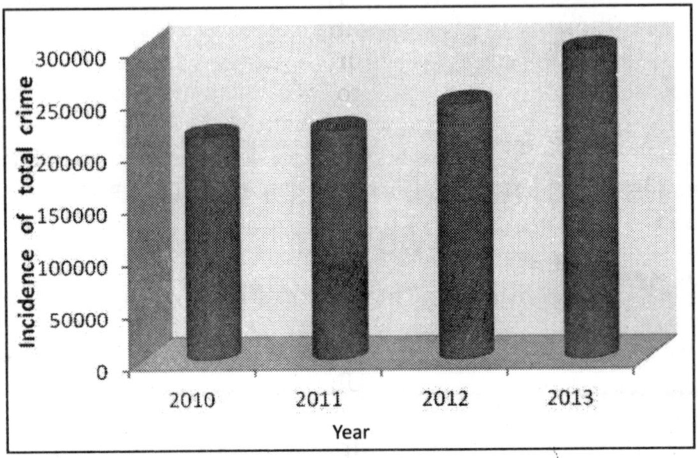

Fig. 7.1: Total Crime Against Women.
Source: National Crime Records Bureau

Background

Primarily, domestic violence emerged as a social issue in USA when Murray Straus and his colleagues (1980) completed their pioneering research and published a book entitled, "Behind Closed Doors: Violence in American Families." Afterwards, prolific researchers from different perspective were done in Western countries. Researchers showed their concern and still are actively engaged to explore the incidence and prevalence rates of women victimization, its root causes and impacts on social and psychological development of victimized women. (Flavia,1988; Ghadially,1988; Jaffe, *et al.*, 2003; Pandey, 2008; 2010; Pandey & Misra, 2000).

In India, domestic violence is found since antiquity. Women are maltreated in many ways, i.e., physically, psychologically, sexually, economically and spiritually and they are bound to live in a very pathetic state. This is rather paradoxical where the concept of *Ardhnarishwar* (symbolizing the sense of balance) is identified in Indian mythology, and also it is stated, *"Yatra Naryastu Pujyante, Ramante Tatra Devatah"—Manusmriti*. There are various forms of crimes against women committed by male counterparts are witnessed in plenty.

Violence against women continues to be a globally epidemic that kills, harasses, tortures and abuses—physically, sexually, psychologically and economically. The domestic violence against women is witnessed in every country cutting across boundaries of caste, community, ethnicity, culture, age, income, education and occupation. No society can claim to be free of such violence; the only difference is in its pattern and trends that exists in countries and regions. Despite this, specific groups of women are more vulnerable including minority, indigenous, migrants, institutionalized or women with disabilities, elderly women, poor or low S.E.S. women and female children respectively. While reliable statistics of women violence are hard to identify, however, studies estimate that from nation to nation 20-50 per cent of women have experienced physical and sexual harassment and mental torture or psychological abuses (UNICEF, 2000). No doubt, this evil is epidemic in our country.

Women are victimized at multiple points, i.e. at workplace, in community or society as well as in the family. The most tragic form of women victimization is domestic violence because it is either unnoticed or ignored considering familial or personal issue but it is quite damaging to a large segment of women population. Therefore, this article focuses on psychological understanding of domestic violence, epidemiology, causative factors and impacts on health status of victimized women.

Concept of Women Domestic Violence (D.V.)

The domestic violence is defined as, "one intimate partner's (spouse) attempt to control, dominate and humiliate the other partner through a variety of means viz.: physical, sexual, psychological, economic and spiritual abuses. Domestic violence goes beyond individual acts of aggression to encompass an overall pattern of behaviour aimed at maintaining full control over the partner" (Jaffe *et al.*, 2003). According to The National Research Council (1993), "Domestic Violence is the intentional infliction of harm or injury by one intimate partner on another."

From legal perspective, domestic violence is defined as: "The physical injury, sexual abuse or forced imprisonment or threat of a family or household member or of a minor child by a person with whom the minor child has had or is having a dating relationship." However, from Social Psychological perspective, domestic violence can occur in the variety of relationship including same sex relationships, extended family relationships, dating, acquaintance and peer relationships. Domestic violence takes place across all groups and cultures. Patterns of violent behavior can be transmitted from one generation to the next. Thus, domestic violence or women abuse is a widespread societal problem. It is form of power and control. It affects the physical, social, emotional and financial well-being of women and children. It can take many forms, including verbal, emotional, psychological, financial, spiritual, sexual and physical abuses. Women from all racial and ethnic backgrounds, sexual orientations, socio-economic classes, religions, ability levels and professions have experienced abuse in their lifetime.

Epidemiology: Worldwide

Domestic violence is both a worldwide and national crisis and has appeared at alarming threshold throughout the world. According to UNICEF study report (2000), 20-50 per cent of women population of the world is victims of domestic violence. The statistics of domestic violence available from various countries evinced the proportion of domestic violence.

The worldwide statistical data of domestic violence indicates that females are more abused than males. According to research report, 1 out of 10 women had confirmed violence at the hands of the one, they loved and three per cent (3%) experienced severe violence including life threatening attacks and injuries (Straus *et al.*, 2003). In 1984, the Department of Attorney General disclosed domestic violence a major social problem that if tolerated allows the seeds of violence to be sown in the next generation. Further in 1992, the American Medical Association reported that women were four times likely to be injured in their homes by their partners than in any vehicle accidents (American Medical Association, 1992).

According to the U.S. National Violence Against Women Survey Report (Tjaden & Thoennes, 2000), 22 per cent of the women and 7.4 per cent of the men surveyed reported that they were physically assaulted by their partners. As estimated, 1.3 million women and 8,35,000 men are physically assaulted by their intimate partners in U.S.

Similarly, statistics from Australia also confirm high rate of domestic violence. The Australian Bureau of Statistics reports that 23 per cent of women experienced violence by an intimate partner in their lifetime (Putt & Higgins, 1997), 12 per cent of women reported that they lived in fear of abuse during their current relationship.

Despite this, males can also be victims of domestic violence. A study conducted by the Canadian Centre of Justice Statistics (2000) reported that 6,90,000 women and 5,49,000 men were victims of some form of spousal assault during a 5 year period in Canada, Australia, New Zealand and around the world, women are far more likely to be killed by their intimate partners than men (Rennison & Welchans, 2000).

The incidence rate of the various forms of domestic violence are reported in the following section:

1. Physical Abuse: A growing body of research studies confirm the prevalence of physical violence in all parts of the globe, including the estimates of 20-50 per cent of women from country who have sometimes or the others, experienced domestic violence. According to UNFPAV World Population Report (2005), in every country where reliable large scale studies have been conducted, between 10 to 69 per cent of women report that have been physically abused by an intimate partner in their lifetime. Similarly in 2002, The World Health Organization surveyed many developed and developing countries and identified the prevalence rate of physical abuse of women at different levels. Figure 7.2 presents the per cent of married women aged 15-49 ever beaten by a spouse or partner.

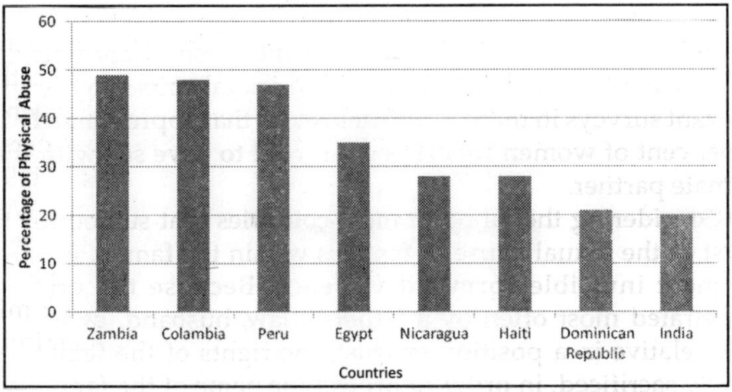

Fig. 7.2: Physical Abuse (aged 15-49) by a Spouse or Partner.
Source: UNFPAV World Population Report (2005).

In a comprehensive survey, respondents of different countries reported having been hit, kicked, stepped, or physically hurt and abused. On prevalence rate of Physical abuse against women, Zambia stood first and India was identified at last but one place and minimum abused victims were identified in Cambodia.

A number of studies on violence against women indicate that:

- The perpetrators of violence against women are almost exclusively men.
- Physical abuse in intimate relationship is almost always accompanied by severe psychological and verbal abuse. In 1 of 4 cases of domestic violence, women also experienced sexual abuse.
- Women are at greater risk of violence from men they know.
- In Australia, Canada, Israel, South Africa and the United States, 40-70 per cent of females were killed by their partners.

Many men and women believe that wife beating is justified. The shame associated with violence against women in the form of domestic violence, rape and other forms of abuse may contribute to the facts that women often suffer it in silence, afraid of repercussion and stigma and never tell anyone.

2. Sexual Abuse: Sexual abuse and rape by husband or an intimate partner is not considered a crime in most countries and women in many societies do not consider forced sex as rape if they are married to or cohabiting with the perpetrator. The assumption is that once a woman enters into a contract of marriage, the husband has the right to unlimited sexual access to his wife. Relevant surveys in many countries reveal that approximately 10-15 per cent of women report being forced to have sex with their intimate partner.

Considering the taboo in most countries that surrounds the incest or the sexual abuse of females within the family, is one of the most invisible forms of violence. Because the crime is perpetrated most often by a father-in-law, husband, or another male relative in a position of trust, the rights of the female are usually sacrificed, in order to protect the name of the family and that of the adult perpetrator. However, studies have shown that from 40-60 per cent of known sexual assaults within the family

Table 7.1: Proportion of physically abused women who sought help from different sources, selected population based studies (WHO, 2002: World Report on Violence and Health, Geneva: WHO)

Country/Area	*Sample*	*Proportion of Physical abuse Women WHO*			
		Never Told %	*Contact Police* %	*Told Friend* %	*Told Family* %
Australia	6,300	18	19	58	53
Bangladesh	10,368	68	-	-	30
Canada	12,300	22	26	45	44
Combodia	1,374	34	1	33	22
Chile	1,000	30	16	14	32*/21***
Egypt	7,121	47	-	3	44
Ireland	679	-	20	50	37
Nicaragua	8,507	37	17	28	34
Republic of Moldova	4,790	-	6	30	31
United Kingdom (UK)	430	38	22	46	31

Notes: * Women who are physically assaulted in past 12 months.
** Refers to the proportion of women who told their family.
*** Refers to the proportion of women who told their partner's family.

Source: Reproduced from reference 25 with the permission of the publisher.

are committed against girls aged 15 years and younger, regardless of region or culture. A recent study in the Netherlands shows that 45 per cent of victims of sexual violence within the domestic sphere are under the age of 18, of these, girls are far more likely to be victims of incest than boys.

Likewise, Population based studies report that from 12-25 per cent of women have experienced either attempted or completed forced sex by an intimate partner or ex-partner at some time in their lives and 38 per cent of sexually abused women were assaulted by their husbands, common law partners or boyfriend (Canadian Panel on Violence Against Women, 1993).

3. ***Psychological/Emotional Abuse:*** Since psychological violence is harder to capture in quantitative studies, a full picture of the deeper and more insidious levels of violence defies quantification. Victim survivors report that ongoing psychological violence—emotional torture and living under terror is often more unbearable than the physical brutality, with mental stress leading

to a high incidence of suicide and suicidal attempts. A close link between domestic violence and suicide has been established based on studies contributed in the United States, Fiji, Papua New Guinea, Peru, India, Bangladesh and Sri Lanka. Suicide is 12 times as likely to have been attempted by women who have been abused than by one who has not. In United States as many as 35-40 per cent of battered women attempt suicide. In Sri Lanka, the number of suicides by girls and women in age range of 15-24 years is 55 times greater than by the number of death due to pregnancy and child-birth.

4. Other Forms of Abuses: Forced prostitution, foeticide or other kinds of economic abuses (commercial exploitation) by male partners or parent are other forms of violence against women and children reported worldwide. Murder of women by their batterers is another phenomenon that should be regarded as a separate category when recording domestic violence. Studies carried out in Australia, Bangladesh, Canada, Kenya, Thailand and the U.S.A. documented the incidence of homicide within the domestic sphere. In Southern Africa, women's groups have begun to document the increasing incident of homicide and data on this issue are available from Boston, South Africa, Switzerland, Zambia and Zimbabwe. A comparative analysis of spousal homicide based on 1991 data, concluded that Russian women are 2.5 times more likely to be murdered by their partners than American women. However, American women are already twice as likely to be killed by their partners as women in Western-European countries.

Women victimization is the most common form of gender based violence. In Northern Ghana girls are 'donated' to priests and/or forced to live as 'wives' and submit sexually to the shrine priests in return for protection of the family. A similar practice called *Devadasi Pratha* exists in Southern India, where young women and girls (*Devadasi*) are 'donated' to serve a temple, and very often end up being prostitute. In a Canadian study, it was found that 21 per cent of women were sexually abused in an intimate relationship and were abused during pregnancy. However, only 26 per cent of women abuse incidents are reported to the police (Statistics, Canada, 1993).

A comprehensive interview was conducted by WHO (2006) with nearly 25,000 women at 15 sites in 10 countries. Researchers found that rates of partner violence ranged from a low of 15 per cent in Yokohama, Japan, to a high of 71 per cent in rural Ethiopia. At six of these sites, at least 50 per cent of women said that they had been subjected to a moderate or severe violence in the home at same point. At 13 sites, more than a quarter of all women said that they had suffered such violence in the past year (World Health Organization, 2006). "In all but one setting women were at far greater risk of physical or sexual violence by a partner than by other people." The report says that rural areas tend to have higher rates of abuse than cities. But no area was immune (World Health Organization Report, 2006).

While researchers and women's groups have long known that domestic violence was widespread and other smaller surveys have supported that notion, the WHO study adds an important dimension to the topic because it provides an unusual amount of quantitative, scientific data on the subject. Whereas, previous studies had focused mostly on developed countries, indeed mostly on the United States, (Claudia Garcia-Moreno, a researchers in the WHO research, 2006).

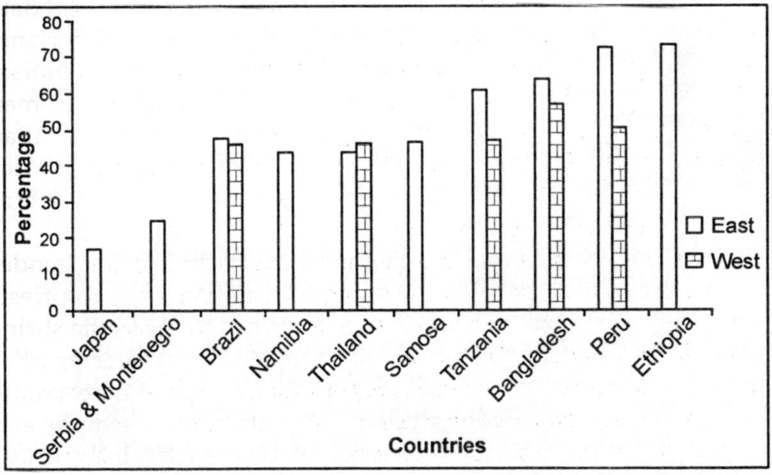

Fig. 7.3: Displays the rate of violence in various residential setting of different countries.

Source: WHO Report, 2006.

The Incidence of Domestic Violence in India

Crime or Violence against women has been recognized as one of the major social indicators in India. At the same time, there is a dearth of information on the magnitude and patterns of domestic violence in India, particularly by way of community based data. Family based data from police, court, hospital and NGO records do exist, but these data remains scattered, hospital and NGO record do exist, but poorly maintained.

Table 7.2 shows the percentage of ever-married women who report different types of acts committed by their current husband if currently married or most recent husband if not currently married. Note that since the different types of violence are not mutually exclusive, women may report experiencing multiple forms of violence.

Table 7.3 shows the percentage of women who have experienced different combinations of physical and sexual violence for India as a whole, according to selected background characteristics and by state.

Thirty-four per cent have experienced physical violence and 27 per cent have experienced physical violence but not sexual violence; 9 per cent have experienced sexual violence and 2 per cent have experienced sexual violence but not physical violence; and 7 per cent have experienced both physical and sexual violence. Overall, in India 35 per cent of women age 15-49 have experienced physical or sexual violence; this proportion is 40 per cent for ever-married women and 17 per cent for never married women. Both types of violence are higher in rural than in urban areas.

The proportion of women who have experienced only physical violence, as well as those who have experienced both physical and sexual violence, or have experienced physical or sexual violence, increases with age till the age group 30-39, but then declines somewhat for the oldest age group. Sexual violence only does not increase linearly with age and is highest for women in the age-groups 15-19 and 20-24.

Women's experience of the different types of violence varies greatly by state. In all states, however, physical violence alone tends to be the most common form of violence. Sexual violence rarely occurs without physical violence. Any sexual violence (with or without physical violence) ranges from 1 per cent in Himachal

Table 7.2: Percentage of ever-married women age 15-49 years who have experienced various forms of violence ever or in the 12 months preceding the survey, committed by their husband. India, 2005-06

Type of Violence	*In the Past 12 months*			
	Ever	*Often*	*Some-times*	*Often or Some-times*
Physical violence				
Any form of physical violence	35.1	4.6	1.6	21.4
Pushed her, shook her, or threw something on her	13.6	1.6	6.6	8.2
Slapped her	34.0	3.8	16.3	20.1
Twisted her arm or pulled her hair	15.4	1.9	7.3	9.2
Punched her with his fist or with something that could hurt her	10.9	1.4	5.0	6.4
Kicked her, dragged her, or beat her up	11.5	1.4	5.1	6.6
Tried to choke her or burn her.	2.2	0.4	0.8	1.2
Threatened her or attacked her with a knife, gun, or any other weapon	1.2	0.2	0.5	0.7
Sexual violence				
Any form of sexual violence	10.0	1.7	5.5	7.2
Physically forced her to have sexual intercourse with him even when she did not want to	9.5	1.5	5.3	6.9
Forced her to perform any sexual acts she did not want to	4.6	0.9	2.4	3.4
Emotional violence				
Any form of emotional violence	15.8	2.9	8.3	11.2
Said or did something to humiliate her in front of others	13.1	2.1	0.7	9.1
Threatened to hurt or harm her or someone close to her	5.4	0.9	2.7	3.7
Insulted her or made her feel bad about herself	8.2	1.7	4.1	5.7

Source: Survey 2005-2006.

Table 7.3: Percentage of women who experienced different combination of Physical and Sexual Violence for India (as a whole) and by State

State	*Violence only*	*Violence only*	*And Sexual Violence*	*And Sexual Violence*
India	26.9	1.8	6.7	35.4
Age				
15-19	18.0	1.8	2.7	22.5
15-17	18.6	1.4	1.6	21.6
18-19	17.2	2.4	4.2	23.8
20-24	24.7	2.4	6.2	33.2
25-29	29.7	1.9	8.4	39.9
30-39	30.8	1.7	8.5	41.1
40-49	30.5	1.3	7.2	39.0
Residence				
Urban	23.5	1.1	4.8	29.4
Rural	28.5	2.1	7.6	38.3
Marital Status				
Ever Married	29.7	2.1	8.3	40.1
Never Married	15.7	0.8	0.3	16.9
North				
Delhi	14.9	0.2	1.4	16.5
Haryana	23.4	1.4	4.3	29.0
Himachal Pradesh	4.1	0.3	1.1	5.6
Jammu & Kashmir	10.1	0.9	1.9	12.9
Punjab	25.0	1.0	4.9	30.9
Rajasthan	27.5	4.6	12.6	44.6
Uttaranchal	22.1	0.4	4.2	26.8
Central				
Chhattisgarh	24.0	0.8	5.3	30.1
Madhya Pradesh	37.0	1.4	8.4	46.8
Uttar Pradesh	30.3	1.1	6.7	38.1
East				
Bihar	38.9	2.9	13.8	55.6
Jharkhand	23.5	2.1	9.2	34.8
Orissa	24.5	3.5	8.2	36.2
West Bengal	19.9	6.2	12.2	38.3
North-East				
Arunachal Pradesh	25.1	2.8	7.5	35.5
Assam	24.7	2.2	9.6	36.5

(Contd.)

State	Violence only	Violence only	And Sexual Violence	And Sexual Violence
Manipur	28.8	2.1	7.9	38.9
Meghalaya	14.6	0.4	1.0	16.0
Mizoram	22.9	0.05	2.1	25.5
Nagaland	12.9	3.1	3.0	19.0
Sikkim	16.8	1.6	2.4	20.9
Tripura	28.9	2.5	13.2	44.7
West				
Goa	12.5	0.6	1.8	15.0
Gujarat	20.7	2.2	4.8	27.8
Maharashtra	27.2	0.3	1.7	29.2
South				
Andhra Pradesh	29.9	0.5	3.4	33.8
Karnataka	16.7	0.2	2.9	19.9
Kerala	12.6	1.3	3.4	17.3
Tamil Nadu	36.1	0.0	2.5	38.7

Source: Survey 2005-2006.

Pradesh and Meghalaya to 16 per cent in Tripura, 17 per cent in Bihar and Rajasthan, and 18 per cent in West Bengal. The prevalence of any violence (physical or sexual) is least in Himachal Pradesh, at 6 per cent, followed by Jammu & Kashmir.

A sizeable number of studies indicate that physical abuse of Indian women is quite high ranging from 22 per cent to 60 per cent of women surveyed (Mahajan, 1990; Rao, 1996). The National Crimes Record Bureau revealed a shocking 71.5 per cent increase in cases of torture and dowry deaths during the period from 1991 to 1995 may reflect increased reporting of violence. In 1995, torture of women constituted 29.2 per cent of all reported crimes against women. In another study, 18 to 45 per cent of married men in five districts of Uttar Pradesh agreed that they physically abused their wives (Narayana, 1996). Kumari (1989) found that one out of every four dowry victims was driven to suicide. A frequent perception of domestic violence against women is that it is limited to physical harm perpetrated on adult women within a marital relationship.

The violence against women was recognized as one of the critical areas of concern by India Government in its 1995 country report, for the Fourth World Conference of Women at Beijing. The numbers of violent cases that are reported give just a small indication of the problem. Torture and cruelty by husband or in-laws constituted the major kind of crime amongst all reported forms of violence against women in 1995 accounting for 29 per cent of all reported cases. Moreover, a study on institutional responses to domestic violence was conducted by the women's studies unit at Tata Institute of Social Sciences, Mumbai in 1997-98 to fill this gap. It was found that the two states of Madhya Pradesh and Maharashtra together accounted for 29.7 per cent of total registered crimes against women. Further, Maharashtra registered the highest number of cases of torture and cruelty by husband and/or his relatives (Mitra, 1999; Pooncha & Pandey, 1999; Visaria, 1999). According to United Nations (UN) population fund report, as many as 70 per cent of married women in India between the age of 15-49 are victims of beating, rape or coerced sex. Similarly, in an on-line survey of the *Tribune*, two third of the women reported some forms of psychological, physical or sexual abuses; 42 per cent experience physical beating or sexual assault, 23 per cent suffer abusive language, belittlement and threats. About 36-38 per cent of women in a Tamil Nadu study and 42-48 per cent of women in Uttar Pradesh study reported violence (Jejeebhoy, 1998). In one village in Punjab, 75 per cent of women from Scheduled Caste households reported regular beating (Mahajan, 1990).

India has one of the highest rates of violence during pregnancy. The Washington based International Centre for Research on Women in collaboration with independent researchers has some alarming statistics to conform this trend. 50 per cent of women interviewed, reported to being kicked, beaten or hit when pregnant. 75 per cent of those who reported repeated violence have attempted to commit suicide.

Recently, a survey study was conducted in eastern districts of Gorakhpur by Mishra (2006). She identified a total of 268 registered cases of domestic violence ranging from physical harassments, sexual harassments to dowry deaths within the last 10 months in Gorakhpur and Basti districts. However, there are more than hundred cases for which women could not ask for the judgment.

The statistics available from I.G. and D.I.G. Offices of Gorakhpur and Basti regions indicate that Gorakhpur is two steps forward in violence against women as compared to Basti district. During January to October 2006, a total of 15 cases of dowry deaths in Gorakhpur, 11 cases in Basti and maximum 22 cases in Kushinagar have been registered. The maximum cases of physical harassments have also been reported in Gorakhpur region (19) as compared to Basti region (09). If we look at the statistics of domestic violence, an increment of 10 per cent per year has been observed in registered cases; however, a numerable number of cases are unreported due to the fear of embarrassment and threats particularly from rural area. A close perusal of statistics available reveals that Domestic violence is now an epidemic in our society and it should be considered as a national emergency. The prolific efforts should be made to check this evil.

Contributing Factors of Domestic Violence (D.V.)

The causative factors of D.V. are multifaceted and can occur at multiple points *viz.*, at Ontogenetic level (abusive personality, stress low I.Q.), Micro system level (marital conflict), Exo-system level (isolated, unsafe neighbourhood) and Macro-system level (patriarchy, cultural acceptance). Earlier studies confirmed that domestic violence is rooted in adults (perpetrator's) psychological disturbances and abusive partners were identified as exposed to D.V. in their own childhood (Kempe *et al.*, 1962). However, later studies evinced the role of multiple causative factors, embedded with each other in the root of violence behind closed doors (Flavia, 1988; Pandey, 2007; Straus *et al.*, 1980). In a classical study, Flavia (1988) identified the cases of D.V. in all strata of society at alarming threshold. She explained it in the perspective of learned helplessness, concept given by Seligman (1975). When women were beaten for the first time they were numb with shock and such humiliation left a permanent scar on their psyche. The repeated assaults threaten their well-being and their survival becomes a major issue. At this stage women seek help but wherever they go are sent back without getting any solution, now they have learnt to accept the violence as something inevitable, a fact to live with and die with Flavia (1988). She interpreted her findings on the basis of "Cycle Theory of Violence". In her study most women had similar stories to recall. The husbands were very considerate after a beating. After some time, the tension begins to mount, small fights leading to a big bang and then the calm, loving husband. These experiences support Walker's (1979) "Three-Phase Theory of Wife Battering", (1) a tension building period followed by, (2) acute battering and,

(3) then the calm-loving respite. The women who have experienced such cycles know the pattern well.

Gender Based Socialization

Kishwar (1994) has rightly pointed out that the real killer of women is rooted in the gender based socialization and imposition of all ill customs on daughters. When a girl is married and sent to her husband's family, her parents and family members say, "We are sending your '*Doli*' today may only your *Arthi* (*Ashes*) emerge from that house (husband's house)". Parents guide their daughters to adapt typical feminine traits, i.e. submissiveness, nurturance, dependency and low achievement orientation to successfully carry out their future roles as obedient daughter and dutiful wife. Studies evidenced that sex stereotype is an universal phenomenon and has direct link with violence behind closed doors (Pandey, 2008; Rao & Rao, 1982; Ward & Sethi, 1983).

Women Empowerment and Domestic Violence

Women empowerment plays buffering role in preventing incidences of domestic violence. Contrary to this, de-empowerment was found closely linked with domestic violence, and poor reproductive health status (Kulkarni, 2000; Mahadevan *et al.*, 2005; Pandey, 2008; 2015; Swift & Levin, 1987; Zimmerman *et al.*, 1997). Empowerment refers to the equal opportunity and equal sharing of views by males and females in decision making. In fact the term "Women Empowerment" has different notions. It has various synonyms such as "Gender Equality for Women", "Modernization of Women" and "Empowerment of Women". The concept of empowerment is an elusive one encompassing within it a myriad of rights. But what does empowerment mean in real terms? At what point can we say, we are "empowered"? Thus, the role and empowerment of women have many facets or angels from which it is being tackled. Empowerment of women involves many things; economic opportunity, social equality, and personal rights. Three major areas of empowerment are : (1) educational empowerment—to increase her awareness and capabilities to participate in society, (2) economic empowerment—to decrease her dependency and increase her participation as an economically productive member of the family and society; and (3) legal empowerment—to ensure that her rights and welfare are safeguarded, and to encourage her participation in various forums as an equal member of the society of humankind. A numerable number of researches have evinced the favourable role of empowerment on health and development of women community (Mahadevan *et al.*, 2005; Pandey & Singh, 2004). Despite this, an inverse relationship between empowerment and family violence has been identified. Researchers have considered domestic violence as a state of de-empowerment of women (Pandey, 2007, 2008; Swift & Levin, 1987).

Marital Conflict and Stress

It is well established that people who are stressed in other areas of their life also report being unhappily married. For example, marital satisfaction has been found to co-vary with a diverse range of negative life, job stress, a variety of dysfunctional personality characteristics, and depression. Straus *et al.* (1980) identified that marital conflict and violence are often associated with domestic violence (Gottman, 1979; Weiss & Summers, 1983). Pandey (2008) found positive relationships of stress and family conflict with various forms of women abuses.

Stress-Violence Relationship

In recent years researchers are showing interest to the studies of stress in family environment (Pestonjee,1992). Investigators interested in clarifying the nature of stress and its relationship to family conflict, domestic violence or child development have evinced that a single stressor, such as sudden financial pressure, that may have triggered an abusive episode is not typically sufficient to account for the development of maladaptive behaviour among abuse victim. In most cases, stress can best be described as a dis-equilibrating event that temporily disturbs the functioning of family members and initiates a chain of adaptive or maladaptive response (Rutter, 1983). Similarly, assuming that domestic violence is a form of stress that is linearly connected to certain negative outcomes warrants cautions. The impact of stress is not uniform and seldom predictable, because it depends on factors such as age prior interactions with perpetrator and her interpretation of acts.

Domestic violence is certainly among the worst and most intrusive forms of stress. It impinges directly on the female's daily life, may be ongoing and unpredictable, and is often the result of action or inactions of person whom the female trust and on whom they depend. However, even traumatic events such as abuse, neglect, emotional deprivation and related forms of maltreatment do not affect females in a predictable, characteristic fashion. Rather, their impact depends on many factors, especially the females make up and available supports (Zahn-Waxler, Cole, Welsh & Fox, 1995).

Consequences of Domestic Violence

A sizable number of studies evinced that domestic violence has prevailed at alarming volume in our society and it has adverse impact on overall development, health and well-being of women and children.

Impact of Domestic Violence on Women Health and Well-being

Violence against women has prevailed at epidemic threshold in our society in many forms ranging from harassment to infanticide and homicides. Women victims to domestic violence are at high risk of poor health and well-being. According to World Bank estimates, the domestic violence account of 5 per cent of the healthy years of life lost to women aged 15 to 44 years. in developing countries. A sizable number of studies reported the damging consequences of domestic violence on physical, mental reproductive health status of women (Mahadeven, 2005; Pandey, 2008; Pandey & Mishra, 1993).

In statewise survey research, Luthra (2006) identified that in Punjab women victims of D.V. showed symptom of depression, anxiety, loss of self-steem, eating problems, obsessive-compulsive disorder and post traumatic disorders. Despite this, fatal outcomes like suicide, homicides, were also explored. Anthropological data also pointed out the common symptoms of depression, hopelessness, exhaustion, anger and fear in victims of domestic violence. In a comprehensive study, Pandey (2008) identified positive link between family conflict, stress, domestic violence and physical illness.

The consequences of domestic violence put severe stress on physical and mental health of women. Pandey (2010, 2011) evinced adverse findings suggest that abused women reported significantly more health problems related to physical and psychological illness than their non-abused counterparts. Physical health problems related to respiratory system, digestive system, nervous system and fatigability were found more in abused women. They also expressed high rate of psychological problems concerned with depression, anxiety, sensitivity and tension. Various forms of abuses were found positively linked with physical and psychological illness.

This finding has sample empirical supports. Lewis and Cooper (1988) identified that family conflict and stress were found associated with decreased life satisfaction and also linked with depression and tension. A sizable number of researches have denoted an exclusively favourable linkage between family conflict and stress with physical and psychological illness. Recently, Pandey (2008) explored that family violence was found the strongest predictor of poor physical and mental health of women and children. In a comprehensive study, Pandey (2007, 2008) evinced that children of abused victims exhibited high stress and poor health status. This study identified close links among family conflict, stress, abuses and illness. The result can be explained on the basis of 'Interaction theory' and attachment theory (Bowlby, 1980), which suggest that poor bonds between wife and husband, in-laws are resulted in the form of domestic violence. Kolko (1992) points out that abusive families are characterized by disturbed pattern of attachment. The insecure pattern of attachment causes high level of stress and domestic violence which in turn leads to decreased health status (Crittenden, 1998; Pandey, 2005, 2007).

Issues and Responses

The findings of present study have raised many issues concerning domestic violence (D.V.) and challenges to prevent this evil. A cursory glance at findings of present study reveals that domestic violence is epidemic in our society. A large portion of women community is in the direct trap of this evil (Domestic violence) and not only damaging the dignity, health and well-being of women community but also ruining the overall development of a large segment of women population around the globe. Therefore, it is a great challenge before us to chalk out intervention programmes combining both reactive and proactive strategies to prevent this evil and promote women health and well-being. Thus, to face these challenges, following intervention devices should be exercised:

Develop Systematic Understanding in Public about the Ingredients of Domestic Violence

Prior to designing any intervention programme, it is essential to systematically scrutinize the causative roots of domestic violence from multidimensional approaches. So, it is suggested to plan innovative and imaginative intervention strategies to counteract the prevalence rate of domestic violence in our society as well to develop understanding of causative factors responsible for D.V., So, that incidence of new cases can be checked.

Promote Women Empowerment and Gender Equality Through Socialisation Process

Present studies proved that majority of women are de-empowered in the family, community and at the workplace. They face blatant discriminatory practices and are deprived of sharing equal opportunity in decision-making. So, it is essential to design and implement intervention strategies to empower women economically, educationally, socially and politically. Simultaneously, public should be sensitized toward gender equality, human rights, and non-violence. Since gender inequality and patriarchy are deep-rooted concepts in our familial system developed through the course of social evolution. Thus, the concept of gender equality and human rights should be introduced in the child rearing practices and education system. Such efforts will be instrumental in making women/girl child empowered and healthy.

Prevent Health Hazards in Abused Victims and Generate Health Services

In present study (Pandey, 2008), it was witnessed that a sizable number of abused victims reported poor health status and emotional disorders, i.e., depression, anxiety and stress reactions. However, in the study setting, no adequate medical facility and counselling centres were observed. Community people were also found ignorant or ill informed about the roots of emotional problems and linkages between physical and mental health. They should be correctly informed about the link of domestic violence, emotional trauma and health hazards through education programme. In addition, concerted efforts should be made by community psychologists, family counsellors, health professionals and community leaders, to contact the family and male members (husband/in-laws) who are violent and encourage them to participate in the whole process which will help them to gain better knowledge and insight and this will in turn, be relevant to change the attitude of these people in the positive direction. Further, intervention programme must integrate comprehensive medical and psychological care for abused victims. It is also suggested to generate emergent health services or local hot line services in community setting so that women/ bystanders can receive calls from women organization or can consult for legal, medical or psychological services. These efforts will be relevant in rebuilding and maintaining health and well-being of women and children.

Generate Knowledge Through Awareness Programme and Strengthen Legal Support System

Present study suggests the essence of sensitizing the public and victimized community about issues related to women rights. Therefore, workshops, conferences, meetings, role play and various communication channels should be exercised to cognize public, disadvantaged community and the victim (in particular) of domestic violence.

Looking at the high increasing graph of Domestic violence, Government of India has taken many steps to prevent D.V. Earlier IPC, i.e., the Code of Criminal Procedure, 1973 and the Evidence Act, 1872 were amended to deal effectively not only the cases of dowry deaths but also the cases of domestic violence. Further, Vienna accord of 1994, the Beijing Declaration and the platform for Action 1995 declared that domestic violence (D.V.), is a human rights issue and serious deterrent development of society. Further, the United Nations Committee on Convention of Elimination of All forms of Discrimination Against Women (CEDAW) has recommended that State parties should act to protect women against violence of any kind. Recently, "The Protection of Women from Domestic Violence Act" has been placed by Government of India (Act No. 43 of 2005) on 13th September, 2005, to provide more effective protection of the rights of women, who are victims of any forms occurring within the family. Thus, it is suggested to cognize public, particularly disadvantaged community about the Act (PWDVA) 2005, and Bills to protect women from various forms of crime and discriminations.

Raise Social Support Network and Bystander Intervention

Social support network has pervasive impact to check the incidence of domestic violence and its consequences. Such efforts create public awareness about the causes, consequences and responses to domestic violence Sometimes, informal groups (neighbours, bystanders) play prominent role as compared to media in activating personal risk of victimization and effort to avoid such victimization (Pandey, 2008; Pandey and Mishra, 2000).

The role of 'Bystanders' in the prevention of D.V., can hardly be denied. They are treated as 'eye to ears' of the police, for such purpose immediate neighbours, friends, relatives, other family members and local residents can serve as bystanders and can help to save victims from crimes. Sometimes, these people ignore to intervene at very early stage because of negative experiences. Public should be sensitised to take initiative and those who intervene should be rewarded and appreciated by the society and Government organizations.

Continue Communication with Global Support System

To check the incidence and prevalence rate of domestic violence, global efforts are essential. Thus, appropriate responses to D.V., should occur from local level (Community or setting) to Government level. Voluntary agencies should also be added with macro level intervention programme. The needs of the disadvantaged group should be kept in the main focus of programme. This combined effort will help to eradicate this evil from our society.

Re-conceptualise Domestic Violence and Develop Innovative Research Strategy and Intervention Programmes

Since domestic violence is considered a universal psycho-social phenomenon, however, the nature and forms of abuse vary from one culture to other culture. There is a need to re-conceptualise domestic violence emphasising contextual and cross-cultural perspectives. Despite this, innovative, imaginative and social action oriented research strategies and intervention programmes should be developed to study the multifaceted dynamics of domestic violence and its damaging consequences on women health and development. It is also essential to bridge the gap between academic and professional roles. This holistic approach will be instrumental to prevent incidence and prevalence rates of domestic violence and promoting health and well-being of women around the world.

References

Flavia, A., (1988). "Violence in the Family: Wife Beating", In: R. Ghadially (ed.) *Women in Indian Society,* New Delhi: Sage.

Ghadially, R. (ed.) (1988). *Women in Indian Society,* New Delhi: Sage.

Jaffe, P.G., Lemon, N.K.D. & Poisson, S.E. (2003). *Child Custody and Domestic Violence: A Call for Safety and Accountability,* Sage, U.K.: London.

Kumari, R. (1989). *Brides are not for Burning: Dowry Victims in India.* New Delhi: Radiant Publisher.

Lewis, S.C. & Cooper, C.L. (1988). "Stress in Dual Career Families", In: Gutek, B.A. Stongberg, A.H., Larwood, L. (eds.) *Women and Work: An Annual Review,* Vol. 31, Beverly Hills, C.A.: Sage Publications.

Mahadeven, K., *et al.* (2005). "Empowerment of Women Through Health Education for Healthy Living of Mother and Children", In: S. Krishna, S.K. Kumar & V.K. Panikkar (eds.), *Health Promotion, Prevention of HIV/AIDS and Population Regulation: Strategies for Developing Countries,* New Delhi: B.R. Publishing Corporation.

Mahajan, A. (1990). "Investigators of Wife Battering", In: Sooshma Sood (ed.), *Violence against Women,* Jaipur: Arihant Publisher.

Mitra, N. (2006). "Best Practices among Responses to Domestic Violence in Maharashtra and Madhya Pradesh", In: N. Duvvury (Project

Director ICRW) *Domestic Violence in India* : A Summary Report, U.S.A.: Washington, DC.

Narayana, G. (1996). *Family Violence, Sex and Reproductive Behaviour among Men in Uttar Pradesh,* India.

Pandey, S. (2005). "Child Abuse: An Impediment to the Development of Creative Potential in Children", *Psychological Studies,* 15, 234-242.

Pandey, S., & Mishra, B. (2000). "Dowry and Status of Women in India". In: K. Mahadevan, GAO Ersheng, Yu Jing Yuan, R. Jayasree, A.K.M. Nurun Nabi, P. Rajaram, F. Bourdier, P.J. Reddy, V.K.R. Kumar and V.M. Sandeep (eds.), *Reproductive Health of Humankind in Asia and Africa: A Global Perspective,* New Delhi: B.R.P.C.

Pandey, S. (2008). *Psycho-Social Aspect of Domestic Violence,* New Delhi: Concept Publishing Company (P) Ltd.

Rao, V. (1996). "Wife Beating in Rural South India: A Qualitative and Economic Analysis", *Social Science Medicine,* 1-12.

Ruttar, M. (1983). "Stress, Coping and Development in Children: Some Issue and Some Questions", In: N. Garmezy & M. Rutter (eds.), *Stress, Coping and Development in Children,* New York: McGraw-Hill.

Sekaran, U. (1985). "Enhancing the Mental Health of Dual Career Family Couple", *Indian Journal of Applied Psychology,* 22, 57-62.

Seligman, C., Bush, M. & Krisch, K. (1975). "Relationship between Compliance in the Foot in the Door Paradime and Size of First Request", *Journal of Personality and Social Psychology,* 33, 517-520.

Straus, M.A., Gelles, R.J. & Steinmetz, S.K. (1980). *Behind Closed Doors: Violence in the American Family.* Beverly Hills, C.A.: Sage.

Visario, L. (1999). "Violence against Women in India: Evidence from Rural Gujarat", In: N. Duvvury (Project Director ICRW) *Domestic Violence in India: A Summary Report,* U.S.A.: Washington, DC.

Zahn-Waxler, C., Cole, P.M. Welsh, J.D. & Fox, N.A. (1995). Psychological Correlates of Empathy and Pro-social Behaviours in Pre-school Children with Behaviour Problems, *Development of Psychopathology,* 7, 27-48.

8

Son Preference and Declining Sex Ratio

Causes and Implications

Manju Mishra

Introduction

The latest Census of India (2011) revealed that the child sex-ratio (number of girls per 1,000 boys among children in the age group 0-6 years old) is at its lowest since 1947, when India gained her independence. India's skewed sex ratio and son preference (Kishor, 1993) have persisted since 1901 and have not eroded despite the tremendous economic strides India has made through liberalization and globalization (Miller, 1981; Arnold, Choe, and Roy, 1998). One of the most alarming trends in India is that son preference, which can be a normal attribute for couples who have only girls, is accompanied by the neglect and death of millions of females through lack of medical care, improper nutrition, infanticide, and sex selective abortions (Arnold, Kishor, and Roy, 2002). This is occurring even among the educated, affluent groups in India (*Times of India*, 2010). Sen (1992, 2003) first addressed this disturbing trend by recognizing that millions of women in India and China are missing because of widespread neglect in nutrition, health care, and prenatal care. India and China are the only countries in the world in which female infant mortality rates are higher than that of males (United Nations, 2011). The skewed child sex ratio in India is a shameful testimony to how girls and women are devalued in India.

This chapter analyses the trend of son preference and declining sex ratio in India. It aims to answer significant questions.

1. What are social, cultural and economic causes favouring son preference?
2. What are consequences of declining sex ratio for the women and the nation itself?

The chapter is divided into three sections:

Section I: This section gives the overview of trends of son preference and neglect of daughters in India.

Section II: This section presents the social, cultural and economic causes of son preference and decline of sex ratio.

Section III: This section presents the implementations of declined sex-ratio and paucity of women in the society.

SECTION I
SON PREFERENCE AND NEGLECT OF DAUGHTERS IN INDIA

A. Trends in Son Preference in India

Table 8.1 shows trends in the child sex ratio among the different states in India from 1981 to 2011 (Census of India, 1981, 1991, 2001, 2011). Table 8.1 shows some interesting trends in regional variations in child sex ratios during the last four decades. Overall, the child sex ratio in India and the six broad regions is declining every year since 1981. The northern and western states have the lowest child sex ratio while the southern and eastern states have relatively higher child sex ratios, and this trend has been consistent for decades. The last column in Table 8.3 shows the relative gains or declines in the child sex ratios from 1981 to 2011 in the individual states. The largest decline in child sex ratios are observable in the northern states of Jammu and Kashmir, Haryana, Punjab, Rajasthan, and Himachal Pradesh in the north, Maharashtra in the west, and Madhya Pradesh in central India. The states of Kerala in south India and Mizoram in North-eastern India show the least decline in child sex-ratios over the last four decades.

Table 8.1: Sex-Ratio (Females per 1,000 Males) of Child Population 0-6 years of age (1981-2011)

India/States	*1981*	*1991*	*2001*	*2011*	*Decline in Sex-Ratio since 1981*
India	**962**	**945**	**927**	**914**	**48**
NORTH					
Delhi	926	915	868	867	59
Haryana	902	879	819	830	72
Himachal Pradesh	971	951	896	906	65
Jammu & Kashmir	964	–	941	859	105
Punjab	908	875	798	846	62
Rajasthan	954	916	909	883	71
Uttarakhand	–	949	908	886	–
CENTRAL					
Chhattisgarh	–	984	975	964	–
Madhya Pradesh	977	941	932	912	65
Uttar Pradesh	935	927	916	899	36
EAST					
Bihar	981	953	942	933	48
Jharkhand	–	979	965	943	–
Orissa	995	967	953	934	61
West Bengal	981	967	960	950	30
NORTH–EAST					
Arunachal Pradesh	997	982	964	960	37
Assam	–	975	965	957	–
Manipur	986	974	957	934	52
Meghalaya	991	986	973	970	21
Mizoram	986	969	964	972	14
Nagaland	988	993	964	944	44
Sikkim	978	965	963	944	34
Tripura	972	967	966	953	19
WEST					
Goa	965	964	938	920	45
Gujarat	947	938	883	886	61
Maharashtra	956	946	913	883	73
SOUTH					
Andhra Pradesh	992	975	961	943	49
Karnataka	975	960	946	943	21
Kerala	970	958	960	960	10
Tamil Nadu	967	948	942	946	21

Sources: Ramaiah *et al.*, 2011; Census of India, 1981, 1991, 2001, 2011.

Table 8.2 shows ten districts in India with the worst child sex-ratio in 2001 and 2011 (Census of India, 2001 and 2011). Most of the districts are located in the northern states of Punjab and

Table 8.2: Ten Districts with the Lowest Child Sex Ratios in India (2001 and 2011)

2001			2011		
District	*State*	*Child Sex-Ratio*	*District*	*State*	*Child Sex-Ratio*
Fatehgarh Sahib	Punjab	766	Jhajjhar	Haryana	774
Patiala	Punjab	777	Mahendragarh	Haryana	778
Manasa	Punjab	782	Rewari	Haryana	784
Bathinda	Punjab	785	Samba	Jammu & Kashmir	787
Kapurthala	Punjab	785	Sonipat	Haryana	790
Sangrur	Punjab	786	Jammu	Jammu & Kashmir	794
Gurudaspur	Punjab	789	Bid	Maharashtra	800
Kurukshetra	Haryana	771	Ambala	Haryana	806
Ambala	Haryana	782	Rohtak	Haryana	807
Sonipat	Haryana	788	Pithoragarh	Uttarakhand	812

Sources: Ramaiah *et al.*, 2011. Census of India, 2001 & 2011.

Haryana, displaying child sex ratios as low as 766 girls per 1,000 boys.

Overall, the northern and western states uniformly show low child sex ratios across decades and demonstrate very high son preference (Bhaskar & Gupta, 2007, Bhat, 2002, Retherford and Roy, 2003). Sex selective abortions in northern and western regions are higher than the national average in India. According to Kulkarni (2007), 19 per cent of expected female births in Punjab during 2001 were aborted.

B. Neglect of Female Infants and Girls in India

One of the reasons behind the declining child sex ratio can be attributed to higher female infant deaths in India. Table 8.3 shows the infant mortality rate for all states and union territories in India in 2010 (Sample Registration Survey, 2011). Infant mortality rate refers to deaths of children from 0-12 months per 1,000 live births (Sample Registration System, SRS, 2010). The overall infant mortality rate in 2008 was 47 per 1,000 live births. The male infant mortality rate of 46 exceeds the female rate of 49. The same pattern of higher mortality rates for girls compared to boys is reflected in all the states in India. The state of Kerala in the south has the lowest

Table 8.3: Infant Mortality Rate by Sex and Residence, 2010 (Death of Children from 0-12 months per 1,000 live births)

India/States	*Total*	*Male*	*Female*
India	**47**	**46**	**49**
NORTH			
Delhi	30	29	31
Haryana	48	46	49
Himachal Pradesh	40	35	47
Jammu & Kashmir	43	41	45
Punjab	34	33	35
Rajasthan	35	52	57
Uttarakhand	38	37	39
CENTRAL			
Chhattisgarh	51	48	54
Madhya Pradesh	62	62	63
Uttar Pradesh	61	58	63
EAST			
Bihar	48	46	50
Jharkhand	42	41	44
Orissa	61	60	61
West Bengal	31	29	32
NORTH-EAST			
Arunachal Pradesh	31	31	32
Assam	58	56	60
Manipur	14	11	16
Meghalaya	55	55	56
Mizoram	37	36	39
Nagaland	23	19	28
Sikkim	30	28	32
Tripura	27	25	29
WEST			
Goa	10	6	15
Gujarat	44	41	47
Maharashtra	28	27	29
SOUTH			
Andhra Pradesh	46	44	47
Karnataka	38	37	39
Kerala	13	13	14
Tamil Nadu	24	23	24

Sources: Registrar General of India, Sample Registration System, 2010.

female infant mortality rate and gender discrepancies in infant mortality rates. Globally, more males are born than females, but biologically female infants have higher survival rates than male infants (Hammond, 1977; United Nations, 2011). However, the opposite trend is observed in India (Das Gupta, 1987) pointing to the possibility of girl devaluation and discrimination, neglect of infants through inadequate nutrition and health care (Pande & Astone, 2003), infanticide, and sex specific abortions. This has led to the growing concern in India and in the international community about the issue of "missing females" (Sen, 1992, 2003; Agnihotri, 2000; Sudha & Rajan, 1999).

The heterogeneity in infant female mortality rates across the different states in India can be challenging for policy-makers. Access to economic resources and economic development of the states cannot explain the differential trends in infant mortality in the various states in India. Literacy and educational attainment are also not correlated with infant mortality trends. Table 8.3 shows that some states, such as Assam, Orissa, Uttar Pradesh, and Madhya Pradesh have very high female and male mortality rates. These states are some of the poorest states in India; hence lack of adequate nutrition, medical care, prenatal care, and illiteracy can partly explain the high mortality rates. On the other hand, the state of Mizoram in the north-east is not very advanced economically, yet the infant mortality rates for females are much lower than the above mentioned states. Among the tribal population in Mizoram, females actively participate in social and family making decisions, and girls are valued as much as boys. The tribes in Mizoram have maintained their culture because they are physically isolated from the Hindus and have not been pressured to change their culture or conform to upper caste Hindu traditions (Mitra, 2008). The state of Kerala in the south has the lowest female infant mortality rate in India. Although Kerala is facing many economic challenges, it has the highest gender and human development index in the country. Affluent and relatively educated states like Punjab and Haryana in the north do not display low infant female mortality rates.

SECTION II
CAUSES OF DECLINING SEX RATIO

Skewed sex ratio cannot be put down to natural or biological factors, but it is most likely due to socio-cultural and economic factors. While deprivation and malnutrition are some of the economic factors that has been used to explain existing imbalances, whereas infanticide, feticide, dowry deaths, infant mortality among female and discrimination in their health care have been understood to be the result of specific socio-cultural practices which are responsible for lasting consequences.

Indian society is patriarchal society, i.e. a male oriented society and there is a strange invisibility of girl child. Based on purely biological factors number of females should exceed or at least equal the numbers of males in a given population. However, this is not the case in India in general and north India in particular. The short-fall of women has termed as missing women or declining sex ratio. India's sex ratio has been declining over century from 972 in 1901 to 940 in 2011, i.e. a drop of 32 points and there are various reasons for such a wide gap between male-female ratios. According to census 2011, the declining sex ratio in India is due to "neglect of the girl child resulting in their higher mortality at younger age, high maternal mortality, sex selective female abortions, female infanticide and change in sex ratio at birth" (Census of India, 2001: 91). Thus, there are number of causes for declining sex ratio in such a complex patriarchal Indian society, where son preference is a deep-rooted social value. It is found that crime against girl children (women) are committed by most impoverished and desperate that is far from true. In the heart of the most prosperous pocket of the country there is a darkness that has manifested it self in some of the most daming statistics to emerge from the 2001 census in previous chapter. As independent India move ahead its attitude toward the girl child has, as the census 2001 suggests, regressed to the Dark Age. What is more revealing is that the imbalance is most pronounced in some of India's wealthiest parts. The worst offenders are Haryana, Punjab, Delhi and Rajasthan. The fashionable and most affluent district of Delhi has witnessed a 50 point drop in the past decade (Desai & Patel, 1985: 20).

In this way, the physical neglect of females, female infanticide, sex selective abortion etc. are evident in Indian society and the degree to which these practices occur can vary from region to region due to various other factors. In north Indian states, there are number of factors which are responsible for such practices like sex selective abortion, infanticide, practice of dowry (bringing girl child is like the watering of neighbouring plant), hypergamous marriage, preference of male child for *moksha* (material and spiritual advancement of their parents) etc. These later practice obviously comprise the lowest level of unequal opportunity by their very nature of threatening existence; however they are categorically different than discrimination and domination because they tend to be motivated by social, economical and religious pressures rather than gender ideologies. It is estimated that 1.20 crore girls are born in India every year, about one-fourth die before their fifteenth birthday because of female infanticide, discrimination in health care and maternal mortality, malnutrition and as a victims of rape, dowry death and molestation (Bhadra, 1999, Ghadially, 1988). Thus, there is a social acceptance of neglect of girl child which is rooted in Indian traditional social structures, institutions and ethos, and this is almost a pan-Indian phenomena. Following are the major causes of declining sex ratio in north India.

Female Infanticide

Female infanticide is an age-old practice among human populations to regulate the numbers of children and eliminate the unwanted offspring. It was prevalent among the Greeks, the Romans etc., and it is little known in India prior to the Britishers. Female infanticide was first noticed by Jonathan Duncan who while residing at Banaras, found it to be prevalent in the Rajkumars and the Raghuvanshi clans of Rajputs of Benaras Division in 1789. He also discovered the same practice among the Rajput of Kathiawar and Kuch. This practice was also noticed by William Carey in 1794, when he witnessed "the dedication of children to Ganges, to be devoured by crocodiles and sharks." Near his home at Ganga Sagar (Calcutta), where a grand festival was held every year, Carey saw that mothers threw their children into the sea. However, since then, female infanticide has been widely prevalent in spite of the Female Infanticide Act, 1870 (The Act). Abolishing the practice of infanticide in India) amongst several communities like the Rajputs, the Khatris, the Gkkhars, the Khochars, the Malhotras, the Seths, the Bedis, the Moyal Brahmans, the pure Pathans, the Mohammendans (Muslims) of Punjab, the Jats (Sikhs of Punjab) etc. (Goswami, 2007: 39-79). Regionally, the practice of female infanticide was/is confined mainly to the northern part of India from Gujarat in the West to the eastern border of Uttar Pradesh, the only example of infanticide from north-eastern India is that of tribal Nagas. Examples from the central (Madhya Pradesh) and south India are very few. These scattered examples of infanticide outside north India are provocative cases demanding their own explanation, that these groups, like so many tribal groups, practiced infanticide primarily because of its "family planning" effects. Thus, daughters /girls are drowned in the basin of milk, poisoned by opium applied to the breast of mothers, and strangulated to death are some of the methods being used by these communities to eliminate the girl child (Miller, 1997).

Historically, the main reasons for this practice in India included the system of hypergamy, whereby women must marry into a social group above their own, a custom which forbids the marriage of a women with a person of lower social standing. This invariably led to the giving of a large dowry to secure a bridegroom of high caste or of high social status, moreover, the marriage customs like the touching of knee or taking hold of the knee of the bridegroom by the bride father, further worsened the whole scenario and hence persons of high caste, unwilling to humble themselves for the sake of a daughter. Thus, the financial burden of marying of a daughter, the social status of high caste and social stigma of having an unmarried daughter at home, forced people to kill (their daughter) infant girl at birth. There were also some superstitious beliefs which lent credence to prevalence of female infanticide. A common belief was that if you kill a female child, the next one is sure to be male. Another belief was that, female children bring ill luck to the family, and could bring possible disgrace to the family honour because of their youthful exuberances. Thus, practice of female infanticide in India in general and north India in particular did not arise from any religious motive. It develops under specific conditions and was conditioned by particular political, social and economic circumstances. It was a practice which arouse out of social customs, clan and marriage (Goswami, 2007).

Sex Selective Abortion Practice of Female Foeticide

The availability of parental sex determination tests and abortions was a boon for those desiring to rid themselves of daughter. Infanticide, although widely practiced, was associated with a certain amount of guilt. Since many Indians believe that the soul does not enter the fetus until the end of the second trimester of gestation, sex selective abortions removes the stain of sin and guilt and is therefore far more morally acceptable.

Sex determination tests became big business shortly after their introduction in India in the 1970s. Billboards stating, "Invest

Rs. 500 now, save Rs. 50,000 later" were designed to encourage prospective parents to abort female fetuses and save on a future dowry (Kusum, 1993). Posters in train stations promoted sex determination together with an abortion for just Rs. 70. Clinics distributed flyers advertising their services. As the number of clinics grew, competition pushed down the prices of the services, making them more affordable to the lower middle class. From 1982 to 1987, the number of clinics for sex determination increased from less than 10 to 248 in Bombay alone. Even more alarming was a study of centres in Bombay which revealed that out of 8000 abortions in sex hospitals preceded by aminocentesis, 7,999 were female fetuses. Between 1978 to 1982, according to one report, 78,000 female fetuses were aborted after a sex determination test (Kusum, 1993; Shah, 1992). In another study, 430 out of 450 female fetuses were aborted in one hospital, while none of 250 male fetuses were aborted even when there was evidence of genetic problem (Ramanamma, 1980).

Social Context

To understand the social context in which the practice of sex selective abortion exists and, in fact flourishes, we should first examine the cultural basis of son preference in India. The reasons behind that has been called "*son mania*" are both multifaceted and deeply imbedded in Indian culture (Ramanamma, 1980). They are also unfortunately inextricably entwined with a corresponding discrimination against daughters. In the ancient Indian text, the *Atharva Veda, mantras* are written to change the sex of the foetus from a girl to a boy. A son's birth is likened to "a sunrise in the abode of gods" and "to have a son is as essential as taking food at least once a day", whereas a daughter's birth is a cause for great sadness and disappointment (Ramanamma, 1980).

Indian society is patrilineal, patriarchal and patrilocal. Sons carry on the family name. They are also charged with the task of supporting their parents in old age. Parents live as extended families with their sons, daughter-in-laws, and grandchildren. Daughters, on the other hand, become part of their husband's family after marriage and do not make any further contributions to their birth parents. Indian sayings such as, "Bringing up a girl is like watering a neighbour's plant", and "The girl who has married is like the spittle which has been spat out, and no longer belongs to the parents", exemplify the feeling of wasted expenditure on raising a daughter (Jeffery, 1984).

Indian men are also responsible for the funeral rites of their parents and are the only ones who can light the funeral pyre. Some feel that they will only be able to achieve *moksha* (transcending the circle of reincarnation via the performance of good deeds) through their sons. Thus, the importance of having sons continues beyond even this life in Indian culture.

A very important factor contributing to son preference is that of economics. Daughters, for several reasons, are an economic liability to families whereas sons are a great asset. One of the most publicized reasons for this disparity is the dowry system. In many parts of India, particularly in the North, the parents of the bride must give money and gifts to the groom's family as part of the marriage agreement. Formerly, dowries were only expected in high caste marriages where the bride would not be expected to work in the fields and was thus presumed to be an economic burden on her husband. The bride's family, therefore, compensated the groom's family with a dowry.

Presumably in an attempt to emulate higher castes, the custom of dowry giving has, over the past several decades, spread throughout the social structure in India. Lower castes, viewing dowry as a status symbol, have adopted the custom with even more zeal than the upper castes: "the Brahmanical form of marriage with dowry is often considered more prestigious and when castes attempt to upgrade themselves they frequently assume this form of marriage payment" (Miller, 1981). The dowries, in present times, frequently cost the bride's family two to three times their yearly income. Refusal to offer a dowry seals a girl's fate as a spinster and shames the family name. Failure to deliver the offered dowry or honor further requests may result in a so-called "dowry death" or "bride burning" in which the groom's family kills the bride to allow the groom to remarry and bring in a more substantial dowry. Furthermore, in some groups, the gift-giving continues after the marriage.

Another economic disadvantage of daughters in India is their relatively low earning potential. As in many other countries, although the women work as hard or harder than their male counterparts, they make very little money. The long hours spent cooking, cleaning, and caring for the children are viewed as "sitting at home all day". Even the time spent in the fields is not considered significant since the men do much of the heavy lifting. Frequently illiterate, due to lack of schooling, women in India are generally unable to obtain high-paying work and are therefore financially dependent on the men in the family. As a result, it is felt to be to a family's economic advantage to minimize the number of daughters.

Since many of the reasons behind son preference are economically based, it is ironic that the most extreme sex ratios are seen in the higher castes who tend to have most of the wealth (Miller, 1981). The reason for discrimination against daughters in these groups seems to be related more to issues of family pride than to concern over money. Indian culture requires that a girl marry into a family with a caste equivalent to or, preferably, higher than her own. She then adopts that caste as her own and is thus "elevated." Boys, conversely, are encouraged to marry below their castes to maximize dowry potential. As a result, it is frequently difficult to find an appropriate husband for a daughter of an upper class family, which has the potential for putting great shame on the household. In addition, some of the higher castes, such as the Rajputs, are Kshatriyas which translates as warriors. These groups take great pride in their fierceness. Daughters do not fit well into their culture and are potentially a source of vulnerability in the family. Sons, on the other band, are a source of pride and strength: "the role of sons in exerting control over farm resources, in protecting the community against dacoits, and in the army of the state...may have been factors militating for the generalized preference for sons" (Machlachian, 1982). The Rajputs and the other warrior castes are cited throughout the literature for their liberal use of infanticide prior to the advent of sex determination techniques (Freed, 1989; Miller, 1981; Machlachian, 1982).

Unsafe Motherhood and Unsafe Abortion

There are no reliable estimates of maternal deaths available for the country. The maternal mortality is calculated as the number of maternal deaths per 1,00,000 live births. This is an indicator of how safe motherhood is. This is also greatly responsible for declining sex ratio in India. India's maternal mortality is highest in south Asia 540 deaths per 1,00,000 live births or one women dying roughly every five minutes. An estimated 1,36,000 women die in India every year due to pregnancy related setbacks. The number of maternity related deaths which occur in a week in India is equivalent to what occur in a whole year in Europe. One of the reason why women in India succumb to reproduction related complication is the lack of timely transportation to the nearest hospital (Azmi, 2007, *Times of India,* 8th March, 2007) the rate of maternal mortality vary from state to state, from 28 in Gujarat to 707 in Uttar Pradesh for the year 1998. But according to the National Health Survey-3, the maternal mortality ratio is estimated to have been declined from 400 maternal death per 1,00,000 live birth in 1997-98 to 300 in 2001-03 (NFHS-3, 2005-6:4). From this statistics, it is clear though the maternal mortality is responsible for declining sex-ratio but female foeticide is much more than it as it reduced by 100 as compared to 1998. Among the direct causes of maternal deaths, obstructed labour due to mal-position and mal-presentation of uterus is the most prominent one. Anaemia along with tuberculosis is among the indirect causes of maternal death. Poor nutrition, inadequate and imbalance diets, stemming as much from economic poverty as from the discriminatory treatment meted out from childhood resulted in the poor health conditions of women as they grow up. Lack of awareness and discriminative attitude towards women are much more responsible for maternal mortality in India.

Child Mortality Rate

According to NFHS-3 Infant Mortality is 57 per 1000 live birth as a whole, it is 56.3 for male children and 57.7 for female children, but the child mortality is 14.2 for male and 22.9 for female children. Thus, it is responsible for declining sex ratio in India, though NFHS-3 recorded decline in infant mortality from 77 in 1998 to 57 in 2005. In this way, there is discrimination among the sexes. Girl child is discriminated against even when it comes to breast feeding, supplementary nutrition and care giving, some time the female baby is never fed by their parents and leave to die due to ill prejudice and bias attached to them and due to the forthcoming fear of dowry. Thus, female disadvantages in child mortality is rightly taken as one of the indicators of gender bias in India and large number of death in early childhood account for the skewedness in the overall sex-ratio.

SECTION III
CONSEQUENCES OF DECLINING SEX-RATIO

Declining sex ratio has many potentially serious consequences. Although there are no historical model by which to learn about the implications of a lack of women relative to men, it is obvious social consequences is that there are not enough women for men to marry and the institution of marriage would lose its relevance. This scarcity of brides might lead to the child betrothal and early marriage (child marriage) to cope with the problem. Increasing numbers of child brides will further contribute to the poor status of women, as will be less likely to finish the school or develop skills before marriage. Young brides and their children are also more likely to suffer from the increased morbidity and mortality associated with early child birth Thus, there are serious socio-economic and health implications of declining sex ratio (Makinson,1985). Another consequence of scarcity of women is the increase in dowry, i.e. payment of exorbitant dowry, daughter are often sold to higher castes and even poor man often pay a bride price to obtain a wife. Among the Jats in particular and various other in general, the scarcity of women led to widespread system of polyandry.

Thus, if this trend of gender imbalance continues one of the serious repercussions would be a rude shock to the institution of marriage in the decades to come. It has severe consequences especially in North Indian states of Punjab and Haryana which are characterized by inability of men in marriageable age to find suitable partner, *The Hindustan Times*, July 12, 2003 read as "in Hathin (Haryana), because of shortage of women men buying brides from other states like Assam, West Bengal and from far away villages of Bihar. The price put on such a girl is much less than what people pay for cattle, after marriage they are condemned to a life of slavery(Jain, 2006: 22).

An associated phenomenon is the abduction and trafficking of girls. Thus, shortage of brides would be resulted in expansion of the sex industry with the magnitude of spreading Sexually Transmitted Diseases (STDs) and deadly disease like HIV/AIDS would increase manifold. In this distorted social scenario marked by growing anti-social behaviour, crimes against women like rape, molestation, eve-teasing, child marriages, forced polyandry etc. is also expected to rise. The state of Haryana has seen a drastic increase in prostitution, violence and rapes against women in recent years (Singh & Mohan, 2005).

Conclusion

On the basis of the discussion above we can conclude that son preference and declining sex ratio has their roots deeply rooted in our patriarchal culture. This is not due to any biological or natural factors, but socio-cultural and economic factors are responsible for the son preference and neglect of daughters in India. Prenatal sex determination test also have contributed in sex selective abortions. Female foetus is being killed in mother's womb after detecting her sex. Infanticide, maternal and child mortality, son preference for attaining *moksha* are some important factors responsible for the decline of sex ratio over the years in India. This skewed sex ratio has serious negative implications for women's health, fertility choices and future well-being of girls. Balancing this gap is very essential for the well-being of women and the nation. Women are essential part of India's labour force. Policy-makers should seriously look into this matter and should do concrete efforts to handle this situation. If this situation will not be controlled, the nation will have to pay serious costs. I sum up the discussion by quoting Barbara Miller's summary of cultural basis of sex selective abortions and infanticide in India:

> "It has often noted that in Indian thought, the process of creation and destruction are inseparable, that one is the necessary counterpart of the other. Indeed, the creation can come only from destruction. Fertility and mortality, growth and decay, female and male are likewise conjoined in a dramatic dynamic that unfolds in this book – (*Endangered Sex*). For this is a story of how the birth of some inexorably brings the death of others, of how the survival of males feeds on the demise of females, of how the intense desire for sons is directly tied to the fatal neglect of daughters. The light and dark of Indian culture, the giving and taking, the benign and malign are simultaneously expressed in a twisted, tortured dance whose tempo continually increases. It is the time for the dance to end."

References

Agnihotri, S.D. (2000). *Sex Ratio Patterns in the Indian Population: A Fresh Exploration*, New Delhi: Sage Publications.

Arnold F., Kishor S., & Roy, T.K. (2002). "Sex Selective Abortions in India", *Population and Development Review*, 28(4), 759-785.

Kishor, S. (1993). "May God give sons to all: Gender and child mortality in India", *American Sociological Review*, 58, 247-265.

Miller, B. (1981). *The Endangered Sex: Neglect of Female Children in Rural North India*, Ithaca: Cornell University Press.

Mitra A. & Singh, P. (2007). "Human Capital Attainment and Gender Empowerment: The Kerala Paradox", *Social Science Quarterly*, 88(5), 1227-1242.

Mitra A. & Singh, P. (2006) "Human Capital Attainment and Women's Status In the Labour Market: The Kerala Puzzle", *Journal of Economic Issues*, Vol. XL, No. 3.

National Sample Registration Survey, 2011.

Sen, A. (1992). "Missing Women", *The British Medical Journal*, 304: 586-587.

Singh, M. & Mohan V. (2005). "The Rise of Sex Selection in India", *Democracy at Large*, (I), 30-32.

Sudha, S. & Rajan., S.I. (1999). "Female Demographic Disadvantage in India, 1991: Sex Selective Abortions and Female Infanticide 1981-1991", *Development and Change*, 30(2), 585-591.

Bumiller E. (1990). *May you be the Mother of a Hundred Sons: A Journey among the Women of India*, New York: Ballantine Books.

Jeffery, R. & Jeffery P. (1984). "Female Infanticide and Amniocentesis." *Social Science and Medicine*, 19(11), 1207-12.

Kusum (1993). "The Use of Pre-natal Diagnostic Techniques for Sex Selection: The Indian Scene." *Bioethics*, 7 (2/3), 149-65.

Machlachian, M.D. 1982. "Comments on 'The Mania for Sons' (Ramanamma)", *Social Science and Medicine*, 16, 879-85.

Makinson C. (1985). "The Health Consequences of Teenage Fertility." *Family Planning Perspectives*, 17 (3), 132-9.

Miller B. (1981). *The Endangered Sex: Neglect of Female Children in Rural North India*, Ithaca, N.Y.: Cornell University Press.

Ramanamma, A. & Bambawale, U. (1980). "The Mania for Sons: An Analysis of Social Values in South Asia." *Social Science and Medicine*, 14B (2), 107-10.

Shah, A. & Taneja, S. (1992). "What do Males and Females of Delhi think about Female Foeticide". *Indian Journal of Social Science*, 5 (1), 81-92.

9

Dowry Victimization and its Impact on Women and Girl Child

Sushma Pandey, Niharika Tripathi and *Pratibha Singh*

Researchers from different disciplines have shown their concern in understanding the nature and problems of dowry in the case of Indian women. It is rather paradoxical that in a country like India where it is said, *"Yatra Naryastu Pujyante Ramantey Tatra Devatah"*—*Manusmriti*—there are plenty of evidences of bride burning and torture of women by men are witnessed.

This chapter is an attempt to derive the social psychological roots of dowry victimization and real status of women in ancient as well as in modern times. At the same time the problems caused by dowry on Indian women and other factors contributing to such downfall along with remedies provided by government and organizations have been its focus.

Conceptualization of Dowry

It is customary in Indian society that the bride's parents give gift (dowry) to the groom and his family at the time of their daughter's marriage. The history of such customs and the general economics involved have been properly documented (Nair, 1978; Pandey & Mishra, 2000; Rajaraman, 1983; Sambrani & Sambrani, 1983; Srinivas,1984). Dowry is defined in terms of, "the property brought by wife at the time of her marriage when she is required to leave her parents home and join the household of her husband". The ancient book *"Smriti"* recommends the giving of suitable ornaments to the bride but the extent of price is left to the desire of bride's parents/guardians. Earlier, the dowry was given in a very simple and voluntary form. In the present time, dowry is not considered as a gift or *'Daan'*, but rather demand for cash and various household goods made by the groom and his family on the bride's parents without any concern for the capabilities of the bride's parents. It is supposed to be all right till it becomes difficult for the bride's parents to meet the demands. Consequently, it leads to dowry deaths and attempts for suicide by young women whose parents fail to fulfill the demands of the groom's parents or the groom himself. Thus, the dowry problem has become a matter of serious concern specially among the upper and middle classes of rural and urban people.

A number of restrictions imposed on people in the name of rules of marriages have also strengthened the continuation of the dowry system. The caste endogamy and clan exogamy and *'anuloma'*, (highpergamy) and *'pratiloma'* (highpogamy) have been misinterpreted and misused and thus, they have restricted the choice of a mate. These systems have insured that marriages take place within one's caste and outside one's clan. Since the parents of girls aspire for the marriage of their daughter with a boy of higher status (*pratiloma*) the boy belonging to higher status becomes a valued object. It leads to higher demands, which result in dowry. All parents want to marry their daughter to a boy of higher status and are prepared to meet the demand made by the boy or his parents either in cash or kind or both. Marriages are fixed with an oral promise to have a 'full paid' certificate by girl's are parents from the boys' parents. In a number of cases marriages cancelled because of less payment and sometimes the girl is subjected to cruelty and torture by the boy or his family members. The nature, gravity and magnitude of dowry problems would be discussed in a later section. A brief structure of dowry from different historical perspectives is discussed in following section.

Historical Background

For centuries women in India were considered as subordinates and given a status inferior to that of men. A number of social evils like infanticide, *purdah*, child marriage, dowry etc., adversely affected the status of women. Out of these social evils dowry was the worst. Altekar (1962) reports that dowry was not so pronounced in the past. Dowry was generally unknown in early societies, castes and communities. Literature and historical researches establish beyond doubt that movement held a position of equality with man during Vedic period. About the importance of women's education, '*Atharva Veda*' asserted that "the success of women in her married life depends upon her proper training during the *Brahmacharya*". As many as twenty women's names are listed who composed the hymns of the '*Rigveda*' and Apala, Lopamudra, Ghosha etc., are among them (Kuppuswamy, 1972).

The conversation between 'Maitreyee' and 'Yajnavalkya' in *Upanishadic* period is very famous. Maitreyee preferred to be highly educated in *Brahmavidya* rather than to get her share of the property from her husband's side. There are examples of women, being free to select their life partners. Instances of love marriages are also found during the period of *Upanishads*. Remarriage of widows, *Anuloma* marriages, were also allowed (Shastri, 1952). According to Dutt (1909), "Hindu women held an honoured place..... were taking shares in sacrifices and religious duties, attended great assemblies and state occasions, they were distinguished in science and literature disciplines and were considered intellectual companions of their husbands".

However, the status of women began to decline after three hundred BC. It was during the Buddhist period that women were not allowed the right of Vedic studies. But the status of women really deteriorated during the Gupta period. Further deterioration took place between A.D. 1206 and 1761. During this period, a number of social evils like; female infanticide, child marriage, *purdah, jauhar, sati* and slavery cropped up and affected adversely the position of women and dowry was the worst evil.

Contrary to Hindu women, Muslim women could inherit property though only half as much as a man could. But the social position of Hindu as well as Muslim women was similar. In both cases women were socially and economically dependent on men. A rare few among them, like Raziya Sultana, Chand Bibi etc. distinguished themselves as more than a man. But, they are exceptions and they could do little for enhancing the status of Indian women. With the advent of Islam during the Turka, Afghan and Mughal period, the Hindu society became very rigid. Hindu women were forcibly converted and married with Muslims. It all promoted early marriages on a large scale. These things made the dowry system to prosper.

It is recorded that dowry originated during the 13th and 14th centuries among the rich Rajput families of Rajputana. In the pre-British period the dowry system did not spread widely among people in general and it did not assume any alarming shape. But during the British period it became an evil of great magnitude. Dowry was treated as the price of the bridegroom for him being married with a daughter of another family. The price of the bridegroom was determined on the basis of his qualification, education, job, high position etc., and the socio-economic status of his family. Because of English education and lucrative jobs, the youth of the British period raised their price in the marriage market. Thus, the rich parents were quite successful in getting their daughters married very easily. The characteristics of girls like beauty, character, education and even their careers were not considered while settling the marriages. The dowry system became a part of religious custom. '*Kanyadan*' was considered as '*Mahadan*' (giving of daughter as precious gift) along with gifts in cash and kind.

In the 20th century, the dowry system took an ugly turn. Many families were ruined due to the exorbitant demands of bridegrooms or their families. Sometimes they have led to the suicide of young brides whose parents were unable to fulfill the demands of bridegrooms. The sensational suicide of Snehalata (1914) can be taken as a representative example. As a result, now the birth of a girl is considered as a misfortune, and she is brought up in relative neglect, which promotes the incidence of child abuse and neglect.

In present era, dowry has become a serious problem and given rise to a number of acts of domestic violence and even deaths. A number of reform societies and religious organizations which have been seized of the menace have come forward to enhance the status of women through education among women and they have advocated widow marriages. The attempts made by Mahatma Gandhi to raise the status of Indian women are particularly noteworthy. He said that the status of women in societies is the main measuring rod of the advancement of civilization. Gandhi fought stoutly against the many wrongs done to our women in the name of tradition, religion and law. Gandhi said, "let us not live with one limb completely or partially paralyzed. We must be incapable of defending ourselves or healthily competing with the other nations, if we allow the better half of ourselves to become paralyzed."

Gandhian views Against Dowry

Gandhi was outspoken against dowry. He said in 1928, "Any young man who makes dowry a condition of marriage discredits his and dishonours womanhood." He advised girls to resist such evil customs by remaining maidens either for life or at least for a number of years until they found understanding grooms. In 1933, Gandhi advised girls to not wear jewellery on their bodies, which he considered an offence to the eye in a country of semi-starvation and insufficient nutrition of many people (*Harijan*, 1933). Actually Gandhi wanted that in their own interest and also in the interest of the society women should not wear ornaments. As reported in *Harijan* (1934), marriages did take place in his *Ashram*, but such ceremonies were very short and simple. Inspite of the efforts made by great persons like Gandhi the dowry system persists in various parts of the country in various forms. Thus, a number of restrictions were imposed on the dowry system prevailing in the society.

With the development of institutions for higher education, colleges and universities, where the students have an opportunity to mix with each other, there is scope for both boys and girls to change their conservative outlook and choose their life-partners on their own. At the same time opportunities for women's employment have widened the scope for women to interact with the people of different strata of society and thus, inter-caste marriages are not exceptions now. Naturally, among such people there is a dislike of the dowry system.

Opposition to dowry has been building up for several decades. On 20th April, 1924, *Tyagi Bhumihar Brahmans* held a conference in Ghazipur under the presidentship of Maharaj Kumar of Kashi and passed a resolution to check the dowry system. According to Chand (1935), a conference was also held at Hyderabad and more than 24 girls declared in writing that they would not marry young men who would demand dowry. In December, 1929 (*Hindustan Review*, 1929) a conference was held at Calcutta where a number of resolutions were passed against dowry and overwhelming majority of speakers spoke against the dowry system and called it the greatest social evil of the time. Such conferences held at different places motivated the people not to take or give dowry at the time of their marriages. Later on the *Swadeshi Andolan* and other political organizations came forward to uplift women's status in our society.

Women's struggle for equality took a big step forward with the coming of independence. The Hindu succession Act of 1956 made the daughter an equal co-heir with the son. Articles 14 and 15 of the Constitution of India (1958) guaranteed complete equality of men and women. The Hindu Marriage Act, 1955 permitted dissolution of marriage on specific grounds. Monogamy was made mandatory for men as well as women. Thus, the social reform movement, the freedom struggle, women's own movements and Constitution of India made a big contribution in this direction. But dowry system has persisted. A proper social climate is yet to be created to check this evil.

Contributing Factors of Dowry

An overview of literature on dowry suggests that the nature and pattern of dowry changed with passage of time. Social influence plays important roles in deciding the presence and persistence of the dowry system. Earlier, dowry was voluntary and it was not demanded. But in medieval India, the Mughal rulers and Nawabs demanded high dowries. The Rajput kings gave dowries to ensure the comfortable living of their daughters after marriage. However, this system was popular among rich Brahmans and ruling Rajputs. The lower castes had a bride price in the place of dowry. Among them daughters, in contrast to the higher castes, were considered as an asset to the family useful for agricultural labour and other traditional occupations. But even the lower castes in imitation of the upper castes adopted dowry. As a result, poor Rajputs unable to give dowry started killing their newly born female children. In course of time it gave birth to dowry killings in different parts of the country. Various social and psychological factors have accentuated the problems of dowry causing poor status of women around the globe.

1. Gravity of Dowry based on Social Structure, Religion, Caste and Community and Culture

Mahatma Gandhi wanted that "Young men who soil their fingers with such ill-gotten gold (dowry) be excommunicated from society". But, it has remained a pious wish only. The growth of industrialization and migration of people from villages to city have changed the magnitude and dimensions of dowry. The number and variety of dowry items demanded have increased because these things have become available in the market. Any attractive thing newly coming into the market is added to the list of dowry items and the girls' parents are to meet such demands if they have to marry their daughters with well-to-do bridegrooms.

The legal facility of a share in the parental property to the girls (Hindu Succession Act, 1956) has not been effective, in the sense that such demands are not made by the girls. Thus, this Act has become redundant. The 1961 Act prohibited dowry. This prohibition Act against dowry is observed only in gross violation of it. Those who are supposed to observe and follow such Acts, they themselves have been promoting dowry directly or indirectly, may be because of family or societal pressures.

Since marriage practice conventions in India differ from one corner to the other corner of the country, there are large variations among them between dowry-givers and dowry-takers. The variations are a socio-cultural phenomenon-urban-rural setup and family background, caste, class, ethnicity, religion and culture.

In Muslim culture the custom of *'Mehar'* is in the practice. *'Mehar'* is the money or property obtained by wife from her husband at the time of marriage (or *Nikah*). In the *'Sunnat'* (deeds by Prophet), *'Mehar'* is of two types, i.e. *'Moajil'* and *'Mohajil'*. *Moajil* is paid just after *Nikah* or Confirmation of marriage. And *Mohajil* can be paid at any time before death. But in practice it is seen that after marriage *Mohajil* is waived by the wife. According to Muslim law marriage is a contract and *'Mehar'* is its essential consequence. The Muslim community treats marriage as a contract in which wife is the property and *'Mehar'* is it's cost or value (Calcutta High Court; *Jakiri Begam* vs. *Sakeena Begam*, 1989). Without any mention of *'Mehar'*, its practice is easily inferred from the marriage taking place.

The dowry system is quite different in some parts of India. For example, in Kerala, the Nayars neither pay bride price nor give dowry. The Nayars are a matrilineal and matrilocal community with an institution of visiting husbands. They occasionally offer normal gifts as token of their love and affection.

On the other hand, the Tiyyars like Nangudi and Vellalars have the system of paternal cross-cousin marriage, thus, the girl is married to her father's sister's son. A girl is given a patch of land as a gift at the time of her marriage. But, these are not variation of dowry. Gradually, the scene is changing in these parts of the country (Pandey & Mishra, 2000).

At present, dowry is not only considered as '*Daan*' (gift), but the '*Haq*' (Right) of a groom and his family. Dowry does not only include cash and material goods for the bridegroom and his parents, but, it also includes gift and cash for all the primary Kinsmen and some other secondary and remote relatives. The groom's father exhibits the dowry to his kinsmen and fellowmen with a sense of pride, expressing his superiority and status. Even after providing a lot of dowry, apart from other reasons, the bride givers do not accept, in some communities even water at the door of their son-in-law as it considered a sin. However, gradually such practices are changing.

2. *Psychological Perspective of Dowry*

Since, social factors provide structural explanation of dowry system however, to understand the gravity of dowry practices and inclination of human being towards dowry; certain psychological factors are discussed in the following section.

(i) Socialization of Women/Girl in India

Female socialization has been viewed as an important causal factor leading to criminal acts towards women. Kishwar (1994) has pointed out that when a girl is married and sent to her husband's family, her family member and others say "we are sending your '*doli*' today, may only your *Arthi* (Ashes) emerge from that house (husband's house)". Kishwar's remark can be appreciated if it is understood that the real killer of women is the dowry. At the same time there is the feeling of parents that the marriage of their daughter should be arranged at any cost.

With women's awareness of their roles and right in society, around the seventies, cases of bride-burning began to be reported by some women reporters in the Newspapers published from Delhi. Thus, the Government had to take a serious view of the problem. In 1987, Lok Sabha was told that out of 3,108 dowry complaints 382 were under Dowry Prohibition Act and India Penal Code. Apart from these complaints registered by the Police, many more were registered by women's organizations. According to one estimate made by a Social Science Research Centre, dowry deaths have raised up to 900 per year in Delhi only. Praveen Garewal of Saheli (A Delhi based Women's Organization) feels that the incidence of dowry related atrocities are rooted in contemporary social developments. According to her, the reasons behind such incidents are upward mobility and aspiration of the newly emergent urban middle class. In such prevailing situation, wife is perceived as a consumer durable. Another reason is the status of working women and their desire for certain amount of independence. Garewal (1994) further believes that women's desire for freedom makes it harder for a woman to accept the subjugation that is expected from her in-laws.

(ii) Woman's Lifestyle

Certain expectations are attributed to the life style of women in Indian society. For example, it is expected that if a girl is married and has some children, she should remain happy for the rest of her life. It is also expected that she should always reflect it in her behaviour. But such expectations become false when a number of psychosocial problems arise out of the dowry system. Apart from the number of such problem related with the rules of marriage or unemployed life-partners, there are other problems such as discrimination towards females, misperception, false cognition, attributional biases of dowry practices and so on.

(iii) Dowry Victimization: A State of Learned Helplessness

A huge amount of literature is available describing the process and strategies adopted in dowry deaths. A number of phases have been observed. For example, if the bride demands or even desires to have something either from her husband or in-laws, she has to listen comments on her parents. Such comments (*Tumhare Pitaji Ne Iskey Liye Rokara Diya Hai zyada bologi to mayake bhej doonga tumhare mayake mein hota hoga*) disturb the bride mentally. When such comments and harassments accumulate, they lead the bride to the second phase where either she herself desire to go to her parents' house or she is sent against her wishes to her parents. In the third phase, the girl's inability to bear any longer such humiliations expresses itself either in the form of suicide or self-poisoning. If this is not possible the in-laws themselves contrive the death of the bride either by burning her or use some other strategies convenient for them. According to one report 50 per cent of the dowry women were burnt alive and 20 per cent were poisoned. These results are supported by a bulk of studies (ICSSR Reports, 1994; *Rashtriya Sahara,* 1995; Khan & Ray 1995; *Sunday Observer,* 1996). According to Khan and Ray (1995) the dowry deaths are a middle and lower middle class phenomenon. Pandey and Mishra (2000) identified a large number of cases of women harassment and dowry victimization in eastern districts of Uttar Pradesh, and no community and class was found immune of this evil. In another study, Pandey (2008) found that out of numerous causative factors of domestic violence, dowry was one of the main reasons.

Now-a-days, every citizen is status conscious and wishes for easy money and luxury goods. This is the most frequent practice in our society of dowry-givers and dowry-takers. Verghese (1995) reports that officers in IAS and Central Service Officials, Doctors, Engineers and others like them make the highest demand in the market. As far as dowry deaths or violence attached to it are concerned, India is not the only country where such incidents take place. According to one estimate even in the USA, most of the time such cases are not reported to the police. The reasons behind such deeds are: (1) Victimization produces fear regarding the safety and security about one's own; (2) Women fear that reporting of such violent actions may result in domestic problems and may break down their relations; (3) such victims perceive themselves helpless; and (4) Victims believe that nobody can change the events taking place in their lives since it is fixed for them. These reasons force them not to register their pains and sufferings. The victim and her family feel that the police and court may further cost them in the form of time, money, energy as well as mental peace, etc. These factors produce self-blaming tendencies (Kidd & Plotkin, 1986). By blaming themselves for the occurrence victims regain a sense of control and feel less need to report to the authorities. Such non-reporting of incidents lead to the death of victims.

Consequences of Dowry

A huge amount of researches indicates adverse consequences of dowry system. The seriousness of such problems can be imagined by looking at the figures presented below, related to total crime against women and dowry victimization in India.

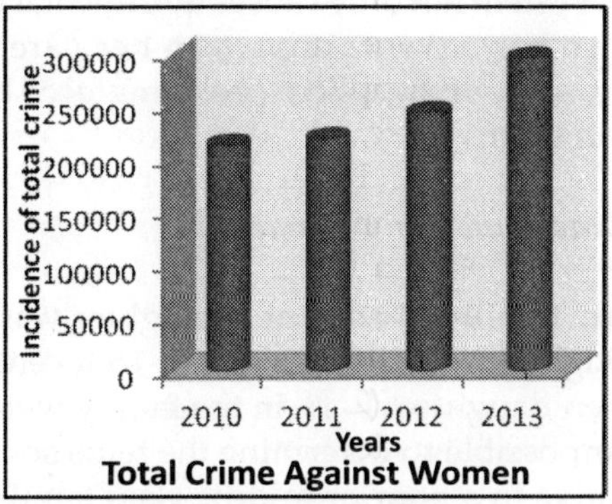

Fig. 9.1: The Details of Crime Against Women During Year 2010-2013
Source: National Family Health Survey, 2005-2006.

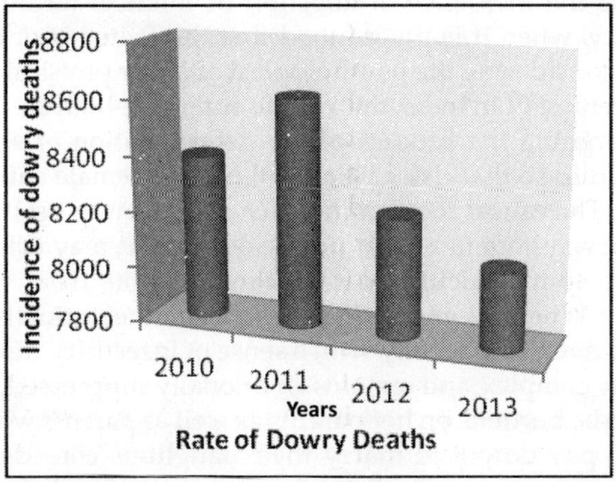

Fig. 9.2: The Details of Dowry Deaths During Year 2010-2013
Source: National Family Health Survey, 2005-2006.

Fig. 9.1 indicates that total crime against women in four years, i.e. 2010-2013 has increased gradually. In 2010, it is minimum whereas, till 2013 it has increased by an alarming rate. However, different pattern is identified in case of dowry death (Fig. 9.2). It is clear from figure; the rate of dowry death of women during these years is random. In year 2010 the death due to dowry rises approximately 8,400. There is sudden increase in 2011 and after that during 2012 and 2013 it is decreased by margin.

The dowry system not only causes detrimental impact on girls (victim) but also has adverse impact on her parents and family members. Here, some of the salient problems faced by target group are discussed in brief:

1. *Impact of Dowry on Girls/Women*

Earlier, in many families, "birth of a daughter was regarded as a curse due to high demand of dowry till 18th century and there were cases when daughters born in the family were put to death. Since, it was impossible to determine the fetus sex and also there was no alternative in a poor or middle class family except to kill the daughter in infancy. Still, Honour killing is in practice in some families. Now, the invention of determination of sex of foetus has increased the incidence of abortion or medical termination of pregnancy, when it is determined that the foetus is of a female, without considering the psychological effect or physical health of "Amniocentesis". In India, the middle or middle-high class families are undergoing the process of the determination of sex, of the coming child so that risk of the child born as female child, can be avoided. The causal root behind such act is dowry itself."

Dowry system is a great pernicious evil. It may orient many girls to commit suicide, to save their parents from economic drudgery. When the engagement is broken due to dowry the girl begins to live in the society with a sense of insecurity, develops an inferiority complex, and remains emotionally suppressed. She feels herself to be burdens on her parents as well as parents who cannot afford to pay dowry to marry their daughters consider them a burden for the family. Similarly, brothers consider their sisters as barriers in the achievement of their aspirations. As a result, many a time the treatment given by parents and brothers to girls in the family disrupts harmony in intra-family relations.

A bulk of literature proves the epidemic cases of dowry deaths. It is defined as "the unnatural death of a woman caused by burns or bodily injury occur if it can be shown that the woman was subjected to cruelty by her husband or her husband's relatives shortly before death in connection with a demand for dowry. Dowry-related violence against women occurs among all subgroups of the population, the rates are higher among the poor and the lower castes. Alcoholism is also associated with increase in violence against women.

The alarming state of dowry death can be estimated on the basis of Survey Report of Dowry Deaths presented by Lok Sabha during 5 Years, i.e. 2005-2010, in five states of the country, i.e. Uttar Pradesh, Bihar, Madhya Pradesh, Andhra Pradesh and West Bengal. As Fig. 9.3 displays, almost increasing order in dowry crimes during five years and Uttar Pradesh is the leading state in terms of total dowry death i.e. 12,254 in between year 2005-10 whereas, West Bengal has the minimum, i.e. 2805 in these years.

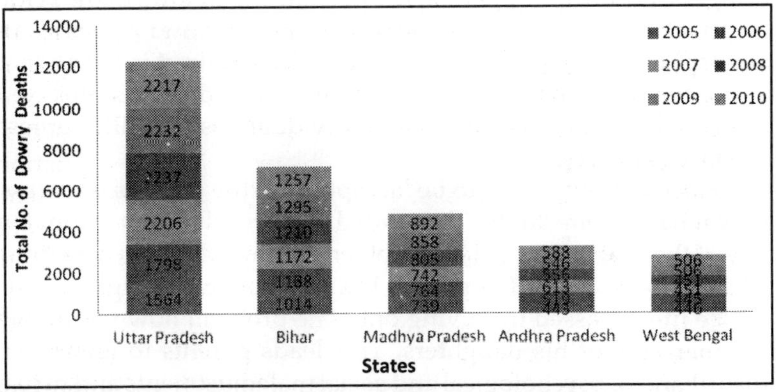

Fig. 9.3: Reported Dowry Deaths (2005-06 to 2009-2010).
Source: National Family Health Survey, 2005-2006.

Though dowry-death is generally understood to involve the murder of a woman on the dowry issue in the family of procreation but before the act of killing, several forms of harassment and humiliation take place against the victim. The humiliation generally will start with criticism, followed by familiar circumstances, abuses and demands for more money. Some women used to put up with victimization because they know that their parents are not in a position to give more and to some other will think that things will change after the birth of a child.

2. Problems faced by Families and Parents of Bride

Dowry system leads to family conflicts. When a mother-in-law does not get dowry to her satisfaction, she maltreats her daughter-in-law and abuses her father, mother and relatives. "The emotional shock on the part of the girl and the authoritarian personality of mother-in-law leads to family conflicts."

Dowry affects the marital relations in a sizeable proportion of married couples. This is mainly so because the present day youths threaten their wives with desertion if they do not bring enough dowry from their parents. This social evil of dowry is the major cause of breakdown of marriages. The boy use to think of himself a dignified individual and views the girl as a subjugated entity with an inferior and degraded status. At parents' house she is treated as a burden and in the matrimonial home, the dowry she brings is more important than her person. The in-laws of the bride in an attempt to extract more and more dowry create an atmosphere of harassment and cruelty. Generally, it is found that a wife coming to the matrimonial home without dowry is subjected to many humiliations. She as an individual has no utility unless she brings dowry.

Earlier, dowry used to be 'accepted' by the grooms party but now it has become to the 'demanded'. The result is that "from the day of the birth of the girl, the problem of dowry haunts the minds of the parents. And if, a person has three or four daughters; his whole life is passed in solving only one problem how to arrange the marriage of his daughters. This leads parents to emotional disturbances, psychological and social maladjustments and to live in a pathetic state throughout their life."

Dowry Victimizations and Downfall of Status of Women

Dowry is considered as a main factor causing deterioration in the status of women in India. It is seriously affecting development and health status of women throughout the world. It is a social evil and it seriously affects those communities especially the salaried class, who are constrained to fulfill the dowry demands. The people from these groups and communities face a lot of problems regarding the amount they have to save for the marriage of their daughters from their tightened economic conditions. Apart from it, the parents of brides face a lot of psychological pressures for ensuring a better life for their daughters. This stressful state sometimes manifests in immoral acts. Day by day the crime rate against women is increasing. Similarly, killings of the female embryo in our society are increasing day-by-day. Cases of female infanticide are still found in some of the communities and the motivation towards such acts is inherent in the dowry practice.

The problem of dowry is interrelated and has psychological, social, demographic and economic dimensions. Female children are reared, in Indian society, in such a way that their roles are restricted and they are trained to learn the art of womanhood and motherhood. They are taught for full devotion and loyalty to the husband and other family members. Male superiority, traditional burdens and paralyzed society create horror where one would fear to make any significant intervention. Although, many efforts have been made to solve this problems yet the solution to this problem is not likely to be found in the near future. The only hope left is self-awareness, and through awareness developed by the mass-media and educational upliftment programmes, women may avail themselves of their rightful place in Indian society. Although women have started participating in the economic, political and social spheres of life, yet their numbers are few. And at the same time many kinds of prejudices, male dominance in society, sex stereotypes, and other discriminations inhibit the upliftment of women in society.

A number of psycho-social factors play inhibiting roles. It is surprising to note that among the dowry victims most of the females were highly educated and placed well. It seems, thus that there is no correlation between crimes related to dowry and education, employment and economic independence. Everybody realizes the need for change in attitudes of the society, but the appropriate styles are yet to be finalized and the amount of effort to be decided.

Dowry Prevention and Cure: Some Recommendations

Looking at the seriousness of dowry problem it is urgently required to chalk out intervention programmes having both curative and preventive devices as well as long-term and short-term devices. The long-term measure should include inculcation of a new ideology and value system. We have to train our young men not to think of themselves in terms of marketable commodities to be sold by their parents to brides' parents in return for dowry. Inter-caste marriages should be encouraged. In short-term preventive devices, effective action should be taken immediately whenever dowry-related crimes occur. The victims should be provided legal and social protection. The media should highlight such incidents with a view to motivating people not to be involved in such incidents. The nature of punishment for those involved in such social evils should be so stringent that others not only learn a lesson but are deterred from indulging in such evils. Despite this, some recommendations are made to prevent this evil:

1. **Social support:** It is a very important factor in mitigating the impact of dowry related stressful situations. Such support is also provided by women's groups and organizations, and neighbours to the victims. Apart from these, women's organizations (57%), community leaders, relatives, college students as par professions and human rights group (41%) play an important role in giving support. According to Taylor (1984) such efforts create public awareness of the crime. The information provided by such supports play a more important role than the mass media in activating personal risk of victimization and action to avoid such victimization.
2. **The role of bystanders:** In preventing such crimes the contribution of neighbours, other family members, relatives etc. can hardly be denied. These bystanders are treated as 'eyes to ears' of the police. For such purpose, immediate neighbours, friends, family and local residents can serve as bystanders and can minimize such crimes. It is said that sometimes these people ignore at the primary stage which later on lead to serious crimes. That is because many times the victims do not seek help from these bystanders. Thus, because of hesitation to disturb the social relations, bystanders are not so active. Parents also dislike, not always, the intervention from outsiders due to fear that they may not find grooms for their remaining daughters.

3. **The role of the police and court:** For the prevention of crimes against women, the police and court should play important role. Sometimes, their role is found vogue and questionable in dowry related crimes. Manushi (1982) quotes from the speech of a police commissioner at a college, who said "Dowry death is not a case rather it is an incident, it is a tragedy. I have five thousand incidents like these. It is a very ordinary matter". Rohrbaugh (1981) reports that the attitude of the police in dowry death cases is similar to the evident cases of wife battering. From these reports it looks as though many dowry death cases are dismissed by the police as cases of suicide rather than murders.

It also takes too much time for a Court to reach a judgement regarding dowry death because of the lengthy court procedures. According to the report by Manushi, despite a huge number of dowry deaths between 1983 to 1985 only 10 cases reached the trial stage and judgments passed by various courts. In only three cases, out of the 10 cases, the accused were sentenced by the session's court to life-imprisonment and one case is in the Supreme Court which is yet to decide on it. The reasons are faulty investigation or some interpretation errors. It seems easier for a court either to acquit the accused or grant bail.

Legal Implications of Dowry

The Indian Government has taken several steps to eradicate the evil of dowry. In this connection a number of Bills have been passed but, contrary to expectation, the number of dowry deaths and crimes has only increased. A brief summary of such Bills and Acts are discussed next.

In order to curb the dowry practice, Indian Government passed, the Dowry Prohibition Act in 1961. This Act was modified with Dowry Prohibition (Amendment) of 1984, which was again modified with Dowry Prohibition Bill, 1986. Although the intentions of such Acts and Bills are beyond doubt, they have remained in theory only and in actual practice, they have not been effective.

Prior to these Bills, the Hindu Succession Act had been passed in 1956. But because of agitation from different parts of the country, especially from Punjab, Haryana etc., a number of points were raised against it and the right of equality was not provided. Also the distinction between dowry and voluntary gifts was not made clear. It is believed that the gift should be of customary nature and not very costly. The whole section in the Act would only legalize any extent of dowry. And interpretation of the dowry amount may be subjective and biased (Vanita, 1984). Provisions were also made for returning the dowry amount back (*Pratibha Rani* vs. *Suraj Kumar* case upholding, 1965, 1982) or dowry (Supreme Court Judgement, 1985). The decision of Supreme Court was highly appreciated by a number of women's organizations. Again in 1996, the Dowry Prohibition Bill was presented in the Rajya Sabha and the provisions of Acts were tightened. But all these Legal provisions have failed to bring about the expected improvements and thus, the deterioration in women's status has gradually increased.

Conclusion

The seriousness of dowry problem and status of women in India and all over the world can be imagined on the basis of considerable attention paid by social scientists, psychologists, government, media, women organizations and social support groups. The reports submitted by these groups have considered dowry as the most significant factor in deterioration of status of women in India. Around the globe, efforts are made to root out this evil. Consequently, U.N. declared the year 1975 as women's year and period between 1975-1985 as women's decade. In 1975 the National Committee on Women's status recommended changes to improve women's status. Inspite of all these efforts the required change in perception and attitude towards dowry and women's welfare is not yet seen. In our society, the expectations from women are very high and they are to be like Sita and Savitri but the treatment given to them is anything but satisfactory. There is a long history of women's sufferings in society. She is required to play a number of varied roles but even those, who are directly benefited by them, do not show proper concern with the problems of women.

The image of women in India is perceived according to the socio-psychological perspective. The sociological perspective defines the expressive function of women and psychological perspective expects her as passive and dependent. Marriage and motherhood are necessary fulfillment for identity formation. This can be labelled as duality of women in Hindu ideology (Susan, Wadley, 1988), i.e. identified with nature; women as birth-giver and protector of children and paradoxically the other view of women sees them as evil and destructive.

A number of recommendations are provided from different schools and organizations for the better status of women, i.e. to bring back to them the status once given to them (*Yatra Naryastu Pujyantey Ramantey Tatra Devatah—Manusmriti*). It is supposed that women should be aware of inequality and oppressiveness. Thus, consciousness raising groups should be organized to raise Indian women to be aware of their problems and utilization of legal supports to solve their problems. The media can play an important role in this regard. The role of psychologists and sociologists can hardly be exaggerated in making women aware of their social reality. It is also suggested that Indian people should change their rearing and socializing styles of their daughters. Employment and economic independence should be made available to them along with higher education. Such efforts will make women empowered and also instrumental in accentuating better status of women in India.

References

Altekar, A.S. (1962). *The Position of Women in Hindu Civilization from Prehistoric Times to Present Day*, New Delhi: Motilal Banarasidass.

Calcutta High Court, (*Jabiri Begam* vs. *Sakeena Begam*) (1989).

Central for Social Science Research (1994). Quoted by Tavleen Singh, "Rising Crimes against Women", *Illustrated Weekly*.

Dutt, R. (1909). *Civilization and Ancient India*.

Gandhi, M.K. (1928). *Women*, Nav Jiwan Publishing House, Ahemadebad, 1964.

Garewal (1994). Quoted by Tavleen Singh, "Rising Crimes against Women", *Illustrated Weekly*.

Gandially, R. & P. Kumar, (1988). "Bride-Burning: The Psycho-Social Dynamics of Dowry Deaths." In: Rehana Ghadially (ed.) *Women in Indian Society: A Reader*. New Delhi: Sage Publications.

Harijan (1933). 22 December.

Harijan (1934). 12 January.

Hindustan Review, April (1929).

Kane, P.V. (1965, 1982). *Dharmashastra Ka Itihaas*. Hindi Bhawan, Lucknow.
Khan, K.S. & R. Ray (1984). "Dowry Death", *Indian Journal of Social Work*, XIV, pp. 303-307.
Khan, R.S. & R. Ray (1995), "Dowry Deaths: A Recent Phenomena", Study. *Times of India*.
Kidd, R.F. & L. Plotin, (1986). "L.N.D. Self-blame and coping with Stressful Life Events", Unpublished Manuscript.
Kishwar, M. (1994). Editor, *(Manushi) Indian Express*.
Kuppuswamy, M. (1972). *Social Change in India*, Delhi: Vikas Publications.
Manushi (1982), Reports.
Manushi (1983), Reports.
Manushi (1985), Reports.
Nair, P.T. (1978). *Marriage and Dowry in India*, Calcutta: Minerva Associates Publications.
Pandey, S. & Mishra, B. (2000). Dowry and Status of Women in India. In: K. Mahadeven *et al.* (eds.). *Reproductive Health of Humankind in Asia and Africa: A Global Perspective*, Vol. 2, pp. 561-582, New Delhi: B.R. Publishing Cooperation.
Pandey, S. (2008). *Psycho-social Aspects of Domestic Violence*, New Delhi: Concept Publishing Company.
Rashtriya Sahara (1995). Rising Graph of Violence Against Women.
Hastakshep information based on National Crime Record Bureau, 8-9.
Rajaraman, I. (1983). "Economics of Bride-price and Dowry", *Economic and Political Weekly*, XVIII, pp. 275-78.
Rohrbaugh, J.B. (1981). *Women: Psychology's Puzzle*, London: Abacus.
Sambrani, B.R. & S. Sambrani (1983). *Economics of Bride—Price and Dowry. Economics and Political Weekly*, Vol. 1, XVIII, pp. 601-603.
Sexena, D.B. (1995). "Dowry Deaths a Recent Phenomenon: Study", *Times of India New Services*.
Shastri, S.R. (1952). *Women in Vedic Age*, Bharatiya Vidya Bhawan.
Snehlata (1914). She was a Bengali girl who burnt herself to death in 1914 as she knew that her father had to mortgage property for expenses including dowry.
Srinivas, M.N. (1984). *Some Reflection on Dowry*, New Delhi: Oxford University Press.
Sunday Observer (1996). Dowry Death in Maharashtra. Speech by the Minister of State for Home Affair in Maharashtra Legislative Assembly.
Tyler, R. (1984). "Assessing the Risk of Crime Victimization : The Integration of personal Victimization Experiences and socially Transmitted Information", *Journal of Social Issue*, 40, 1, pp. 27-28.
Vanita, R. (1984). "Nominal Changes", *Manushi*, pp. 24, 29-31.
Verghese, I. (1995). "Dowry Deaths: A Recent Phenomenon: Study", *Times of India*.

10

Mental Health Issues of Domestically Abused and Violence Victimized Old Women

Anubhuti Dubey

> Abuse of older women is not generally age based, rather it is often "domestic violence grown old—a continuation of violence started earlier in life".
>
> —*Lazenbatt, Devaney & Gildea* (2010)

The number of the elderly in India is growing and it is estimated that approximately 90 million older persons are living in India, presently. Life expectancy has increased from 40 years in 1951 to 64 years. Growth rate of elderly (3.09) is higher than that of the general population (1.9). At age level of 60+, the proportion of widows (54%) is more than widowers (16%). Such demographic transitions have posed tremendous challenges for healthy ageing.

Domestic violence tends to be considered as a problem of younger aged women, but evidences suggest that violence against women doesn't stop as they grow older; it is just less visible. Studies found that domestic abuse/violence is experienced by women of all ages, however older women are overlooked. Domestic violence, also known as domestic abuse, spousal abuse, family violence, and intimate partner violence (IPV), can be broadly defined as a pattern of abusive behaviours.

Domestic violence has many forms including physical aggression (hitting, kicking, biting, shoving, restraining, slapping, throwing objects), or threats thereof, sexual abuse, emotional abuse, controlling or domineering, intimidation, stalking, passive/covert abuse (e.g. neglect), and economic deprivation. It can be perpetrated by any person in an ongoing relationship with the victim. For older women, this can include a spouse, partner, adult child, other family member or caregiver.

Domestic violence can be defined as any act of gender-based violence that results in, or is likely to result in physical, sexual, psychological or financial suffering to women, including threats of such acts, coercion or arbitrary deprivation of liberty, and denial of human rights, often in combination of one another (Phillips, 2000; Garcia-Moreno, 2000; Hightower *et al.*, 2004; Straka, 2006). In addition, it also includes neglect, self-neglect, and forms of social abuse (Zink *et al.*, 2005). Studies revealed that physical violence victimization may actually be products of non-physical abuse, which almost always accompanies physical violence (Follingstad & DeHart, 2000).

Domestic abuse on older women is likely to be similar to those on younger women; however, the effects are likely to be more severe, the longer the abuse has occurred. The 1992 British Crime Survey found that less than 4 per cent of women over 60 said that there had been any physical violence in their relationships. The British Crime Survey (2001) suggests that older women are more likely than younger women to define an event as 'domestic violence' contradicting the view that older women do not report Domestic Violence as they fail to recognize it as 'abuse' (Walby & Allen, 2004; Pritchard, 2000).

The interface between these two social problems has received only slight attention in domestic violence or elderly abuse research (Aronson, *et al.*, 1995; Brandl & Raymond, 1996; Seaver, 1996; Harris, 1996; Vinton, *et al.*, 1997; Phillips, 2000). The distinction between 'domestic violence' and 'elder abuse' and operational definitions of the terms means that often domestic violence against this group of women is subsumed under the heading of 'elder abuse' (Aronson *et al.*, 1995; Whittaker 1995; Seaver, 1996; Harris, 1996; Vinton 1999; Sedger, 2001; Hightower, 2002). Positioning domestic violence within the context of elder abuse assumes that there is a type of abuse particular to older people, an abuse due to dependency and physical fragility, even though research indicates that even in old age, victims of physical abuse most commonly are women, and perpetrators are most commonly men.

Domestic violence against older women can be part of an ongoing phenomenon taking place within a marriage or family for many years. Long-term violence and abuse can take its toll on older women who may suffer health problems over and above their chronological years and affect their capacity to cope with everyday life. Lazenbatt, Devaney and Gildea (2010) did a qualitative research to understand the experience of domestic violence of older women of Northern Ireland. The stories and narratives conveyed in this study provide a powerful picture of the lifelong domestic violence experienced by older women and how they make sense of their violent experiences. The major findings from the study highlight how their 'well-being' is weakened by living in a domestically abusive context. Key findings from the research indicate that older women are less likely to seek help due to social expectations and a lack of specialist services for older victims, and that they are more likely to resort to misusing alcohol and prescription drugs in order to cope, with significant consequences for their mental and physical health. Psychological abuse had the strongest impact on their physical and mental health such as long-term depression and anxiety (94%), the use of psychoactive medication (100%), and the likelihood of becoming a heavy drinker and experiencing alcohol dependence (22%). The findings suggest that depression through the life course may play some role in increasing the chance of becoming a victim of interpersonal violence, and may make it even harder to leave an abusive relationship.

Domestic violence against older women was also likely to co-exist with society's prejudice against older people, rendering older women's suffering and needs invisible. In the domestic violence framework, violence against women is viewed as gendered abuse of power, while ageing is perceived as a subset of abuse against older persons, ignoring the particular experiences of older women. A study of older female victims of psychological violence conducted in Quebec, Canada, found that control behaviour was a central category of psychological abuse and that such behaviour on the part of the perpetrator increased at retirement (Montminy, 2008).

Older women may be more reticent to tell others about their experiences. The shame of experiencing violence is often deeply embedded and many women blame themselves for the abuse: for not being a good wife, or for expecting too much. Taboos, fear and feelings of guilt and shame also account for a high rate of nonresponsiveness and of hiding the truth (Ruiz-Perez *et al.*, 2007). Older women face greater risk of physical and psychological abuse due to discriminatory societal attitudes and the non realization of the human rights of women. As Compared to younger women, older women are more likely to have lived in their home for several years and have accumulated possessions which are not easy to leave behind. Once a woman becomes a grandmother and her role includes caring for grandchildren this also makes it difficult to leave an abusive relationship because of issues such as feeling responsible for providing child care.

Studies also found they were taught a keen sense of privacy about family matters and a strong commitment to family loyalty and solidarity (Aronson *et al.*, 1995; Seaver, 1996; Smith and Hightower *et al.*, 2001). Finnish National Survey (Piispa, 2002) revealed a substantial group of older women who reported that physical violence had diminished over the years, but was replaced by more pernicious psychological abuse. In some cases, the violence may actually worsen with age as its effects may in fact become more severe with increased fragility and vulnerability of the victims (Alcalde, 2006).

Older women are statistically more likely than younger women to have health problems, reduced mobility or other disabilities (Hightower, Smith and Hightower, 2001). Images portrayed on TV, films and magazines show abused women as younger women with children, and may convey the impression that domestic violence doesn't occur in mid or later life. It is often assumed that injuries, confusion etc., are the results of age-related conditions. (Mullender, 1996). Older women in particular often feel that revealing Domestic Abuse may disrupt the family, and worry about their children's reaction. Fears that they will not be believed or even blamed often discourage women from disclosing.

While age and gender are the primary issues in addressing abuse in later life, socio-economic status, religion, ability, and ethnicity are among the factors affecting in important ways how a woman defines herself and how she seeks and how she receives help (Alcalde, 2006). If research and service provision to this point has focused only on women up to age 50 then virtually the entire older half of the female population at risk of Domestic Violence (those aged 50 to 85 years) will, or has been ignored (Scott *et al.*, 2004; Scott, 2008). Older women are reluctant to report cases.

Research suggests that in up to 25 per cent of cases where adult women are abused, the perpetrator is an adult child. This could make seeking help even harder.

Prevalence of Domestic Violence among Elderly Women: Studies and researches on domestic violence/abuse had been being carried out on a wide spectrum internationally, but only few to found in Indian scenario. Swedish prevalence data comes from a sample of women aged 18 to 64 (Lundgren *et al.*, 2002), and, according to the Crime Victim Compensation and Support Authority, data for women older than 64 are not available. Data on prevalence of violence against older women in Finland and Sweden revealed that Faith, Hope, Battering, of women 55 and over, 13.4 per cent were victims of partner violence in the year prior to reporting (Heiskanen & Piispa, 1998). Statistics from Australia indicate that one-third of all current victims of Domestic Violence are older women, but over 60 per cent of this group do not seek professional help (Mouton *et al.*, 2004). A longitudinal study in Melbourne reported that 28 per cent having experienced emotional, physical, or sexual domestic violence in their lifetime, and 6 per cent had suffered serious physical abuse in the past year (Mazza *et al.*, 2001). In 2007, a prevalence study on elder abuse undertaken by the Department of Health and Comic Relief estimated that 2,27,000 older people had been neglected or abused in their own homes in the previous year and that domestic violence accounted for a significant proportion of that figure. Data from the Scottish Police show that only 1.2 per cent of reported Domestic violence was the victim aged 61 or older, with a further 5.2 per cent aged 51-60 years at the time of the incident (Scott *et al.*, 2004; Scott, 2008). Study in U.K., *Older Women and Domestic Violence* (Blood, 2004), highlights that women aged over 60 who are victims of Domestic violence are suffering silently because the problem is ignored by professionals and policy-makers. The most recent evidence that indicates that one in four women who have experienced an incident of physical violence in the past 12 months is aged 45 years and older (Australian Bureau of Statistics, 2006).

Women seemingly appear to enter a violence-free zone between the ages of 45 and 65 years old, to reappear in studies of 'elder abuse' with recorded rates of abuse two and a half times the rate of men (Boldy *et al.*, 2002).The most recent studies have estimated a lifetime prevalence of physical assault or psychological abuse (e.g., verbal threats) ranging from 18.1 per cent in women aged 60 or over (Fritsch *et al.*, 2005) to 32 per cent in women aged 50–79 who participated in the Women's Health Initiative observational study component (Mouton *et al.*, 1999). In studies that used broader definitions of partner violence, rates of past-year physical and verbal partner violence were 3.5 per cent and 21.7 per cent, respectively, in women aged 70-79 (Mouton, 2003). The National Elder Abuse Incidence Study (NEAIS, 1998) estimated that in 1996, 4,49,924 older adults were abused or neglected in domestic settings. Perpetrators were adult children or spouses in two-thirds of the incidents.

Context of Domestic Violence against Women in Later Life: It occurs in two main contexts. The first is late-onset domestic violence, which begins for the first time in later life, either in a new or existing relationship. The second is domestic violence "grown old", where women have experienced domestic violence throughout a relationship lasting into their later years. Studies indicate that the latter category—domestic violence "grown old"—is the most common. Both contexts can involve a range of behaviours, including financial, emotional, physical abuse.

Risk Factors: The findings of the studies on older women and abuse/violence conducted in the European Union as part of the DAPHNE III AVOW Project identified some risk factors and eliminated others (Luoma *et al.*, 2011). Women in the youngest old-age cohort (60-69 years of age) who were married, not fully retired, reporting poor physical and mental health – and who, when faced with stressful and difficult situations more often used a disengagement behavioural coping style – reported significantly higher prevalence rates of abuse (Luoma *et al.*, 2011) than older women in the '70-79 years of age' and '80 years of age and above' old-age cohorts who were not married (widowed, separated or single), had reported good mental health, and did not usually adopt a disengagement behavioural coping style.

Domestic Violence/Abuse and Effect on Mental Health: Mental illness can be co-morbid with abuse and present additional challenges when present alongside patterns of abuse. The health consequences of violence against elderly women are often immediate and acute, long-lasting and chronic, and/or fatal. Many of the times older women's are more likely to suffer severe physical injuries than younger women; injuries that can be exacerbated by pre-existing health conditions linked to age, such as arthritis, diabetes or osteoporosis. Older women are more likely to have a range of mental health problems. Research consistently finds that the more severe the abuse, the greater its impact on women's physical and mental health. In addition, the negative health consequences can persist long after abuse has stopped. The consequences of violence tend to be more severe when women experience more than one type of violence (e.g. physical and sexual) and/or multiple incidents over time despite being very likely to suffer from specific health conditions such as depression, anxiety, digestive problems, and chronic pain.

Marshall (1994) noted that subtle 'psychological' abuse may actually be more effective in controlling an abuse victim than physical violence. Anxiety disorders are the most frequently occurring mental disorders. Decreased self-esteem is also associated with victimization. Golding's (1999) meta-analysis found that about 48 per cent of abused women reported symptoms of depression. In 1999, Mouton and colleagues published reports of a pilot study regarding associations between health and domestic violence in older women. This study documented that domestic violence has a negative relationship to mental and physical health. In a more recent study Mouton (2003) concluded that domestic violence continues across the life span and again documented that exposure to abuse affects older women's mental health.

Coker and Colleagues (2002) documented that physical Domestic Violence was associated with increased risk for chronic poor health, substance use, developing chronic disease, injuries, cuts, bruises, and broken bones or mental illness. Research by Morgan Disney (2002) documented that older women reported that the effect of abuse on their mental health was one of the factors that prompted them to leave. Mental health consequences most frequently mentioned were anxiety (75%), depression (77%), eating issues (40%), fears and phobias (51%), panic attacks (40%) and loss of confidence (82%).

Older women's difficulties worsen by a general lack of awareness about domestic violence. Researches revealed that older women experiencing domestic violence/abuse may not report increased ill-health, although they face enormous effect on mental health. Studies found that older battered women faced an increased risk of psychological problems like panic attacks and acute anxiety.

Older abused women subjects reported feeling frustration, anger, helplessness, hopelessness, and low self-esteem as negative mental health consequences of family relationships. It is now well accepted that women abuse in old age is often the main factor in the development of depression, anxiety, and other mental health disorders and may lead to sleep disturbances, self-harm, suicide eating disorders and substance misuse.

Studies reveal that psychological health effects are more dangerous than physical health effects. Battered women can experience depression, panic anxiety, nightmares, restlessness, eating problem, psychogenic diarrhoea and other social dysfunction. Study reported that battered women also experience suicidal thoughts (Sometimes commit suicide) and homicidal thoughts more frequently than normal women.

Despite the evidence from available data that older women are at greater risk of abuse and violence, older women have not been mainstreamed into ongoing research and discussion on violence against women.

Barriers to Older Women Victims Seeking and Getting Help: Barriers to seeking help by older women victims of violence/ abuse may be both internal (feelings of hopelessness and concern for the abuser, for example), or external, such as lack of services specifically designed for older women victims' needs. Victims felt not only the need to keep the abuse secret, but also abuser behaviour, self-blame and emotional.

Blood (2004) had carried out a research by Help the Aged, and the housing trust HACT, study suggests that older women face serious barriers to accessing support and are offered few appropriate services when they manage to enter the service system. These barriers include: cultural and professional assumptions that older women are not experiencing domestic violence; traditional attitudes about the meaning of 'abuse'; fear, stigma and shame; disability and health problems; lack of independent income; member of ethnic minority groups; isolation from and lack of knowledge of resources and with community services. Awareness of the problem is also low, and many professionals lack training, accept ageist stereotypes, discourage disclosure, and are less likely to identify the signs of domestic violence accurately in older women.

Older women have been socialized with more traditional attitudes and values, particularly relating to gender roles, marriage, and family (Zink *et al.*, 2003).These values can prevent them from discussing family problems such as domestic violence with others.

Financial barriers may be even greater for older women, as many are not in paid employment, and thirdly ageing health problems and disability may make them dependent on someone for care and this may be the perpetrator (Straka & Montminy, 2006).

Lack of support from others as their social networks may have been severely reduced due to ill health or death of peers (Wolf, 2000); a lack of knowledge regarding services available preventing women from knowing what help is available to them. Many older women often assume that services are only for younger women with children (Pitchard, 2000; Scott *et al.*, 2004). Older women may be the main caregiver for their abusive spouse partner or disabled child making it extremely difficult for them to leave the family home (Seaver, 1996; Wolf, 2000; Blood, 2004).

Many older women also suffer from health problems themselves making it difficult to live alone (Morgan Disney *et al.*, 2000; Hightower *et al.*, 2001; Scott *et al.*, 2004; Scott, 2008). Some older abused women have no formal education or economic resources and are more economically vulnerable and more likely to be financially dependent on their abusers than younger women.

1. **External Barriers:** External barriers included the fear that adult children and other family members would reject them, concern that law enforcement and the courts would not provide needed assistance and would possibly cause more harm, by not protecting the victim and therefore exposing her to more violence (Hightower *et al.*, 2006). Older battered women reported being estranged from their adult children who had witnessed their being abused when they were growing up, especially if the abuse occurred during serial relationships. Some children were also subjected to abuse when young. This was perceived by women as leading to a loss of support from adult children. Abuser tactics or behaviour can also create barriers to older women victims leaving a violent situation (Beaulaurier *et al.*, 2007). These tactics can include isolating the victim from extended family and friends, intimidating

the older woman victim by threatening to harm her. Financial barriers to leaving an abusive living situation may be greater for older women than for younger women, and older women victims were more likely to have health, mobility and vision problems.

2. **Internal Barriers:** While seeking help has been identified as the critical step that older battered women needed to take in order to achieve a violence-free life, there were found to be significant internal barriers to taking this step (Beaulaurier *et al.*, 2007). Internal barriers were identified as the self-perception of powerlessness, isolation, self-blame, the felt need to keep the abuse secret, feeling intimidated, and feelings of hopelessness.

Conclusion

It can be concluded that there is a need to classify domestic violence as a major health problem. An effective preventive programme that could eliminate domestic violence could hope to achieve a reduction in the prevalence of poor mental health in the total population, a fact that underscores the need for culturally acceptable and sustainable intervention strategies to deal with this social *malaise*.

References

Alcalde, M.C. (2006). "Migration and class as constraints in battered women's attempts to escape violence in Lima Peru", *Latin American Perspectives*, 33(6), 147-164.

Aronson, J., Thornewell, C. & Williams, K. (1995). "Wife assault in old age—coming out of obscurity", *Canadian Journal on Aging*, 14(S2), 72-88.

Beaulaurier, R.L., Seff, L.R., Newman, F.L. & Dunlop, B. (2007). "External barriers to help seeking for older women who experience intimate partner violence", *Journal of Family Violence*, 22(8), 747-755.

Beaulaurier, R.L., Seff, L.R., & Newman, F.L. (2008). "Barriers to help-seeking for older women who experience intimate partner violence: A descriptive model", *Journal of Women & Aging*, 20(3-4), 231-248.

Bhardwaj, U. (2014). "Domestic Violence Against Women Causes and Cure", In: Jane Ellis, & Ravi K. Thiara (eds.) *Preventing Violence*

Against Women and Girls: Educational Work with Children and Young People. London: Policy Press.

Blood, I. (2004). "Older women and domestic violence", *Help the Aged*. gatesheadolderpeoplesassembly.co.ukgatesheadolderpeoplesassembly.co.uk

Boldy, D., Webb, M., Horner, B., Davey, M., & Kingsley, B. (2002). Elder Abuse in Western Australia. Report of a Survey Conducted for the Department for Community Development—Seniors' Interests, Curtin University of Technology, Division of Health Sciences.

Bow, H. (2011). Domestic Violence 'Grown Old': The Unseen Victims of Prolonged Abuse.

Brandl, B., & Raymond, J. (1996). "Older abused and battered women: an invisible population", *Wisconsin Medical Journal*, 95(5), 298-300.

Coker, A.L., Davis, K.E., Arias, I., Desai, S., Sanderson, M., Brandt, H.M., & Smith, P.H. (2002). "Physical and mental health effects of intimate partner violence for men and women", *American Journal of Preventive Medicine*, 23(4), 260-268.

Disney, M. (2000). *Two Lives—Two Worlds: Older People and Domestic Violence*, Volumes 1 and 2; Council on the Ageing, Status of Women, Partnerships Against Domestic Violence, Australia.

Follingstad, D.R., & De Hart, D.D. (2000). "Defining Psychological Abuse of Husbands Toward Wives: Contexts, Behaviours and Typologies", *Journal of Interpersonal Violence*, 15 (9), 891-920.

Fritsch, T.A., *et al.* (2005). "Intimate partner violence against older women in Kentucky", *Journal of the Kentucky Medical Association*, 103, 461-463.

Garcia-Moreno, C. (2002). "Violence against women: Consolidating a public health agenda", *Engendering International Health: The Challenge of Equity*, Cambridge: MIT Press.

Golding, J. (1999). "Intimate partner violence as a risk factor for mental disorders: A meta-analysis", *Journal of Family Violence*, 99-132.

Harris, S. (1996). "For better or for worse: spouse abuse grown old", *Journal of Elder Abuse & Neglect*, 8, 1-30.

Heiskanen, M., & Piispa, M. (1998). *Faith, Hope, Battering: A Survey of Men's Violence against Women in Finland*. Helsinki: Statistics Finland.

Hightower, J., Smith, M. & Hightower, H. (2001). *Silent and Invisible—A Report on Abuse and Violence in the Lives of Older Women in British Columbia and Yukon B.C./Yukon Society of Transition Houses*, Vancouver, B.C.

Hightower, J. (2002). *Violence and abuse in the lives of older women: is it elder abuse or violence against women? Does it make any difference?* United Nations International Research and Training Institute for the Advancement of Women.

Hightower, J., & Smith, M.J. (2004). "Gender violence: Voices of older women" in Newsletter of older woman abuse.

Hightower, J., Smith, M.J., & Hightower, H.C. (2006). "Hearing the voices of abused older women", *Journal of Gerontological Social Work,* 46(3-4), 205-227.

Kumar, R. (2012). "Domestic Violence and Mental Health", *Delhi Psychiatry Journal,* 15 (2), 275-278.

Lazenbatt, A., Devaney, J., & Gildea, A. (2010). *Older Women's Lifelong Experience of Domestic Violence in Northern Ireland.* Changing Ageing Partnership (CAP), Queen's University, Belfast.

Lundgren, E., Heimer, G., Westerstrand, J., & Kalliokoski, A.M. (2002). "Mens violence against women in "equal" Sweden—A prevalence study", *Umea: Astroms tryckeri AB.*

Luoma, M.L., *et al.* (2011). *Prevalence study of abuse and violence against older women: results of a multicultural survey in Austria, Belgium, Finland, Lithuania, and Portugal* (European Report of the AVOW Project). Finland: National Institute of Health and Welfare (THL).

Marshall. (1994). *The Concise Oxford Dictionary of Sociology,* New York, NY : Oxford University Press.

Mazza, D., Dennerstein, L., & Dudley, C., *et al.* (2001). "The physical, sexual and emotional violence history of middle-aged women: a community based prevalence study", *Medical Journal of Australia,* 199-210.

Mouton, C.P. (2003). "Intimate partner violence and health status among older women", *Violence Against Women,* 9, 1465-1477.

Mouton, C.P., *et al.* (2004). "Prevalence and three year incidence of abuse among post-menopausal women", *American Journal of Public Health,* 94 (4), pp. 605-12.

Montminy, L. (2008). "Older women's experiences of psychological violence in their marital relationships", *Journal of Gerontological Social Work,* 46, 2, 22.

Mullender, A. (1996). *Rethinking Domestic Violence: The Social Work and Probation Response,* London: Routledge.

National Family Health Survey 3-Domestic Violence, p. 501.

Neglect, Abuse and Violence Against Older Women, United Nations, New York, (2013) (/undesadspd.org/Ageing.aspx).

Phillips, L. (2000). "Domestic Violence and Aging Women", *Geriatric Nursing,* 21 (4), 188-195.

Piispa, M. (2002). "Complexity of patterns of violence against women in heterosexual partnerships", *Violence Against Women,* 8(7), 873-900.

Pritchard, J. (2000). *The Needs of Older Women: Services for Victims of Elder Abuse and other Abuse.* Bristol: Policy Press.

Ruiz-Pérez, I., Plazaola-Castaño, J., & Vives-Cases, C. (2007). "Methodological issues in the study of violence against women", *Journal of Epidemiology and Community Health,* 61(Suppl 2), ii26-ii31.

Seaver, C. (1996). "Muted lives: older battered women", *Journal of Elder Abuse & Neglect,* 8, 3-21.

Sedger, R. (2001). "Is it aged abuse or domestic violence?", *Australian Domestic Violence & Family Violence Clearinghouse Newsletter,* 3-4.

Scott, M., McKie, L., Morton, S., Seddon, E., & Wosoff, F. (2004). "Older women and domestic violence in Scotland... and for 39 years I got on with it", *Edinburgh: Health Scotland.*

Scott, M. (2008). "Updating older women and domestic violence in Scotland", *Edinburgh: Centre for Research on Families and Relationships and Health.*

Smith, M.J., (Greta) & Hightower, J. (2000). "Office for the Prevention of Domestic Violence", New York State, http://www.opdv.state.ny.us/index.html.

Straka, S., & Montminy, L. (2006). "Responding to the needs of older women experiencing domestic violence", *Violence against Women,* 12, 251-267.

"Understanding and Addressing Violence Against Women", World Health Organization, http://www.who.int/

Vinton, L., Altholz, J.A.S. & Lobell Boesch, T. (1997). "A five-year follow up study of domestic violence programming for older battered women", *Journal of Women and Aging,* 9, 3-15.

Vinton, L. (1999). "Working with Abused Older Women from a Feminist Perspective", *Journal of Women and Aging,* 11 (2/3), 85-100.

Walby, S., & Allen, J. (2004). Domestic violence, sexual assault and stalking: Findings from the British Crime Survey, London: Home Office Research Study, 276.

Whittaker, T. (1995). "Violence, gender and elder abuse—Towards a feminist analysis and practice", *Journal of Gender Studies,* 4, 35-45.

Wolf, R.S. (2000). "The older battered woman", *National Violence Against Women,* http://www.vawprevention.org/research/olderbattered.html. Retrieved, 2(26), 06.

Zink, T., Regan, S., Jacobson, C.J. & Pabst, S. (2003). "Cohort, Period, and Aging Effects A Qualitative Study of Older Women's Reasons for Remaining in Abusive Relationships", *Violence Against Women,* 9(12), 1429-1441.

Zink, T., Fisher, B. & Regan, S. (2005). "The prevalence and incidence of intimate partner violence in older women in primary care practices", *Journal of General Internal Medicine,* 20, 884-888.

11

Psycho-Social Factors Related to Inequality and Violence against Indian Women

Ravi P. Pandey and *Purnima Awasthi*

Introduction

The perspective of gender looks at the impact of gender on people's opportunities, social roles and interactions. Implementation of the policy, programme and project goals of international and national organizations is directly affected by the impact of gender and, in turn influences the process of social development. Gender is an essential component of every aspect of the economic, social, daily and private lives of individuals and societies, and of the different roles ascribed by society to men and women. As a developing country, India is plagued with societal issues related to socio-cultural control and gender inequality that result in inequalities of income and opportunity (Comyn, Kemmis and Smith, 2014). Gender equality, representing the equal value of the roles of women and men, is considered vital for the progress and development of a nation (Hussain & Kirmani, 2010); however, women lag far behind from men in most measures of human development (e.g., literacy rate, health). It is almost stupidity to think that a nation can fully develop when almost half of its population remains deprived (Madhok, 2014). This is especially true for the women in India, who comprise 48.2 per cent of India's population of 1.22 billion (Census of India, 2011).

In workplace, to increase the representation and participation of women, organizations must systematically break down the barriers inhibiting women's participation. Human resource development (HRD) professionals, for example, could facilitate the improvement of existing recruitment and selection and access to training and development opportunities—related policies, procedures, and practices. Successfully removing the barriers to women's participation would stimulate transformation of the male-dominated culture in most corporate organizations (Bilimoria, Joy, & Liang, 2008). Still, HRD professionals must remain mindful that existing notions of gender roles are socially and culturally constructed and tend to be rigidly predefined across social, economic, and political domains (Sinha, 2013). Thus, the barriers to participation in the workplace are consistently accepted as the norm in Indian society in general, even to the familial level by the women themselves (Sinha, 2013). Undoubtedly, HRD can have an important role in promoting the development of women in the workplace and ultimately contributing to the good of the nation as it seeks to meet the needs of its citizenry.

Causes of Gender Inequality in India

Gender inequality in India arises from social construction of unequal power within a relationship, creating a distinct convention of male domination and female subordination in most spheres of life, including the workplace (Esteve-Volart, 2004). This socially constructed male domination supports the idea that the tasks, roles, functions, and values contributed by men are decidedly more beneficial than similar contributions from women, encouraging societal and workplace norm of gender inequality. Although India has made significant economic advances as a nation, growth in human development (e.g., access to resources for good health, access to educational opportunities, and a decent standard of living) has been painfully slow in most areas (Arora, 2012). Patriarchy is one such norm in India, particularly applying to women as their lives are dictated and monitored by the male members of the family from birth to death (Chada & Sinha, 2013; Razvi & Roth, 2004). A woman cannot possess any assets of her own or displease her husband, as she would be held in violation of her wifely duties. In addition to taking care of husband's needs, she must handle and be responsible for the housework and children, perform religious duties, prepare all the food, provide male children, and be loyal and faithful to her responsibilities towards her home, all the while subduing her own needs, thoughts, and actions (Razvi *et al.*, 2004).

Gender inequality takes on many forms in India, arising from different social practices viewed as normal from a religious or cultural standpoint (based on deep historical roots), resulting in women being disproportionally underrepresented in the economic mainstream. These social practices have profound economic consequences because they do not allow society to take advantage of the talent inherent in women (Menon-Sen & Shiva Kumar, 2001; Sivakumar, 2008). Women in India have existed in predominantly patriarchal environments, facing discrimination in terms of social, political, educational, and economic opportunities due to their perceived inferior status, resulting in the continued dominance of the patriarchal practices in Indian society.

Gender Inequality in Various Spheres in India

In India Gender inequality exists in terms of access to health, education, and employment. Menon-Sen and Shiva Kumar (2001) stated that gender inequality in India exists in the cultural framework. The female child receives less nurturing, care, and parental attention than males, thus, making them far more vulnerable than boys to disease and infections, leading to poor health and a shorter life span (Chand & Mehrotra, 2012). Men outnumber women in India, aged 21 and above. For instance, in 1991, there were 927 women for every 1,000 men, and according to the 2011 Census, the number has slightly increased, and the gender ratio for Indian adults aged 21 or above is 940 women for every 1,000 men (Census of India, 2011). The preferential treatment for males permeates all social classes in India, which sets the gender inequality standard for girls throughout their life span. Roy and Vecchio (1998) argued that education in India is gender discriminatory, too, with males obtaining more access to education, as can be seen from their literacy ratios of 82.14 per cent and 62.46 per cent, respectively (Census of India, 2011).

Indian girls are primarily groomed for marriage, parents always prefer to invest in a boy's education (Roy & Vecchio, 1998). A common belief in everyone is that when girls marry, they belong to their in-laws (Chada & Sinha, 2013), so the return of investment for education or other things is certainly too low. Families with low income with limited resources, education for girls becomes unaffordable. Because male views dominate in Indian households, girls often do not gain access to educational opportunities, and the type of education they receive is often functional and basic; such as reading, writing, maintaining personal hygiene, and effectively conducting household chores. The ideology of Indian society is to keep a woman within the walls of the home and isolated, education is not considered necessary (Roy & Vecchio, 1998). Gender discrimination in the workplace reduces the availability of talent to an economy, leading to negative economic consequence (Esteve-Volart, 2004). In India, many social practices, perceived as orthodox from a religious or cultural standpoint, push women away from the economic mainstream, not allowing the nation's economic development to include the inherent talent women could provide.

Violence against Women

The United Nations Organization was formed in 1945 and women's rights have always been important to the UN. The UN's charter aims to "to reaffirm faith in fundamental human rights, in the dignity and worth of the human person, in the equal rights of men and women."

Despite this aim, violence against women did not start to gain the attention of the UN and the world until the 1980s (World Health Organization, 2017). Violence against women is always discussed and acknowledged not only as a global public health issue, but also as a human rights violation. At the Millennium Summit in 2000, a set of goals was formed to address extreme poverty, and these were called the Millennium Development Goals (MDGs). Three of the eight goals addressed women—to achieve universal primary education; promote gender equality and empower women; and improve maternal health.

There are many terms used commonly to indicate violence against women. Some of these are intimate partner violence (IPV), gender-based violence (GBV), and domestic violence (DV). The World Health Organization (WHO) defines intimate partner violence as "the behaviour by an intimate partner or ex-partner that causes physical, sexual or psychological harm, including physical aggression, sexual coercion, and psychological abuse and controlling behaviours" (World Health Organization, 2016). The European Institute for Gender Equality defines gender-based violence, as violence inflicted by men on women and girls, and highlights the fact that violence against women is an expression of power inequalities between women and men (European Institute for Gender Equality, 2017).

Domestic violence is probably the biggest of the terms because it includes children and other family members. The Merriam-Webster dictionary defines domestic violence as "the inflicting of physical injury by one family or household member on another; *also*: a repeated or habitual pattern of such behaviour" (Merriam Webster, 2017). The United Nations Declaration on the Elimination of Violence against Women (1993) defines violence against women as "any act of gender-based violence that results in, or is likely to result in, physical, sexual or psychological harm or suffering to women, including threats of such acts, coercion or arbitrary deprivation of liberty, whether occurring in public or in private life" (UNICEF, 2017).

Violence against Women in India

In recent years there has been more media reporting on violence outside the home in India. The levels of public harassment, sometimes known as "eve teasing" and number of violent crimes against women, such as rape have increased. This may be due to increased awareness and reporting, especially since the highly publicized brutal gang rape and death of a medical student in Delhi in 2012. There is proof that street harassment, rape and other forms of violence have been a problem for decades. Street harassment, "eve-teasing" has not been taken seriously in the past and in Indian films it is the most common type of sexual violence depicted (Dhillon & Bakaya, 2014).

There is much debate and speculation regarding the cause of this increase, including increasing sex-ratio balance, too few police, few female police, acceptance of violence, low status of women and minimal convictions of these crimes (*Washington Post*, 2012). Violence against women inside the home is a major issue. This requires an understanding of the family structure in India.

Arranged marriage remains the norm in India. Marriage is considered a relationship and understanding between two families, not just two people. Most of the Indians consider this type of marriage as more stable and desirable because it assures shared religion, socio-economic status, and caste. In their book, *Violence and Crime in the Family: Patterns, Causes and Consequences,* Krishan and Subramaniam (2015) describe Indian families as patrilineal.

Violence against women becomes an even more difficult issue to tackle in countries with a high Gender Inequality Index (GII). India's GII is 0.53, and the HDI ranking is 131 (UN 2016). To compare, the World GII is 0.449, the United States' GII is 0.203, and United States' HDI rank is 11 (UN 2016). Within the context of this gender inequality, leaders in India recognized the need for legislation regarding violence against women. In 2006, after years of fighting and lobbying by those involved in the women's movement, the Indian Parliament enacted The Protection of Women Against Violence Act (*Nyaaya,* 2017). This Act was meant to protect women from physical violence and other abuse, including restricting activities or access to family finances. It is difficult to say how effective the law has been. There are some review studies, including the one discussed below, and some smaller studies in the literature, however the large countrywide surveys are conducted infrequently (every 5-10 years) and then the data must be analysed.

Violence against Women during Pregnancy in India

India is a large and extremely diverse country, which makes measuring and understanding VAW challenging, especially during pregnancy. Martin and Tsul (1999) studied five geographic districts in Uttar Pradesh and found that 5.4 to 13.0 per cent of men reported harming their wives during pregnancy. Peedicayil and Sadowski (2004) found similar results, although with a wider range, 0.9 per cent to 20 per cent of women experiencing violence during pregnancy and 40-60 per cent of women who had previously been victims of violence reported that violence continued during pregnancy. In four districts in Nepal, 19.8 per cent of women experienced violence during pregnancy (Silwal, 2012).

Policies and Practices in India to Improve Gender Inequality

Gender inequality is a most difficult challenge for India, and it is unlikely to be solved merely by legislation; however, gender-friendly and gender-neutral policies can help accelerate positive social change (*The Developing World's Missing Women Workers*, 2013). One of the most important factors to initiate gender equality in India, apart from women's safety, is equal access to educational opportunities for females.

Policies and Programmes to Improve Educational Opportunities

The Governmental and Non-governmental Organizations (NGOs) are making consistent efforts to ensure literacy and learning among females in India. Several Governmental programmes, with gender equality education as a key component, have been initiated since independence; the programmes of Social Education, including literacy, was introduced as part of the Community Development Programme in 1952 (Nayar, 1960). Many years later, the Kothari Commission on Education (1964-1966) emphasized the importance of accelerated literacy growth. The 1968 National Policy on Education, in addition to endorsing the recommendations of the Kothari Commission, also outlined the importance of development and implementation of adult and continuing educational programmes as matters of priority (Bhargava, 2008).

India's former Prime Minister, the late Rajiv Gandhi, recognizing illiteracy as a major impediment to India's holistic development initiated the National Literacy Mission (NLM) in 1988 as one of the five technology missions in India with a focus on functional literacy, primarily for women, to strengthen literacy growth. NLM was given the mandate of imparting functional literacy to the 15 to 35 year age group. In the Indian context, the definition of functional literacy included life skills, skill development, and a general awareness of the rights of citizens and their environment, leading to a silent empowerment of the disadvantaged sections of the community (Bhargava, 2008).

The Post Literacy Programme (PLP), a sub-campaign of the NLM, went beyond functional literacy and concentrated on the holistic development of women to enable neo-literates to convert their newly acquired literacy skills into a problem-solving tool. In other words, the goal was to make their acquired knowledge pragmatic for their living and working lifestyles (Loomba & Matthew, 2007).

The Continuing Education Programme (CEP) provided lifelong learning opportunities for women on a range of issues, including income-generating programmes, skill development, and quality of life improvement programmes (Bhargava, 2008). Some of the objectives of the CEP campaign included the following:

- Facilitating opportunities for neophytes to apply their acquired skills to inspire an enhanced quality of life;

Coordinate short-term training and orientation programmes to upgrade vocational skills and thereby attempt to improve the economic conditions of Indian women, including provision of library and reading room facilities to create an environment conducive to literacy and a learning society, and organizing cultural and recreational activities with effective community participation (Singh & Sween, 2002).

In addition to the NLM, Sarva Shiksha Abhiyan (SSA, Education for All), SSA, was a flagship programme introduced by the Indian Government, mandated by the Eighty-Sixth Amendment to the Constitution of India, facilitating free and requisite education for children 6 to 14 years of age. The programme was an attempt to catalyze timely universalisation of elementary education (UEE), the primary goal of the SSA (2007).

The academic endeavours of the SSA have extended to a subsidiary programme called the Mahila Samakhya (Education for Women's Equality). This programme works in conjunction with individual State Governments to be primarily focused on women's education and empowerment for those women in rural areas, particularly women from socially and economically marginalized groups (Hay, 2012). In addition, the Mahila Samakhya implements alternative paradigms to strengthen women's mobilization and empowerment, and successfully shift focus to economic interventions as the principal outcome (Jandhyala, 2003).

The Governmental and Non-governmental Programmes mentioned above primarily focus on reducing gender inequality by providing equal educational opportunities for the Indian female population. However, results thus far have demonstrated, at best, a moderate amelioration in terms of development and implementation among women in India (Arora, 2012).

HRD Policies in India

The origins of human resource (HR) functions in India can be traced to the pre-independence era (in the early 1920s), where the Tata Group implemented basic employee welfare policies, such as provident funding (e.g., retirement) and paid time off (Singh, 2002b). Post-Independence, the 1950s saw the inception of two professional HR bodies, namely, the Indian Institute of Personnel Management (IIPM) and the National Institute of Labour Management (NILM) (Singh, 2002b).

HR functions in India expanded in the 1970s and 1980s to focus on improved organizational efficiency and effectiveness, including training and development activities to support effective management of individual-level worker outcomes such as morale, motivation, and job satisfaction. In recent years, the emphasis on structured HR policies can be attributed to the competition Indian organizations face with their overseas counterparts to build a highly skilled and effective workforce equipped with the requisite tools required to compete in the global market (Budhwar & Sparrow, 1997; Krishna & Monappa, 1994; Ratnam, 1995).

Policies to Improve Employment Opportunities for Women

The Ministry of Human Resource Development (MHRD; 2012) was created on September 26, 1985, to support gender equality through the One Hundred Seventy-Fourth Amendment to the Government of India. The MHRD, in addition to focusing on female education through their Department of School Education and Literacy, mainly focuses on providing flexible options for Indian women to participate in the workforce. MHRD set up a committee to improve the status of women by analyzing causes of gender inequality and identifying factors, and delineate fundamentals to diminish gender inequality.

The Committee on Status of Women in India (CSWI), in its first report, identified distinct demographic trends of wide disparities in access to literacy, education, and livelihood between males and females (Sharma & Sujaya, 2014). The findings of the Committee gave impetus for the women's movement to raise issues and push for further reforms and change. Some of the policies revisited included the following: protecting women against sexual harassment, allowing women to work the same hours as men, earning equal salaries as their male counterparts for the same amount of work, ensuring equal access to training and learning opportunities, and establishing the same retirement age for men and women (Cahn, Kelso and Miller, 2012; Rohila & Sharma, 2012). In addition, further steps were taken by several state governments to incorporate similar policies leading to women's empowerment. Efforts to set up effective institutional establishments to address women's issues are prevalent both at state and national levels (Sharma & Sujaya, 2014).

Conclusion

The studies all-over the world on VAW, have consistently found few significant relationships between violence and socio-demographics. VAW is now considered a public health problem by most countries and communities, there are many ways to address it. Making awareness about VAW at both the community level and with medical providers is important.

There are many ways to go about this including billboards or posters and newspaper and television advertisements. Special health fairs or health awareness days may be planned by public health workers and community health workers, with input from physicians to raise awareness. Activities may include plays (*pathnatyas*), role-plays, talks, and pamphlet distribution. There is so much innovation occurring around the world to develop both technological and low or no tech methodologies to fight gender inequity and violence against women. Culture in the developing world is changing rapidly about what is tolerated so there is reason to be hopeful about reducing VAW and its consequences.

Gender inequality is an important issue worldwide. We focus on India because research suggests that this issue is particularly pronounced there, and the role that HRD could play in reducing its likelihood in the workplace is profound. We identify a number of social and cultural causes that cannot be separated from a historical context. Gender inequality exists in India because historically, in a paternalistic society, it has been socially and culturally acceptable to undervalue women's contributions to society and in turn the workplace.

These norms are deeply rooted in Indian culture and are

seemingly almost unshakable, but that is not necessarily so. Strong efforts to lead the nation to correct this inequality issue have already been put in place through important and impressive legislation. Nonetheless, much more effort is required that originates from within organizations, not because the government legislated it, but because it is the right thing to do. HRD may play a very significant role in leading such efforts to reduce gender inequality in Indian organizations. Recruitment and selection practices, training and development activities, and reward systems could be aligned through policies and procedures at the organization to promote gender equality.

The Government of India has committed to eliminating violence against women and girls through numerous policies, laws, and programmes, yet one in three women aged 15 to 49 years experiences some form of physical or sexual violence during her lifetime. In order to strengthen the process of gender budgeting, the Ministry of Women and Child Development has been undertaking various capacity building measures for the officials of the State Governments by organizing training programmes/ workshops regularly. In order to improve employability a separate Ministry of Skill Development and Entrepreneurship has been created. Equal Remuneration Act, 1973 provides for payment of equal remuneration to men and women workers for the same work of similar nature without any discrimination. In order to ensure social security to the workers including women in the unorganized sector, the Government has enacted the Unorganized Workers' Social Security Act, 2008. The Sexual Harassment of Women at Workplace (Prevention, Prohibition and Redressal) Act, 2013 has been enacted, which covers all women, irrespective of their age or employment status and protect them against sexual harassment at all workplaces both in public and private sector, whether organized or unorganized. These policies and schemes may be useful in India to overcome the gender inequality and violence against women.

References

Arora, R.U. (2012). "Gender inequality, economic development, and globalization: A state level analysis of India", *The Journal of Developing Areas, 46*, 147-164.

Census of India (2011). *Number of literates & literacy rate*. Retrieved from http://censusindia. gov.in/Census_Data_2001/India_at_glance/ literates1.aspx

Chand, S., & Mehrotra, M. (2012). "An evaluation of major determinants of health care facilities for women in India", *Journal of Humanities and Social Science*, 2(5), 1-9. doi:10.9790/0837-0250109.

Bhargava, A. (2008). *Functional Literacy in India: A Progress Report*, Toronto, Ontario: Canadian Education Association.

Bilimoria, D., Joy, S., & Liang, X. (2008). "Breaking barriers and creating inclusiveness: Lessons of organizational transformation to advance women faculty in academic science and engineering", *Human Resource Management*, *47*, 423-441. doi:10.1002/hrm.20225

Budhwar, P., & Sparrow, P. (1997). "Evaluating levels of strategic integration and development of human resource management in India", *The International Journal of Human Resource Management, 8*, 476-494. doi:10.1080/095851997341568.

Cahn, N., Kelso, M., & Miller, B. (2012). *Gender equality in employment: Policies and practices in Switzerland and the U.S.* Washington, DC: George Washington University.

Chada, R., & Sinha, K.D. (2013). "Indian family systems, collectivistic society and psychotherapy", *Indian Journal of Psychiatry*, 55, 299-309.

Comyn, P., Kemmis, R.B., & Smith, E. (2014). "How can the expansion of the apprenticeship system in India create conditions for greater equity and social justice?", *Australian Journal of Adult Learning, 54*, 369-387.

Dhillon, M. & Bakaya, S. (2014). "Street Harassment: A Qualitative Study of the Experiences of Young Women in Delhi", *SAGE Open* 4(3), 1-11. doi: 10.1177/2158244014543786

Esteve-Volart, B. (2004). *Gender Discrimination and Growth: Theory and Evidence from India*. London, England: London School of Economics and Political Science.

European Institute for Gender Equality. (2017). Gender-based Violence. Retrieved from http://eige.europa.eu/gender-based-violence/what-is-gender-based-violence.

Hay, K. (2012). "Engendering policies and programmes through feminist evaluation: Opportunities and insights", *Indian Journal of Gender Studies*, 19, 321-340. doi:10.1177/097152151201900208

Hussain, N., & Kirmani, M. (2010). "Gender differences: A case study of Malda district of West Bengal, India", *Pakistan Journal of Women's Studies: Alam-e-Niswan, 17*, 75-96.

Jandhyala, K. (2003). *Empowering Education: The Mahila Samakhya Experience*. Retrieved from http://portal.unesco.org/education/es/ file_download.php/ea8dc35fd1a0a150c7f436b3 ba0380af Empowering +Education.+ The+Mahila+Samakhya+Experience.doc

Krishna, A., & Monappa, A. (1994). "Economic restructuring and human resources management", *Indian Journal of Industrial Relations, 29*, 490-501.

Loomba, S., & Matthew, A. (2007). "India's National Adult Education Programme", In *Literacy, Knowledge and Development: South-South Policy Dialogue on Quality Education for Adults and Young People* (pp. 91-115). Mexico City, Mexico: INEA (National Institute for Adult Education) and UNESCO (United Nations Educational, Scientific and Cultural Organization) Institute for Lifelong Learning.

Madhok, D. (2014). *Missing Women: India's Record in Women's Participation in the Workforce is Depressing*. Retrieved from http://qz.com/238484/indias-record-in-womens-participation-in-the-workforce-is-depressing/

Martin, S. & Tsul, A. (1999). Domestic Violence in Northern India. *American Journal of Epidemiology*, 150 (4), 417-426.

Merriam Webster Dictionary Website. (2017). Retrieved January 26, 2017 from: https://www.merriam-webster.com/dictionary/domestic%20violence.

Menon-Sen, K., & Shiva Kumar, A.K. (2001). *Women in India: How free? How equal?* New Delhi, India: United Nations Development Assistance Framework.

Nayar, B.R. (1960). *Community Development Programme: Its Political Impact*. Retrieved from http://www.epw.in/system/files/pdf/1960_12/38/community_development_programmeit_ political_impact.pdf

Nyaaya. (2017). The Protection of Women from Domestic Violence Act, 2005. Retrieved from: http://nyaaya.in/law/557/the-protection-of-women-from-domestic-violence-actn 2005/#section-1.

Peedicayil, A., & Sadowski, L. (2004). "Spousal physical violence against women during pregnancy", *BJOG: An International Journal of Obstetrics and Gynaecology, 111.*, 682- 687.

Ratnam, V. (1995). "Economic liberalization and the transformation of industrial relations policies in India", In: A. Verma, T. Kochan, & R. Lansbury (Eds.), *Employment Relations in the Growing Asian Economies*, pp. 121-144. London, England: Routledge.

Razvi, M., & Roth, G. (2004). "Socio-economic development and gender inequality in India", In: T.M. Egan, M.L. Morris, & V. Inbakumar (Eds.), *Proceedings of the Academy of Human Resource Development*, pp. 168-175. Bowling Green, OH: Academy of Human Resource Development.

Rohila, A., & Sharma, A. (2012). *Impact of Liberalization in Services on Higher Education*. Retrieved from http://papers.ssrn.com/sol3/papers.cfm?abstract_id=2022792

Roy, K., & Vecchio, N. (1998). *Poverty, Female-headed Households, and Sustainable Economic Development*, Westport, CT: Greenwood Press.

Sivakumar, M. (2008). *Gender Discrimination and Women's Development in India*. Erode, India Munich Personal RePEc Archive. Retrieved from http://mpra.ub.uni-muenchen.de/10901/

Singh, A., & Sween, D. (2002). "Lifelong learning for women empowerment", In: M.K. George (ed.), *Lifelong Learning for Social Development: A Review of Global Perspectives—Conference Proceedings*, pp. 30-35. Kerala, India: Loyola College of Social Services.

Singh, K. (2002b). "Strategic HR orientation and firm performance in India", In: T.M. Egan (Ed.), *Proceedings of the Academy of Human Resource Development Conference*, pp. 3-10. Bowling Green, OH: Academy of Human Resource Development.

Sharma, K., & Sujaya, C.P. (2014). *Towards Equality: Report of the Committee on the Status of Women in India*. New Delhi, India: Pearson.

Silwal, P. (2012). *"Violence during Pregnancy among Young Married Women in Nepal"*, Retrieved from UConn Digital Commons.

Subramaniam, M. & Krishan, P. (2015). *Violence and Crime in the Family: Patterns, Causes, and Consequences*. Bingley, UK: Emerald Group Publishing.

Sinha, M. (2013). *The Gender-Mainstreaming: Bridging Gender Inequality in India*, Munich, Germany: Verlag. Retrieved from http://www.grin.com/en/e-book/265536/the-gendermainstreaming-bridging-gender-inequality-in-India.

United Nations International Children's Emergency Fund (UNICEF). (2017). *Domestic Violence against Women and Girls*, UNICEF, Retrieved January 26, 2017 from https://www.unicefirc.org/publications/pdf/digest6e.pdf.

United Nations Development Programme (UNDP). (2016). *Human Development Reports, Gender Inequality Index and Human Development Index*. Retrieved from: http://hdr.undp.org/en/content/gender-inequality-index-gii.

Washington Post (2012). "Ten Reasons India has a Sexual Violence Problem." Retrieved from: https://www.washingtonpost.com/news/worldviews/wp/2012/12/29/india-rape-victim- dies sexualviolence-proble/?utm_term=.e9577e54fd48.

World Health Organization (WHO). (2017). *No to Violence Against Women*. Retrieved from: http://www.create4theun.eu/how-did-violence-against-women-become-a-human-rights- concern/.

World Health Organization (WHO). (2016). *Violence against Women, Intimate Partner and Sexual Violence Against Women*. Retrieved from: http://www.who.int/mediacentre/factsheets/fs239/en/

12

Adjustment Problems of Women Working in Educational System

Sushmita Upadhyay

Introduction

Adjustment is a vast phenomenon of a human being. It is a capacity of an individual personality to function efficiently in relation to other people around us. To adjust actually means doing different things in different situations to different people in different societies (Sechrest & Wallace 1967). Successful adjustment is necessary to continue living. Adjust or die is the law of life (Gray 1954).

The spread of education made the women get more knowledge, more thinking power. Only educated woman is able to think nationally. In one of their study B. Sandhya Rani and M. Sharada Devi (2008) found that the role stress of working and non-working women in recreational, social and job life result indicates that majority of the working and non-working women express stress regarding participation in social functions and in religious activities. Stress reduces brain functions such as memory intellectual efficiency and even brings premature old age. It affects our learning and concentration all of which are central to effective performance at work. Pascal (1992) defines stress in term of perceived environmental situation which threatens and gratification of needs.

Some of the findings also indicated that working women feel maladjusted due to the non-cooperative attitude of the husband

and family members. Adjustment is a process that helps a person to lead a happy and contented life while maintaining a balance between his needs and his capacity to fulfil them.

For the empowerment of the women, Constitution of India made the provision under article 15(1), 16(1) and 16(2) that the state shall not discriminate against its citizens on ground of religion, race, caste, sex, place of birth or any of them. Singh, Thind and Jaswal (2006) studied assessment of marital adjustment among couples with respect to women educational level and employment status. The study also investigated that education and employment of the Indian women has got significant implications not only for their own lives but for all the lives and relation linked with them.

Shirin's (2009) studies had analyzed research on the impact of work on mother's health in Tehran (Iran) with a role of analytic framework. Three main explanatory factors were examined alongside a range of mental and physical health outcome variables. In the West, where women paid work is generally associated with better health. Statistically, significant differences between working and non-working women were not found in Tehran.

In one of the studies to determine life stress among working and non-working women in relation to anxiety and depression, the researcher found that in India, among working women positive life changes are related to depression, whereas among non-working women positive life changes are related to anxiety and negative life changes to depression.

Canlon (1986) has examined the sexual dysfunction and disorder patterns of 218 married working and non-working women. Result indicated that women who were pursuing careers of an ongoing, developmental nature were twice as likely to present with the primary complaint of inhibited sexual desire than women who were unemployed outside of the home. Hasmi (2007) in one of her studies found highly significant relationship between marital adjustment, depression and stress. The findings also show that working married women have to face more problems in their married life as compared to non-working married women. Further, the result also reveals that highly educated working and non-working married women can perform well in their married life and they are free from depression.

Objective of the Study

To compare the family adjustment in working women between private sector and government sector.

Hypothesis

Women who are working in government sectors may have better family adjustment on the different dimensions of adjustment like personal, partner, family, work, school etc. as compared to women who are working in private sector.

Method

Participants

The participants for the present study comprised of 50 women. Among them, 25 women were selected from government sector and 25 from private sector or intermediate school, located in Gorakhpur (U.P.), for example—A.N.E Railway Girls Inter College, A.D. Girls Inter College, Ratna-Prakash Memorial School and Little Flowers School.

Measures

Multi-Problem screening questionnaires were administered to access the family adjustment of women. It was developed by Watter W. Hudson (1997). The questionnaire had 65 items designed to obtain information about problems experiencing in eight different areas of personal and social functioning. Seven points rating scale was used to know about the family adjustment. The responses were ranging from (None of the time) to 7 (all of the time). To access the adjustment of different areas of M.P.S.Q. are as follows:

1. **Personal Adjustment:** 14 items are involved in this dimension (item no. 1 to 14). It responded personal thinking for the adjustment.
2. **Partner Relationship:** It consists of 8 items (item no.15 to 21) dealing with the partner adjustment.
3. **Family Adjustment:** This dimension had 9 items (item

no. 22 to 30 which are related to adjustment between job and family.

4. **Work Adjustment:** There are 7 items in this dimension (item no. 31 to 37) which are related to the management of the work in official problems.
5. **School Adjustment:** This dimension consists of 8 items (item no. 38-45).
6. **Social Adjustment:** This dimension consists of 7 items (item no. 46 to 52) which are related to emotional feelings of women.
7. **Financial Problems:** This dimension has 8 items (item no. 53 to 60) which are related to financial management.
8. **Play Leisure:** It contains 5 items (item no. 61 to 65) which are related to measure the enjoyable and leisure time.

Procedure

Before administration of the test the permission to collect the data from school teachers was requested from the principal of the school of Gorakhpur, then the testing schedule was conducted personally from the teachers one by one asking them to follow the instruction of the questions.

Statistical Analysis

Keeping in view the hypothesis of the study discipline statistics consisting of mean, standard deviation, standard error of mean, and t-test was computed to identify the significant differences between the women working in private sector and government sector on multi-problem screening questionnaire (M.P.S.Q.) regarding the adjustment of SPSS system was used to data analysis.

Result

The result is indicated in Tables 12.1 and 12.2 of M.P.S.Q. The result reveals that amongst the eight dimensions only three dimensions shows the significant difference between the women working in government sector and private sector namely personal adjustment ($t = 3.15$, $p < 0.05$), school adjustment ($t = 2.69$, $p < 0.05$) and financial problem ($t = 6.23$, $p < 0.001$). Table 12.1 shows the mean score and standard deviation valves of government and private sector of women in personal adjustment (M = 37.60, 31.40; SD = 6.80, 7.14) respectively. However, no. of significant differences were found among them in partner relationship (t = 1.53, p < 0.001). The mean scores and standard deviation valves of government and private sector of women in partner relationship were (M = 14.00, 11.32; SD = 7.14, 5.06), family adjustment were (M = 13.80, 13.12; SD = 6.90, 7.09) and work adjustment were (M = 18.32, 15.60; SD = 4.90, 6.04) respectively. Further, Table 12.2 shows that on the dimension of school adjustment and financial problems, significant differences were found between government and private sector working women. However, no. of significant differences were found on social adjustment (t = 1.37, p > 0.001) and play leisure (t = 1.78, p > 0.001).

Table 12.1: Result of M.P.S.Q.

Dimensions of M.P.S.Q.	*Govt. Sector*		*Private Sector*		*t-value*
	Mean	*S.D.*	*Mean*	*S.D.*	
Personal adjustment	37.60	6.80	31.40	7.14	3.15**
Partner relationship	14.00	7.14	11.32	5.06	1.53
Family adjustment	13.80	6.90	13.12	7.09	0.34
Work adjustment	18.32	4.90	15.60	6.04	1.75

Note: ** Significant at .01.
Source: Author's own data.

Table 12.2: Result of M.P.S.Q.

Dimensions of M.P.S.Q.	*Govt. Sector*		*Private Sector*		*t-value*
	Mean	*S.D.*	*Mean*	*S.D.*	
School adjustment	31.96	7.32	26.72	6.40	2.69**
Social adjustment	21.48	4.05	19.68	5.17	1.37
Financial problems	28.48	4.49	18.76	6.38	6.23***
Play & Leisure	17.16	7.14	13.84	6.02	1.78

Note: ** Significant at .01. *** Significant at .01.
Source: Author's own data.

The mean score and standard deviation value of government and private sector women in school adjustment were (M=31.96, 26.72; SD=7.32, 6.40), social adjustment were (M=21.48, 19.68; SD=4.05, 5.17), financial problems were (M=28.48, 18.76; SD=4.49, 6.38) and the last dimension, that is, play and leisure were (M=17.16, 13.84; SD=7.14, 6.02) respectively.

Disscusion

Results revealed that women working in government sectors were significantly higher than their counterparts working in private sectors on three dimensions of M.P.S.Q. namely, personal adjustment, school adjustment and financial problems. No significant difference was found between them on partner relationship, family adjustment, work adjustment, social adjustment and play and leisure. Here, before the implification of the result must be clear that higher score means poor adjustment and low score means better adjustment. Thus, the result indicates that in the private sector they provide different facilities as compared to government sector. They give attractive salary, so that they could lead better personal adjustment. According to "Egunyonis (2009) higher continuing education seeks to build highly individualized and flexible programmers of learning and largely make use of untapped resource for teaching and learning."

Further, as it was hypothesized about school adjustment, supported here. In the private sector women score will be lower than the women working in government sectors. Many studies indicate that those in private sector are also engaged in multiple extracurricular activities as well as different notes. On the other hand, in government sectors they feel relaxed about their job security as well as they use monotonous techniques which do not make their positive effort for recent informations about their job category. Therefore, they score high on the scale as compared to private sectors.

Findings also indicate that financial problems are less with private working women. It is universally observed that doing jobs in private sectors specially in education system, due to their attractive salary they always try to upgrade their living standards, they use to invest their earnings for the better education of their children, to provide more facilities to the members of their family to achieve good health and technical knowledge.

Kazeem (1998) and Olomukaro (2005) have opined that higher education can be viewed as a mean of acquiring knowledge that will enable the individual to keep up with the rapid social, cultural, economic, political, industrial and technological changes taking place in the environment in which the individual himself/herself to be.

As the result indicates that on the dimension of partner

relationship, family adjustment, work adjustment, social adjustment and play and leisure, no significant differences were observed. In both conditions, women face more or less same problem according to adjustment. Therefore, feeling of stress and depression takes place.

Many researchers threw light on the basis of different reasons or the important causes of this kind of stress and depression which are lack of time and multiple role of women. Singh (2002) studied the level of stress in working and non-working women, which reveals that the working women have more stress than non-working women. Bhattacharjee *et al.* (1983) studied on family adjustment of married working women and non-working women. No significant differences in adjustment or neuroticism were found between them. So, this study concluded that a women adjustment, Weather employed or not, is a function of her own personality traits, expectation and perception combined with those of her spouse and family members.

Therefore, it can be concluded that adjustment is a phenomenon which reflects the basic nature of a woman. As it works everywhere, so it can be managed by the basic originality of a woman in which some original qualities involve, i.e. impurity, peacefulness, calmness, tolerance etc.

References

Ahmad, S.N. (2009). "Women work and health in Iran : A comparison of working and non-working mothers", *Social Science and Medicine,* 54(5), 753-765.

Bhattacharjee, P., Bhatt, K.K. (1983). "Family adjustment of married working and non-working women", *Indian Journal of Clinical Psychology*. Vol. 10(2), 497-501.

Calon, B. (1986). "Sexual dysfunction and disorder patterns of working and non-working wives", *Journal of Sex and Marital Therapy,* Vol. 12 (2), 93-107.

Gray, J.S. (1954). *Psychology Applied to Human Affairs,* New York: McGraw Hill Ltd.

Hashmi Ahmad Hina, Maryan Khursid & Ishtaiq Hassan (2007). "A Study on Marital Adjustment", *Journal of Medical Update*. Volume (2).

Pascal, (1992). *Stress and Coping: The Indian Experience,* New Delhi: Sage.

Rani, B.S. & Devi, S.M. (2008). "Role satisfaction of working and non-working women in marital life and family life", *Asian Journal of Psychology and Education,* 41 (5-6), 10-15.

Sechrest, L. & Wallace, (1964). *Psychology and Human Problems,* Ohio: Charles and Memil Publishing Company.

Singh, M. (2002) *Stress Scale.*

Singh, R.; Thind, S.K. & Jaiswal, S. (2006). "Assessment of marital adjustment among couples with respect to women educational level and employment status", *Anthropologist,* 8(4), 259-266.

13

Constraints of Women Development in India

Ruchi Chandra

The objective of the study is to highlight the major social and financial constraints encountered by rural women entrepreneurs in Lucknow, Uttar Pradesh. In the history of human development, woman has been as important as man and the status, employment and work performed by them in society are the indicator of a nation's overall progress. They are playing a vital role in socio-economic development of the country, however, there are few constraints that women face during their journey of life and their pursuit of getting recognition. Indian women are considered as the source of power (*Shakti*) since ancient times. In this dynamic world, women entrepreneurs are a significant part of the global expedition for sustained economic development and social progress.

The study is mainly based on the primary data collection from the women of lower working class and village girls, defining the Constraints of Women Development in India. It covers the major verticals which acts like a barrier in development of the country women. The research mainly focus on the domains like social taboos and the belief system of the society, the widow's remarriage, treatment of the rape victims and their acceptability in the society, The Health constraints, Education factor, Economic and Social condition of a particular strata.

The tools used for data collection are questionnaire, in-depth interviews and informal interaction with the respondents. The in-depth interviews of 10 respondents were conducted in order to gain better understanding of their operations. Questionnaire was prepared for the respondents including open and close ended questions. The study looks at the socio-cultural and financial barriers to women towards their journey of empowerment.

The status of **women in India** has been subject to many great changes over the past few millennia. From equal status with men in ancient times, through the low points of the medieval period to the promotion of equal rights by many reformers, the history of women in India has been eventful. Devi is the female goddess in India by the majority of Hindu community as the source of primordial power, the symbol of piety and purity. Yet, in a country of such great tradition and culture, Indian women are in the news globally for all the wrong reason : sexual harassment and societal subjugation. In the past decade with the information boom having touched all corners of the globe, unfiltered news about India is available to all. It has meant that the focus in the past two years has been on crimes against women in India rather than on women achievers from India. All the rich G20 nations, India has been the worst place to be a woman. But how is this possible in a country that prides itself on being the world's largest democracy. (world news/the Guardian) The world looks upon India as an emergent power and it is impossible for India to be a power in this region with half of its population lagging behind. In modern India, women have held high offices in India including that of the President, Prime Minister, Speaker of the Lok Sabha and Opposition. But still women in India are suffering lots of atrocities and sufferings. Women when given with suitable environment and opportunity do flourish and fly high up to the sky but they are not safe, secure, powerful, happy and hearty yet.

45 per cent of Indian girls are married before the age of 18, according to the International Centre for Research on Woman (2010), 56,000. Maternal deaths were recorded in 2010. UN Population Fund and Research from UNICEF 2012, found that 52 per cent of adolescent girls and 57 per cent of adolescent boys think it is justifiable for a man to beat his wife. According to the National Crime Records Bureau in India, there was a 7.1 per cent hike in recorded crimes against women between 2010 and 2011. The biggest leap was in cases under the **"Dowry Prohibition Act"** up to 27.7 per cent of kidnapping and abduction up to 19.4 per cent year on year and rape up to 9.2 per cent. A preference for son and fear to pay a dowry has resulted in 12 million girls being aborted over the past three decades (*World News*). We worship

goddesses and yet fail to protect women from these crimes and the blame too.

So many constraints of development of women are found in India, *i.e.* social, economic, self-help and personal level constraints and legal constraints are also found frequently, these are the barriers of the development from person to nation. Women in Indian society face many barriers and constraints. But in spite of these barriers and constraints they are continuously striving for their identity. The following constraints have been discovered through various tests and interviews.

A. Social Constraints

(i) Discrimination: Gender is a common term whereas gender discrimination is meant only for women, because females are the only victims of gender discrimination. Females are nearly 50 per cent of the total population but their representation in public life is very low. From birth to death females are facing lots of discrimination against them. Some of them are:

Abortion of female foetus with the help of scanning: The National Family and Health Surveys (NFHS) show that the sex-ratio for children under the age of seven has declined with time during the past years. This decline can be explained by the access to technology which enables sex-selective abortions.

(ii) Case Study: Soni and Manokamini told us during the interview that they were compelled to abort their baby because it was diagnosed as a female foetus. Their husband and in-laws compelled them to get rid of the pregnancy because they wanted a male child.

Educational constraints (Denial of higher education): The female literacy rate is eventually improving but even then many young girls are not admitted in schools and even if they are admitted for some time they are made to leave it before completing their basic primary education. In small towns and cities, the girls are compelled to drop studies after completing high school and intermediate because it is considered that after getting higher education, the search of suitable groom will be difficult. Our research showed that almost 70 per cent of the women left their education because their parents believe that no boy likes to get married to a girl having higher education than him.

(iii) Mobility Restraints: Mobility is a variable showing a woman's freedom of movement. It is based on if she is able to visit different places without the permission of a family member and if she can go to these places alone. These places include the local market, health care centre, fields outside the village, a temple, relatives and friends as well as a nearby city.

(iv) Health Care Issues: Women and men have many of the same health problems, but they can affect women differently like women may have different symptoms of heart disease. Some diseases or conditions are more common in women, such as osteoarthritis, obesity and depression. And some conditions, such as menopause and pregnancy, are unique to women. Women's health area provides information on a broad range of women's health care topics for women young and old alike covering pregnancy, baby care, beauty and make-up tips, child, gynecological and skin diseases with symptoms treatment. Women do not get proper health care and treatment for their illness. Pregnant women are still deprived of medical guidance and care. They even do not get nutritional diet during pregnancy. The data shows that about half of the women interviewed had the freedom to go to the market or a health facility alone. Seventy nine per cent of women from the highest education (bachelor degree) brackets and only about 30 per cent of lower education bracket women were allowed to go to the market and visit the doctor alone. About 60 per cent women accepted that they give milk, fruits and good diet to their sons only and do not prefer it to the girls because boys need to be strong and healthy. The son-preference shown to be present in many parts of India is important to investigate when it comes to women's empowerment.

In its 2009 report, UNICEF came up with shocking figures on the status of new mothers in India. The maternal mortality report of India stands at 301 per 1000, with as many as 78,000 women in India dying of childbirth complications in that year. Today, due to the burgeoning population of the country, that number is sure to have multiplied considerably. The main causes of maternal mortality are:

- Haemorrhage : 30 per cent
- Anaemia : 19 per cent
- Sepsis : 16 per cent
- Obstructed Labour : 10 per cent
- Abortion : 8 per cent
- Toxaemia : 8 per cent

(v) Early marriage: Early marriage is a major reason for the girls to leave their studies. Insecurity also impairs a country's education system, which particularly limits educational opportunities for girls: parents often keep their daughters home from school to ensure their security. But hindering education further contributes to both early marriage and to increased poverty. The research shows parents resort to early marriage as a protection against both real and perceived risks, because they believe they have no alternatives. However, it is found that girls who are married in young age are more at risk of violence, malnutrition and devastating complications in childbirth.

Family Responsibility: Women assuming multiple roles results in work family conflict because time and energy are shared, clubbed and even extended across the two spheres of activity. When a housewife enters into gainful employment outside home she not only finds a change in her role and status within the family and outside it, but she also finds herself under increasing pressure to reconcile the dual burden of the two roles at her home and her workplace because each is a full time job. Coping up with the situation requires not only additional physical strength, personal ability and intelligence on the part of a working woman but also requires the members of her 'role set' to simultaneously make necessary modifications in their expectations. When conflict between the two life domains occurs, the consequences are reflected in both organisation and domestic life.

(vi) Violence, Eve-teasing, Rape and Sexual Harassment: Despite the policies, laws, and initiatives by civil society institutions, violence against women in India is widespread and the consequences for perpetrators rarely match the crime. Enforcement of laws and sentencing of perpetrators are long and arduous processes, and the gaps in these processes are further widened by corruption. In our research almost 70 per cent of the ladies were found ignorant about the domestic violence law and other laws for protection of women during our interview. A gap in implementing laws and policies on violence against women is the inaccessibility of information on victims' rights among rural and less educated women. Additionally, social stigma and the fear of abandonment by the family play a big role in women and girls' ability or inability to access laws and policies to address sexual and physical violence.

(vii) Dowry: Dowry is eating our society like a tremor. This also gives birth to many evils and other social issues. Dowry is an accepted social custom in our Indian society. As long as there are givers and takers of dowry, there will be victims of dowry. Problematic part is that it made its way to all sections, classes, castes, societies and communities. It permeated even to tribal societies known for primitive egalitarianism and gender equality and to Muslim community too.

In our study it has been discovered that almost 98 per cent of women are affected with the dowry. Some of them faced troubles due to the demands before the marriage and pressure on their parents. Some few told us that their parents are still under huge debt due to the dowry given in their marriage. Nearly 45 per cent of women in the interview informed that they face sarcastic comments for not fulfilling their husband's and in-law's demands of dowry.

Case Study: Meera (name changed) a helper in SRMGPC informed us that she was subjected to cruelty in her in-laws house for 7 years just because her parents could not give her husband a motorbike and at last she was compelled to leave her husband's home and now get divorced on the charge of bad character.

Rape victims are not accepted in society: In India there are lot of cases of crimes in which women are the victims. The National Crime Records Bureau made a report in 1998 that by the year 2010, the rate of crimes in India against women will be more than the rate at which population is growing. Usually, the cases of rape are not reported because it would result in the women not having any respect in society. Rape victims in India face double punishment because on one hand they are victims of cruelty and exploitation and on the other hand they face social condemnation and disrespect in society instead of getting support and respectful acceptance in society

(2) Cultural Values

Cultural norms and values play a major role as a constraint for women in Indian society. These are:

(i) Caste System: About 65 per cent of women answered yes for believing in caste system in the questionnaire based test which has yes or no option only. About 65 per cent of women are found caste bias though 35 per cent of the women are liberal for the caste discrimination. These 35 per cent women who have a liberal approach for caste system are mostly intermediate pass or graduates. Women who believe in caste system hesitate to mingle with others and believe in the prevailing orthodox customs in their class.

Religious Beliefs: Due to lack of proper education people interpret their religion in a wrong way and thus behave redundantly. The Indian women still seems to find her day-to-day societal 'self' or 'location' within the religious *samskara* of marriage. Sometimes, these women are the sole breadwinners of the family, either economically independent of their husbands or abandoned by them — and yet none of these women seemed to have moved beyond the marriage ritual as their personally defining act. The ability to do so, the path to take to be more than just a married person, is there in the religious teachings and in the culture, but is invariably assigned solely to men. Why are none of these women interested in emulating these paths, in order to gain for themselves, both as individuals and as a group, more autonomy? Early marriage, not providing higher education and freedom of movement and expression is related with religious taboos in our Indian society.

(ii) Family History and Honour: For the sake of the family honour and to maintain the so-called past family glory people do not allow their daughters to come out of their home and go to various places alone. They do not want their daughters to get mingled with the boys and thus avoid co-educational institutions. *Khaap Panchayat* and honour killing are still prevailing in our society. *Khap* is a cluster of villages united by caste and geography.

B. Economic Constraints

(i) Hindrances for women in sharing property rights in the family: Mostly in India women do not own land and do not get the opportunity to buy it. The laws are supporting to women but these laws are well implemented. According to the amended law in India, women have a right in their parental property but they are denied to get it. Women are not even given proper share in parent's property. Due to social criticism they cannot even fight back properly for their property rights.

(ii) Case Study: Sarla, who is working as an office co-coordinator is a divorcee with three female children. She belongs to a good middle class family but her brothers denied her for the right in her father's property and thus she is compelled to work at such a profile in a private organization with a meager salary. She could not get higher education because her parents preferred to educate their sons. She got married after completing graduation though she was interested in higher education. But the relief is that she is earning because she could complete her graduation.

(iii) Ownership of property and family income is generally in the hands of Males: Still in 95 per cent homes the family income even the income of the earning wife is in the possession of the males. The women do not have a right to spend the money she has earned herself.

(iv) Parents having limited resources, give priority to educate the male child instead of the girl: It is very common that parents give priority to educate their male child when they have economic restraints. They feel that the male child will take care of them in their old age whereas the girl has to go to somebody else's home. Son is considered as "Budhaape ki Laathi" whereas a daughter is liable to take care of someone else's family, which is a wrong concept.

(v) Workforce participation: Quite opposite to the common approach many women in India do work. According to the national data collection agencies, the number of women believed to be working is not properly kept record of. Even though a lot of women are working in India they are not paid properly. Their salaries cannot be compared with that of men.

C. Self-Help and Personal Level Constraints

Sometimes, women themselves are not interested in their development because they give up due to the circumstances around them. Women lose their confidence due to the adversities they face, and for the sake of proper adjustment in the family they sacrifice their wishes. These constraints are:

(i) Poor Self Image: Just because of being a girl and the condemnations faced from their *naanis* and *daadis* many girls create a poor self image since childhood.

(ii) Lack of Motivation and Confidence: Due to lack of

support from parents and the environment around women lose their confidence and thus become demotivated to progress ahead. In our study almost 39 per cent of the women left their studies because they got demotivated and non-co operation of their family and fraternity.

(iii) Role Conflict: Conflicts arise when one or the other party is not able to reach to an agreement. It is the stage where disagreement crops up. Role conflict is an outcome of conflicts in number of roles performed by an individual. Women assuming multiple roles results in work family conflict because time and energy are shared, clubbed and even extended across the two spheres of activity. When a housewife enters into gainful employment outside home she not only finds a change in her role and status within the family and outside it, but she also finds herself under increasing pressure to reconcile the dual burden of the two roles at her home and her workplace because each is a full time job. Coping up with the situation requires not only additional physical strength, personal ability and intelligence on the part of a working woman but also requires the members of her 'role set' to simultaneously make necessary modifications in their expectations. When conflict between the two life domains occurs, the consequences are reflected in both organization and domestic life.

Inability to Maintain Work-Life Balance: In a discussion that has gone viral on the Web, PepsiCo's India-born CEO Indra Nooyi, counted among the world's most powerful women, has acknowledged that it is difficult to maintain a work-life balance. "I don't think women can have it all. I just don't think so. We pretend we have it all. We pretend we can have it all", 58-year-old Ms. Nooyi told David Bradley, owner of the Atlantic Media Company. Ms. Nooyi said she has died "with guilt" several times as she tried to bring up her two daughters with her husband of 34 years. She recounted that she felt guilty for not being able to attend several activities at her daughters' school as she could not take time off from work.

D. Legal Constraints

It is very well said that "Justice delayed is justice denied". Same is the case with the women who are deprived of the judicial help and justice because of the delayed procedure and corruption.

Delayed Justice: Justice delayed is justice denied, is an old but wise saying. And this is the reason for most of the Indian women avoid seeking help of the court. People in India have lost faith in judicial remedies because of the prolonged and unending process. Women bear the atrocities and avoid going to the court.

***Case Study*:** Sushila narrated us a story about her friend during the interview—Ajanta was subjected to mental and physical cruelty continuously for 5 years in her in-law's place but her parents neither supported her nor brought her back safely, rather they insisted Ajanta to stay to her in-laws to save family's respect. As a result, after suffering from so much of trauma Ajanta committed suicide.

Ignorance of legal Rights: Majority of people in India are not aware of their fundamental legal rights. Women do not know about the **Domestic Violence Act, 2005** and other laws like:

- The Immoral Traffic (Prevention) Act, 1956;
- The Dowry Prohibition Act, 1961 (28 of 1961) (Amended in 1986);
- The Indecent Representation of Women (Prohibition) Act, 1986;
- The Commission of Sati (Prevention) Act, 1987 (3 of 1988);
- The Protection of Women from Domestic Violence Act, 2005; and
- The Sexual Harassment of Women at Workplace (Prevention, Prohibition and Redressal) Act, 2013.

Almost 85 per cent of the women in our survey were unaware about these laws and thus they never get courage to seek the help of judicial system in our country.

Recommendations: To enlarge their participation in small and medium segments a stronger coordinated role of Indian Government, financial institutions, voluntary agencies and educational institutions with an integrated approach is necessary. Young female entrepreneurs should share their success stories in the world of e-commerce to speed up entrepreneurial movement in India. Women entrepreneurs will be better understood and encouraged by studying and focusing: (i) their social and cultural background including family system; (ii) religion and caste; and (iii) location where they are staying.

We need to educate our women and conduct awareness programmes to change the mindset of people so that the women can secure the path of development.

Conclusion

There has been a steady increase in the participation of women in public and private sectors in India. From the point of view of performance, it was observed that the women in India have made significant contribution towards generation of employment, gross output, asset creation and services.

It may be concluded that women have shifted traditional assumptions about their roles and capabilities. There has been a marked change, and it has been for the better. The most important measure of women success should be the extent to get enabled a woman to interpret, apply and enforce laws of their own making, incorporating their own voices, values and concerns.

Our study shows that most of the women (almost 90%) have an urge to grow and develop. Even some of them are willing to enhance their knowledge by adding degrees to their education. This is a positive sign that willingness already exists in the bosom of the women, we only need to provide proper environment, information and facilities to these women.

To conclude, in the words of Former President A.P.J. Abdul Kalam "Empowering women is a prerequisite for creating a good nation, when women are empowered, society with stability is assured".

References

Chakrapani, C., S. Vijaya Kumar (1994). *Changing Status and Role of Women in Indian Society*, M.D. Publications Pvt. Ltd.

Devendra, Kiran (1994). *Changing Status of Women in India.*

www.womenempowermentinindia.com

en.wikipedia.org/wiki/Women_in_India

www.ifad.org/gender

Why is India so bad for women ?/*World News/The Guardian.* *www.theguardian.com.world jul*

14

The Psychological Effect of Infertility Treatment

Shilpi Singh

Infertility primarily refers to the biological inability of a person to conceive. Infertility may also denote to the state of a women who is unable to carry a pregnancy to full term. There are many biological causes of infertility (Markar *et al.*, 2002). This means that the individual's reproductive system is not functioning in fullest capacity.

"To be mother were women created and to be fathers, men" these lines are from the *Manusmriti,* one of the ancient scriptures that directs and guides the code of conduct of human life in Hindu society (Kumari, 1988). The definitions of infertility varies between cultures and the biomedical definition cited above may not capture variations in cultural perceptions of childlessness. The prevalence of infertility is hard to estimate and varies between culture.

In India, it is estimated that one out of five couples is childless and their numbers are growing. There was a 50 per cent jump in infertility rate in urban India since 1981. WHO estimated that in India, the prevalence of primary infertility is to be between 3.9 and 16.8 per cent (Infecundity, infertility, and childlessness in developing countries, 2004). Estimates of infertility is differ widely among Indian states from 3.7 per cent in Uttar Pradesh, Himachal Pradesh and Maharashtra, to 5 per cent in Andhra Pradesh, and 15 per cent in Kashmir (Kumar *et al.*, 2007). Moreover, the prevalence of primary infertility has also been shown to vary across tribes and castes within the same region in India (Unisa *et al.*, 1999; Adamson *et al.*, 2011).

Infertility has been described as a disease, disorder, disability, handicap, illness, syndrome, condition or condition caused by a disease. There is a disadvantage in calling infertility as a disease because falling pregnant does not necessarily cure infertility. It is possible for one to fall pregnant and bear a child using reproductive technologies. There is nevertheless some advantage to regarding infertility as a disease, which is thereby placed within the medical model which could for example assist infertile individuals in acquiring insurance coverage for their treatment. The medical community considers infertility to be a clinical problem for which they can sometimes offer a remedy.

Infertility primarily refers to the biological inability of a person to conceive. Infertility may also denote to the state of a women who is unable to carry a pregnancy to full term. There are many biological causes of infertility (Markar *et al.*, 2002). This means that the individual's reproductive system is not functioning in fullest capacity.

The etiology of infertility is divided into four categories; the female factor, the male factor, combined male and female factor and infertility of undetermined causes (Stanton & Dunkel-Schetter, 1991).

Infertility in women is due to three primary biological causes. First, the women may not be producing and releasing mature eggs due to hormonal problems or ovarian cysts. Second, scarring or adhesions may interfere with the fallopian tubes being able to properly transport the egg from the ovary to the womb. Third, structural abnormalities or hormonal problems may result in the fertilized egg being unable to properly implant in the uterine lining.

Male infertility is due to the male producing an insufficient number of sperm and/or sperm of poor quality and poor sperm production can be caused by hormonal problems (William *et al.*, 1992).

There are a lot of risk factors for infertility. In present era, delay of first pregnancy by choice contributes to inability to conceive and maintain pregnancy. Exposure to toxins, sexually transmitted diseases, and other environmental causes can reduce couples fertility (Eupnu, 1995; Mabasa, 2002).

Only one intensive infertility work up can determine the specific causes of infertility. These include several physical examinations, frequent review of basal body temperature and intercourse records, laboratory tests, surgery, and trials of medical treatment (Eupnu, 1995).

For women, the evaluation should include examination of the cervical, uterine, tubal, peritoneal, ovarian and immunology functioning. These diagnostic and treatment procedures can be physically and emotionally invasive for the couple. They are time consuming, often continuing over a number of years, and often rigidly tied to some event (such as ovulation) in the reproductive cycle (Eupnu, 1995; Williams *et al.*, 1992).

In recent years, the number of couples seeking treatment for infertility has considerably augmented due to the factors such as postponement of childbearing in women, development of newer and more successful techniques for infertility treatment and increasing awareness of available services. This rising participation in fertility treatment has raised awareness and inspired investigation into the psychological ramification of infertility. Consideration has been given to the psychological impact of infertility *per se* and of the prolonged exposure to intrusive infertility treatment on mood and well-being (Anderheim *et al.*, 2005).

Infertility includes psychological, social and physical suffering. Infertile individual may direct his/her anger towards their spouses, themselves, other family members or their friends, couples with children, their doctors or towards society. Feeling of guilt, self-blame or personal responsibility are mentioned in 68 per cent of the articles (Domar & Seibel, 1990). Some couples feel guilt because of sexual practices, contraceptive method, or lifestyle that they believe helped produce their infertility or because they delayed trying to have children. Other feel guilt that they have no specific source, or feel guilt over a previous transgression for which infertility is seen as the punishment.

Infertile couple are anxious about the treatment they are undergoing, and particular about whether or not they will be successful in becoming parents. There are two responses to infertility which involve loss of control.

- First type of control loss is the control over event that are current including a loss of control over one's daily activities, bodily functions, and emotion (Merari *et al.*, 2002).

- The second concern control of the future, and to meet life-goals. Although some articles mention a loss of both types of control, the two types appear to be distinguishable. Infertility is accompanied by a real or perceived loss of control over the present because of chronic stress associated with infertility, some individual feel that they are unable to control their emotions and some complain of mood inability (De Ridder, 2000).

Infertility treatment may indicate the scheduling of work-related or social activities and thereby individual may feel they have surrendered and control over these domains as well (Edelman *et al.*, 1994). The diagnosis of infertility treatments were associated to self-esteem or engenders feeling of failure and inadequacy (Fleming & Burry, 2002). Many of these articles add that feeling of low self-worth are not limited to reproductive function, but they extend to "sexual function and desirability, physical attractiveness, performance, and productive in other spheres as well" (Dyer, *et al.*, 2005).

Infertility is an experience that occurs within a social structure (e.g., marriage, family, community, and culture) and context (e.g., culture or religion) (Nassier, 2000). Although infertility can be a painful psychological trauma and life-altering phenomenon that is isolating and stigmatizing, it is not simply an individual psychological experience but a social experience that occurs within the context of the individual's or couple's life and social milieu. As such, infertility is better understood as a 'process' rather than a single event or series of isolated events (Honea-Fleming, 1996).

Infertility is reduction in the concept of self-esteem and self identity. Nearly 70 per cent of the descriptive article includes reports of individuals questioning their gender identity, their role performance and emotion expectations. Some infertile people also mention difficulty into their self-view and some articles report negative body images held by individuals who are infertile (William, 1997).

The impact of infertility on a couple is largely determined by gender role expectations in society, and thus the experiences of women may be significantly different from that of men. Ulrich and Weatherall (2000) suggest that women experience infertility as an unanticipated life-course disruption. Martin-Matthews and Matthews (2001) focus on the sense among infertile women that time is slipping away and explore the interaction between familial and societal timetables, body timetables and treatment timetables (Earle & Letherby, 2007).

Childlessness thus attracts stigma and profound negative consequences especially for the women. The ability to have children is perceived to be a woman's most unique and important role as well as her obligation to society (Izugbara, 2000). This is particularly true of most developing countries where a woman's status is often defined by her reproductive capacity and womanhood is equated with motherhood (Giwa-Osagie, 2001).

Some studies showed that gender roles take greater precedence in shaping women's experience of infertility than the actual physical problem. That is, instead of 'infertility' being understood as a socially defined life crisis, it is mistakenly transformed into an individual (feminine) trait (White *et al.*, 2006). Women are made to feel and are more likely to feel anxious, guilty, frustrated and depressed. Further, women are largely blamed for infertility, and the negative consequences for them can range from denial of food and health care to being thrown out of the house so that a man can take a second, presumably more fertile wife (Singh, Dhaliwal and Kaur, 1993, 1996; Dyer, 2002).

Few studies in this field suggest that men's experiences of infertility are connected to threats to their masculinity, potency and manhood as well as feeling of role failure (Nachtigall *et al.*, 1998; Edelman *et al.*, 1994). Studies indicated that woman experience global stress (Beutel *et al.*, 1998). Cultural, religious, and environmental factors (e.g., natural or man made disasters such as hurricanes or terrorist attacks) that can and do intensify or somehow influence the infertility experience for individuals and couples (Pasch *et al.*, 2002).

Conclusion

The discussion presented above indicated that infertility is one of the global challenges for millions of couples. Both men and women bear the brunt of the social, emotional, and physical consequences of childlessness. A number of review articles indicated that negative emotional responses proved to be strongly related to the outcome of the fear of failure and threat of treatment. So, the present review chapter would be the next step in this area.

Infertility or inability to have children generally viewed as painful condition for the individual and couples it affects. The present chapter is conducted on psychological consequences of infertility.

References

Adamson, P.C., Krupp, K., Freeman, A.H., Klausner, J.D., Reingold, A.L., & Madhivanan, P. (2011). "Prevalence and correlates of primary infertility among young women in Mysore, India", *The Indian Journal of Medical Research*, 134(4), 440.

Anderheim, L., Holter, H., Bergh, C. & Moller, A. (2005). "Does psychological stress affect the outcome of *in vitro* fertilization?", *Human Reproduction*, 20(10), 2969–75.

Beutel, M., Kupfer, J., Kirchmeyer, P., Kehde, S., Köhn, F.-M., Schroeder-Printzen, I., Gips, H., Herrero, H.J.G. & Weidner, W. (1998). "Treatment-related stresses and depression in couples undergoing assisted reproductive treatment by IVF or ICSI", *Andrologia, 31*, 27-35.

Domar, A.D., & Seibel, M. (1990). "The emotional aspects of infertility", In: M. Seibel (ed.), *Infertility: A Comprehensive Test*, pp. 23-35, Appleton House.

Dyer, S.J., Abrahams, N., Hoffman, M. & Van der Spuy, Z.M. (2002). "Men leave me as I cannot have children: women's experiences with involuntary childlessness", *Human Reproduction*, 17(6), 1663-1668.

Dyer, S.J., Abrahams, N., Mokoena, N.E., Lombard, C.J., & Van der Spuy, Z.M. (2005). "Psychological distress among women suffering from couple infertility in South Africa: A Quantitative Assessment", *Human Reproduction*, 20(7), 1938-1943.

De Ridder, D. (2000). "Gender, stress and coping: Do women handle stressful situations differently from men", *Women, Health and the Mind*, 115-135.

Dunkel-Schetter, C., & Label M. (1991). "Psychological reaction to infertility", In: Stanton, A.L., & Dunkel-Schetter, C. (eds.) *Infertility: Perspectives from Stress and Coping Research*, pp. 29-60, New York: Plenum.

Earle, S., Letherby, G. (2007). "Conceiving time? Women who do or do not conceive", *Sociology of Health & Illness*, 29(2), 233-250.

Edelmann, R.J., Connoly, K.J. & Bartlett, H. (1994). "Coping strategies and psychological adjustment of couples presenting for IVF", *Journal of Psychosomatic Research, 38*, 355-364.

Eupnu, D.L. (1995). "The impact of infertility and treatment guidelines for couple's therapy", *American Journal of Family Therapy*, 23(2), 115-127.

Fleming, J., & Burry, K. (2002), "Coping with infertility", In: D. Valentine (ed.), *Infertility and Adaption : A Guide for Social Work Practice*, pp. 37-41, New York: Haworth.

Giwa-Osagie, O. (2001). "Social and ethical aspects of assisted conception in Anglophone Sub-Saharan Africa", In: E. Vayena, P. Rowe & D. Griffin (Eds.), Report of a meeting on *Medical, Ethical and Social Aspects of Assisted Reproduction,* pp. 50-54, Switzerland: Geneva.

Hanea-Fleming, P. (1996). "Psychological components in obstetric/ genealogic condition with a special consideration of infertility", *Alba Medical Journal of Medical Sciences,* 23, 27-30.

Infecundity, infertility, and childlessness in developing countries (2004). DHS Comparative Reports No. 9. Calverton, Maryland, USA: ORC Macro and the World Health Organization; World Health Organization.

Izugbara, C.O. (2000). "Women's understanding of factors affecting their reproductive health in a rural Ngwa Community", *African Journal of Reproductive Health,* 4 (2), 62-68.

Kumar, D. (2007). "Prevalence of female infertility and its socio-economic factors in tribal communities of Central India", *Rural Remote Health,* 7, 456.

Kumari, R. (1988). *Female Sexuality in Hinduism,* New Delhi: Indian Society for Promoting Christian Knowledge.

Mabasa, L.F. (2000). "Stigma, Community support and therapy methods of infertility in South Africa: A cultural perspective", In: Madu, S.N., Baguma, P.K. & Pritz, A. *Psychotherapy and African Reality,* pp. 62-71. Petersburg: UNIN Press.

Makar, R.S. & Toth, T.L. (2002). "The evaluation of infertility", *American Journal of Clinical Pathology.* 117 (Suppl): S95–103. PMID 14569805.

Martin-M.A., & Matthews, R. (2001). "Living in time: multiple timetables in couples' experiences of infertility and its treatment", In: Daly, K. (ed.) *Minding the Time in Family Experience: Emerging Perspectives and Issues,* New York: JAI and Elsevier Science.

Nachtigall, R., Castrillo, M., Shah, N., Turner, D., Harrington, J. & Jackson, R.A., (2009). "The challenge of providing infertility services to a low-income immigrant Latino population", *Fertility & Sterility, 92,* 116-123.

Nasseri, M. (2000). "Cultural similarities in psychological reactions to infertility", *Psychological Reports,* 86, 2, 375-379. Singapore.

Pasch, L.A., Dunkel-Schetter, C. & Christensen, A. (2002). "Differences between husbands' and wives' approach to infertility affect marital communication and adjustment", *Fertility and Sterility,* 77(6), 1241-1247.

Singh, A., Dhaliwal, L.K. & Kaur, A. (1996). "Infertility in a primary health centre of northern India: A follow up study", *Journal of Family Welfare,* 42, 51-56.

Stanton, A.L., Tennen, H., Affleck, G. & Mendola, R. (1991). "Cognitive appraisal and adjustment to infertility", *Women Health,* 17, 1-15.

Ulrich, M. & Weatherall, A. (2000). "Motherhood and infertility: viewing motherhood through the lens of infertility New Delhi. *Feminism & Psychology, 10* (3), 323-326.

Unisa, S. (1999). "Childlessness in Andhra Pradesh; India: treatment seeking and consequences", *Reproductive Health Matters, 7*(13): 54-64. New Delhi: University Press

White, L., McQuillan, J., Greil, A.L. & Johnson, D.R. (2006). "Infertility: Testing a help seeking model, New Delhi. *Social Science & Medicine,* 62, 4, 1031-1041.

Williams, M.E. (1997). "Toward greater understanding of the psychological effects of infertility on women, New Delhi. *Psychotherapy in Private Practice, 16*(3), 7–26.

Williams, L., Bischoff, R. & Luds, J. (1992). "A biopsychosocial model for treating infertility, New Delhi. *Contemporary Family Therapy, 14*(4), 309-323.

15

Depression and Self-esteem among Rape Victims

Aradhana Shukla and *Rupali Joshi*

Rape is one of the most severe of all traumas, causing multiple long term negative outcomes such as post-traumatic stress disorder (PTSD), depression, substance abuse, suicidality, repeated social victimization and chronic physical health problems (Kilpatric & Acierno, 2003; Koss, Bailey, Yuan, Herrera and Licher, 2003).

Defining Rape

In law, rape is defined as vaginal or anal penetration in the absence of lawful consent. However, the source of penetration (e.g., penis, finger or objects), object of perpetrator and victim and definition of consent varies greatly across jurisdictions. Rape is considered to have occurred when her consent has been obtained by putting her (or any person in whom she is interested, e.g., children, close relatives) in fear of death or of hurt, the administration by him personally or through another of any stupefying or unwholesome substance (so-called "date-rape") or when the age of the victim is below 16 years. Moreover, Indian Law (Section 375 of Indian Penal Code) specifically states that if a woman consents to sex, that consent is invalid and rape is still considered to have taken place if the woman is suffering from "unsoundness of mind or intoxication" so that she is unable to understand the nature and consequences of that to which she gives consent.

Types of Rape

(a) **Penetrative Rape**—The vagina is penetrated by penis, finger or other objects.
(b) **Statutory Rape**—The penis is touched on vagina, but no penetration takes place. This type of rape does not exist Indian statures yet.
(c) **Marital Rape**—When rape occurs within a marriage. This is not yet recognized in Indian law.
(d) **Gang Rape**—When more than one person rapes the victim.
(e) **Date Rape**—When rape occurs during an exploratory platonic romantic meaning between man and woman, where often an intoxicating agent is mixed in the food or drink of the victim.

Rape, sexual assault and verbal abuse of females of all ages and socio-economic strata have become common in incidents in India. Such crime distresses countless women and challenges their well-being. A new U.N. report has highlighted around 20 million girls around the world, close to one in 10, have been raped or seriously assaulted by the time they turn 20 years (UNICEF, 2014).

United Nations Statistical report has shown about 65 countries completed data from government sources (registered cases only) that annually more than 25,000 cases of rape or attempted rape were recorded by police (UNO, 2000).

Jagori and UN Women reports, 2010 have found that in New Delhi about 66 per cent of the women reported having experienced sexual harassment between two or five times during the past year. Rape cases showing an incremental trend on day by day basis in major cities in India.

Generally, people believe that the primary cause of rape is an aggressive desire to dominate the victim rather than an attempt to sexual fulfilment (Jagori and Women, 2010).

Rape is the fourth most common crime against women in India (Kumar, 1993), (Crime in India 2012 Statistics). According to the National Crime Records Buréau (NCRB) annual report, 2013, a total of 24,923 rape cases were reported across India in 2012 (Crime in India, 2012 Statistics). Out of these 24,470 were committed by someone known to the victim (98% of the cases) (Vasundhara,

2014). A large number of rape cases go unreported. (Lora & Sarah, 2014).

According to the *Indian Express* dated 15 December, 2013, National Crime Records Bureau of India reviews that there has been an eight-fold increase in the number of rapes in the last four decades. The rise in the number of rape cases is the most rapid compared to other serious crimes such as murder, robbery and kidnapping (Sardar, 2013).

For every one hour 2.84 cases of rape were reported in country in which on an average 3.55 persons were arrested during the year 2012 (NCRB, 2012).

Table 15.1: Crime against Women (Up to December, 2015).

Crime Heads	*2012*	*2013*	*2014*	*2015*
Rape	706	1,636	2,085	2095
Molestation	727	3,515	4,182	5,192
Eve-teasing	214	916	1,282	1,444
Dowry death	134	144	147	119
406/498-A IPC	2,046	3,045	3,005	3,301
Dowry Prohibition Act	15	15	13	18
Kidnapping	2,210	3,609	3,887	4,160
POSCO Act	—	136	104	82

Source: *Delhi Police*, 2015.

The number of rapes in Delhi registered a rise in 2015, with data suggesting an average of six cases every day. As many as 2,095 cases of rape were reported in 2015 till December 15, compared to 2,085 cases during the same period in 2014.

Last year's statistics are the highest in 15 years. "Most likely, the highest ever", said an officer, adding he was speaking from experience and had not pondered over data prior to 2001.

Data also revealed that 5,192 cases of molestation and 1,444 cases of eve-teasing (euphemism for sexually-colored remarks, street harassment etc.) were reported till December 15, 2015, compared to 4,182 molestations and 1,282 eve-teasing cases in the corresponding period in the previous year.

At least 34,651 cases of rape were reported across India last year, statistics released by the country's National Crime Records Bureau (NCRB) have revealed.

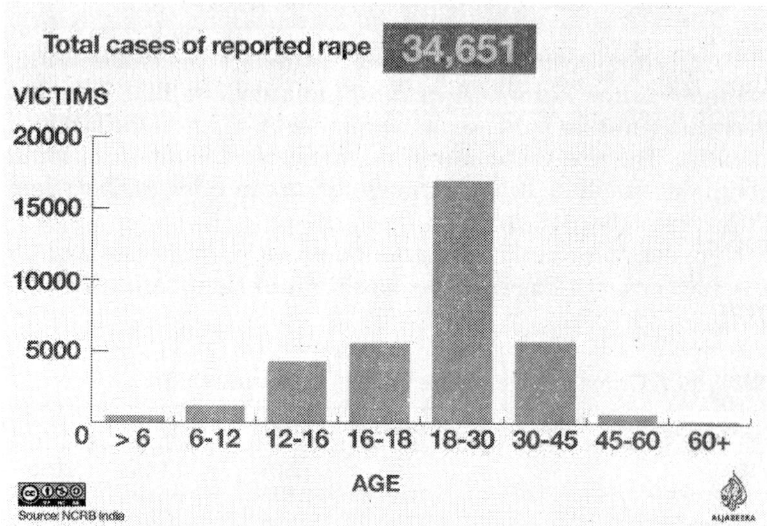

Fig. 15.1: India: Female Victims of Rape: Total cases of reported rape in 2015, divided along age groups.

Source: NCRB India.

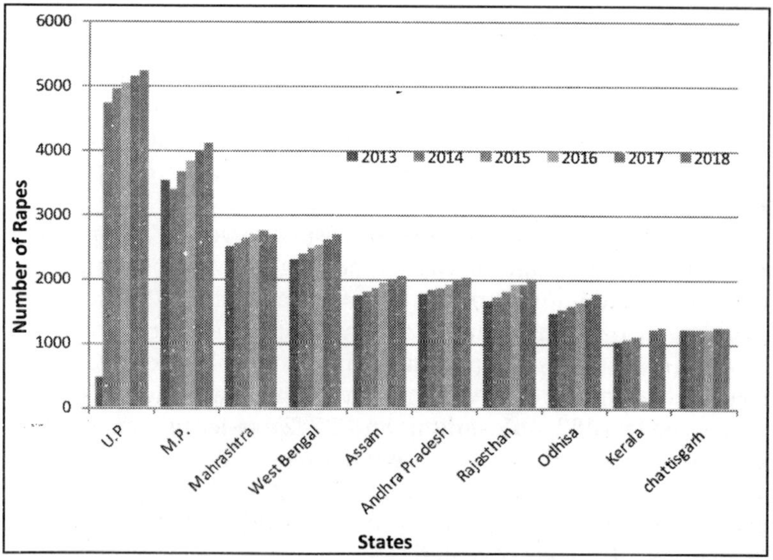

Fig. 15.2: Projected Rapes in India – Higher Incidence.

The released figures showed that victims ranged from female, children younger than six years old to women over 60 years, with those aged between 18 and 30 reporting the largest number of rape attacks—totaling almost 17,000.

Victims knew their alleged rapists in 33,098 of the 34,651 reported rape cases, or 95.5 per cent, according to the figures, which also showed a slight decrease as compared to the 36,735 rape cases reported in 2014.

There were also 4,437 cases of reported attempted rape last year.

Despite the fact that rape is regarded as heinous and criminal in nature, the number and the level of inhumanity of this crime has been on a rise. Be it in affluent or frugal, educated or non-educated contexts; or open or closed societies, this crime is on a rise.

Studies that have continued to assess rape victims over time (Resick, 18 months, Kilpatrick & Veronen, 1983 for 3 years) or have assessed women after an extended period (Burgers & Holmstrom, 1978 after 6 years, Elis, Atkinson & Calhoun, 1981 from 16 years) have found continued problems with fear of depression.

Depression

Depression is a common and serious mental illness that negatively affects how you feel, the way you think and how you act. Depression causes feelings of sadness and or loss of interest in activities once enjoyed. It can lead to a variety of emotional and physical problems and can decrease a person's ability to function at work and home.

Two groups of researchers have focused primarily on the assessment of depression in rape victims.

Frank, Turner and Duffy (1979) administered the Beck Depression Inventory (BDI, Beck, Ward, Mendelsohn, Mock & Rebought, 1961) to 34 rape victims within one month of their assaults. They found that 44 per cent scored in the moderately or severely depressed range. A later study with a larger sample (n=90) resulted in similar findings (Frank & Stewarch, 1984). On the BDI, 56 per cent of those subjects fell in to the moderately or severely depressed range and 43 per cent of the women were diagnosed as suffering from a major depression based on a semi-structured interview.

Atkinson *et al.* (1982) examined depressive reactions in rape victims compared to non-victims over a 1-year period using the BDI and the Hamilton Psychiatric Rating Scale for Depression (HPRS, Hamilton, 1960). They found that both the BDI and HPRS scores for the rape victims were significantly different than non-victims at 2 weeks, 1 month and 2 months post assault but not at the later assessment periods. On the BDI, at 2 weeks post crime 75 per cent of the victims reported from mild to severe symptoms of depression.

Other studies have found similar levels of depression initially (Kilpatrick & Veronen, 1984, Resick, 1988, Rothbaum *et al.*, 1992) using the BDI, the Depression-Dejection scale from the Profile of Mood States Scale (POMS, McNair, Lorrr & Droppleman, 1971) on the Depression subscale from SCl-90R or BSi. However, Kilpatrick and Veronen (1984) continued to find differences between victims and non-victims for 1 year after the crime on both the depression subscales between robbery and rape victims at the 1, 3, 6 and 18 month sessions but not the 12-month session, on a cross-sectional analysis, but found no differences at any session on a longitudinal analysis with a smaller sample.

Finally, the level of suicidal ideation and attempts among rape victims is notable. Although the rates of suicidal behaviour are not very high in the first month after victimization, Elis *et al.* (1981) found that 50 per cent of their long-term sample had considered suicide. Kilpatrick, Best *et al.* (1985) found in their random survey that 44 per cent of rape victims had suicidal ideation and that 19 per cent had suicide attempt.

Rothbaum, Foa, Murdock, Riggs and Walsh (1992) have studied early patterns of reaction by assessing 95 victims of rape or attempted rape weekly for 12 weeks following the crime. They found a consistent pattern with most of the assessment measures they used. At 1-week post-crime, 94 per cent of the subjects met the symptoms of criterion for post-traumatic stress disorder, stress disorder and were clinically depressed.

Abrahamas, Jewkes and Mathews (2012) interviewed 140 participants who were recruited from public hospital service medication. A structured questionnaire was used to collect data on socio-demographic and sexual assault characteristics including perpetrator. Depressive symptomatology was measured using the Centre for Epidemiological Studies Depression Scale. Results showed 84.3 per cent (95%) women were found to have high level of depressive symptoms but lower levels were found among women raped in circumstances in which there was a lesser likelihood of blame such as those raped by stranger rather than intimate partners. Receiving support and severe sexual assault were not associated with depression.

Patrica (1993) studied to review the literature on the psychological impact of rape on adult female victims. Typical patterns of recovery were all reviewed. The problems were fear and anxiety, post-traumatic stress disorder, depression, poor self-esteem, social adjustment issues and sexual dysfunctions.

Choudhary, Smith and Bossarte (2011) aimed to identify patterns in the associations between sexual violence victimization and depression and anxiety symptoms using data from the sexual violence and DA Behavioural Risk Factor Surveillance System (BRFSS) modules. Among all 61,187 participants more than 5 (n=3, 240) were victims of sexual violence, out of which 18.82 per cent reported being diagnosed with depression and anxiety, 8.37 per cent reported an anxiety disorder and 29.28 per cent reported being diagnosed with Depression and Anxiety Disorder.

Self-esteem among Rape Victims

Self-esteem reflects an individual's overall subjective emotional evaluation of his or her own worth. It is the decision made by an individual as an attitude toward the self. Self-esteem encompasses beliefs about oneself, as well as emotional states. Self-esteem is attractive as a social psychological construct because researchers have conceptualized it as an influential predictor of certain outcomes. Psychologists usually regard self-esteem as an enduring personality characteristic.

Given the debilitating psychological impact of rape, it is reasonable to hypothesize that victimization would have a negative impact on victim's self-esteem. Janoff-Bulman and Friezee (1983) have identified self-esteem as a relevant clinical issue for rape victims.

While several authors have suggested that rape victims experience a reduction in self-esteem (Wortman, 1983), there are few data available in this area. Data that are available are limited by an absence of comparison groups of non-victims; nevertheless, they provide preliminary support for low self-esteem among rape victims. Resick (1987a) administered the Tennessee Self Concept Scale (TSCS; Fitts, 1965) to rape-robbery victims. She found that overall, rape-robbery victims had lower self-esteem than both the other groups at all assessment sessions up to and until one-year post rape.

Murphy *et al.* (1998) conducted a study on 204 recent rape victims and a matched comparison group of 173 women to determine the short and long term effects of rape victim's self-esteem. Research participants were assessed at 6-21 days, 1 month, 3 months, 6 months, 1 year, 18 months and 2 years post assault. Findings suggest that victims experience short and long term problems in self-esteem, relationships with others, work satisfaction, relationship with authority, hope for the future and happiness with life, reality and parents compared with non-victims. Victims reported impaired relationships with significant others at 1 year, post assault significantly, lower self-esteem and 18 months post assault and lower satisfaction in relation with their parents at the 2-year post assault assessment.

Abdullah, Sallesh, Mahmud, Ahmad and Ghani (2011) investigated the relationship among cognitive distortion, depression and self-esteem. Self-Cognitive Distortion Scale (SCDS), Beck Depression Scale (BDI) and Rosenberg Self-Esteem Scale (RSES) correlation indicated a positive correlation between cognitive distortion and depression with self-esteem. Results also concluded that rape victims are likely to experience a certain degree of cognitive distortion.

Periloux, Duntley and Boss (2012) examined costs experienced by victims of completed rape (n=49) and attempted sexual assault (n=91) using quantitative analysis of domains: health, self-esteem, self-perceived attractiveness, self-perceived mate value, family relationship, work life, social life, social reputation, desire to have sex, frequency of sex, enjoyment of sex and long term committed relationship. Compared to victims of an attempted sexual assault, victims of rape reported significantly more negative outcomes in 11 of 13 domains. The most negatively affected domains were self-esteem, sexual reputation, frequency of sex, desire to have sex and self-perceived mate values.

Krahe (1988) presented a longitudinal analysis of the links between sexual assault, victimization, depression and sexual self-esteem by examining their cross-legged paths among both men and women. The sample comprised of 2,425 male and female college students. The study consisted of three data waves in their first, second and third year of university separated by 12 months' interval, with sexual assault at one-T1 since the age of 14 and at T2 and T3 for the last of 12 months. Depression and sexual self-esteem were measured at each level. Random intercept cross-legged panel analysis controlling for individual differences in depression and sexual self-esteem showed that sexual assault at T1 predicted depression whereas T2 predictor is associated with depression and lower self-esteem. The T3 predictor is related with sexual assault victimization as well as sexual assault victimization by undergoing depression at T2. Both depression and lower sexual esteem at T1 were indirectly linked to sexual victimization at T3. Sexual assault victimization was shown to be a risk factor for both depression as a general mental health indicator and lowered sexual self-esteem as a specific outcome in the domain of sexuality.

Vianna (2006) conducted a qualitative study to show the results of workshops held with health workers and public health users (raped women) aimed at raising these women's self-esteem and creating awareness among health workers who attend them. Neuro-Linguistic Programming techniques were used to bring back life experiences which contributed to re-reading and to minimize causal factors of low self-esteem. Results showed that experiences lived at home and with loved and admired people and carrying experiences resulting from the rape were responsible for low self-esteem.

Conclusion and Recommendation

According to several studies, the number of rape cases is increasing in India. The disturbing trends of increased attempts and rate of rape across various females of various age groups and states are also visible. Rape victims suffer with spectrum of physical and psychiatric disorders naming lower self-esteem, depression, victimization and sexual and physical health to name a few, resulting in higher health care use. In the domain of psychology, review of the literature indicates that rape is associated with multiple psychological disorders including anxiety, depression, PTSD, eating disorders, sleep disorders and low self-esteem.

The tailing after-effects of rape *viz.* social stigma, alienation and trust deficit are the another layer of negative consequences of the trauma. Rape victims need extensive post assault attention and understanding and may turn to multiple social systems for assistance. Approximately 26 per cent to 40 per cent victims report the assault to the police and pursue prosecution through the criminal justice system, 27 per cent to 40 per cent seek medical care and medical forensic examination and 16 per cent to 60 per cent obtain mental health services.

The literature studied and various patterns and trends related to the rape victims examined along with the after-effects they experience, implies that the victims need a sophisticated and multi-pronged strategy encompassing the medical, physical, mental and legal intervention. The traumatic and inhuman crime warrants the need for the victims to be able to receive the medical intervention (physical and clinical), psychological assistance and legal follow-up in empathic, supportive manner, thus, facilitating the urgently needed recovery process.

References

Abdullah, S., Salleh, A., & Abdul, S. (2011). "Cognitive distortion: Depression and self-esteem among adolescent rape victims", *World Applied Science Journal, 67*(7), 1067-71.

Abraham, N., & Jewkes, R. (2005). "Effects of South African men's having witnessed abuse of their months during childhood on their levels of violence in adulthood", *American Journal of Public Health, 95,* 181-196.

Atkinson, B., Cathoun, K., Resick, P., & Elis, E. (1982). "Victims of Rape: Repeated Assessment of Depressive Symptoms", *Journal of Counselling and Clinical Psychology, 50,* 96-102.

Bohner, G. & Lamprides, E. (2004). "Expecting to meet a rape victim affects women's self-esteem. The moderating role of rape myth acceptance", *Group Processing and Intergroup Relations, 7,* 77-87.

Bulman, R.J. & Frieze, I.H. (1983). "Theoretical perspective for understanding reactions to victimized understanding reactions to victimization", *Journal of Social Issues, 39*(2), 195-22.

Choudhary, E., Merideth, S. & Bussente, R.M. (2011). "Depression, anxiety and symptom profile among female and male victims of sexual violence", *American Journal of men's Health, 6*(1), 28-36.

Crime against women, *Crime in India 2012 Statistics,* National Crime Records Bureau (NCRB), Ministry of Home Affairs, Government of

India, p. 81, archived from the original (PDF) on 16 January, 2016.

Frank, F., Turner, S.M. & Duffy, B. (1979). "Depressive symptoms in rape victims", *Journal of Affective Disorder*, 269-277.

Jagori & Women, U.N., 2010. Report on the baseline survey, https://jagori.org.

Kilpatric, D.G. (1985). *The Sexual Assault Research Project: Assessing the Aftermath of Rape Response*, 8, 20-24.

Kilpatric, D.G. & Aciernnao, R. (2003). "Mental health needs of crime victims epidemiology and outcomes", *Journal of Traumatic Stress, 16*, 119-132.

Koss, M.P., Bailey, J.A., Yuva, N.P., Herrera, V.M. & Litcher, E.L. (2003). "Depression and PTSD in survivors of male violence: Research and training initiatives to facilitate recovery", *Psychology of Women Quarterly, 27*, 130-142.

Krate, B. (1998). "Sexual aggression among adolescents", *Psychology of Women Quarterly*, 22, 37-54.

Kumar, R. (2003). *The History of Doing: An Illustrated Action of Movements for Women's Rights and Feminism in India, 1800-1990*. New Delhi: Kali for Women, p. 128.

Lora, P. & Sarah, P. (2014). *The Fear that Stalks: Gender Based Violence in Public Spaces*, Zubaan Books, p. 79.

Mathew, S., Jewkes, R. & Abraham, N. (2011). "I had a hard life: Exploring childhood adversity in the shaping of masculinities among men who killed an intimate partner in South Africa", *British Journal of Criminology, 51*(4).

McNair, D., Lor, M. & Droppleman, L. (1971). *Manual Profile of Mood States*. San Diego: SA Education and Industrial Testing Service.

Murphy, S.A. & Patrica, A.R. (1997). "The psychological impact", *Journal of Interpersonal Violence*.

Murphy, S.A. (1988). "Mediating effects of intrapersonal and social support on mental health and 3 years after a natural disaster", *Journal of Traumatic Stress, 1*, 155-172.

Patrica, A.R. (1993). "The psychological impact of rape", *Journal of Interpersonal Violence, 6*, 223-255.

Perilloux, C., Duntley, J.D. & Buse, D.M. (2012). "The costs of rape", *Archives of Sexual Behavior, 41*(5), 1099-1106.

Resick, P.A. (1988). *Reactions of female and male victims of rape and robbery*. A Final report (Grant no. 85-IJ-(X-0042) Washington DC: National Institute of Justice.

Rothbaum, B.O., Merdock, T., Riggs, D.S. & Walsh, W. (1992). "A prospective examination of post-traumatic stress disorders in rape victims", *Journal of Traumatic Stress, 5*, 455-475.

Sardar, K. (2013). "A year after Nirbhaya, rapid rise in number of rape complains", *The Indian Express*.

Sirnate, V. (2014). "Good laws had bad implementation", *The Hindu*, Chennai, India. Retrieved 1 February, 2014.

Staff Writer (9 May, 2017). NCRB Data shows 955 rape victims in India known to offenders, Madhya Pradesh tops the list First. Chennai, India. Retrieved 27 October, 2017.

Vasundhara, S. (1 February, 2014). "Good laws, bad implementation", *The Hindu*, Chennai, India. Retrieved 1 February, 2014.

Vianna, L., Bomfem, G.F. & Chicone, G. "Self-esteem of raped women", *Rev Latino- and Enermager* 14(2), 695-701.

Section C

Consequences of Social Justice in Women: Existing Status and Promoting Psychological Health

16

Mental Health: Some Issues Related to Women

Shagufta Afroz and *P.S.N. Tiwari*

Mental health is described by World Health Organization as: "a state of well-being in which the individual realizes his or her own abilities, can cope with the normal stresses of life, can work productively and fruitfully, and is able to make a contribution to his or her community". Good mental health is essential for the well-being of individuals, their families, and the community.

This chapter studies the mental health problems of women, especially in the Indian context. Women's experience of health and disease differ from those of men, due to unique biological, social and behavioural conditions. Biological differences vary all the way from phenotype to the cellular, and manifest unique risks for the development of ill health. The World Health Organization (WHO) defines health as "a state of complete physical, mental and social well-being and not merely the absence of disease or infirmity" (WHO 1948). Women's health is an example of population health, the health of a specific defined population NLM (2015). As per World Health Organization (WHO) estimates, depression is expected to be the second largest contributor to disease burden by 2020, and with one in every three women worldwide being afflicted by common mental disorders including depression, the mental health of women is a serious issue indeed. While studying the psychological construct of mental health, we come to understand that it is deeply embedded within an individual's social and socio-economic relationships. Since women worldwide, and more so in India, face gender-based discrimination at every stage of their lives, their psychological well-being becomes a cause for great concern for us. This note attempts to explore the various risks and protective factors affecting the mental health of women. Gender differences have an impact on mental health and the experience and course of women's mental illness. For this reason, women's (and men's) mental health can only truly be understood by considering not only the biological and physiological, but also the social, cultural, economic and personal contexts of their lives. The purpose of this chapter is to discuss why gender disparities persist and to reveal what areas of the health care system need to be reformed to incorporate social justice into health for women. Women are often the primary caregivers to children, spouses, elderly and disabled relatives. They have the responsibility of recognizing ill health and seeking medical care when a health problem emerges.

Some Facts about Women's Mental Health

- Unipolar depression, predicted to be the second leading cause of global disability burden by 2020, is twice as common in women.
- Depression is not only the most common women's mental health problem but may be more persistent in women than men.
- Depressive disorders account for close to 41.9 per cent of the disability from neuro-psychiatric disorders among women compared to 29.3 per cent among men.
- Leading mental health problems of the older adults are depression, organic brain syndromes and dementias. A majority are women.
- An estimated 80 per cent of 50 million people affected by violent conflicts, civil wars, disasters, and displacement are women and children.
- Lifetime prevalence rate of violence against women ranges from 16 per cent to 50 per cent.

Women face many injustices and inequalities globally, both in terms of economic factors and human rights. An often overlooked aspect of this phenomenon is their health. For example, the World Health Organization points out that "maternal mortality has barely changed since 1990." This fact points to the great need for a specific focus on women's health issues. Some mental health conditions occur more often in women and can play a significant role in the state of a woman's overall health (Astbury and Cabral, 2000). While men and women both experience higher rates of mental illness, mental health conditions are more common in women as shown below:

- **Depression**—Some 10 to 15 per cent of women will experience depression at some point in their lives—double the number of men who will. Women go through significant biological changes across their lifespan, more so than men, so these cyclic shifts can disrupt, malfunction, or create disease. Hormonal flux in particular can wreak havoc on women's mental health. Hormones play a significant role around the time of childbirth, which has resulted in terms like postpartum blues and postpartum depression. Social issues also come into play, as we are raised to internalize our thoughts and feelings, as compared to men, who are encouraged to "shake things off" and "tough it out." Women are taught to be mindful about our thoughts and feelings, not to mention our appearance. Then there are environmental or cultural factors, including the fact that women still tend to bear the brunt of housework and caregiving and maintain the family's social schedule, even if they work outside the home full time, Kristin Carpenter, Ph.D., Director of Women's Behavioral Health at The Ohio State University, Wexner Medical Centre notes that women also tend to earn less than their male counterparts, she adds, "which can cause financial strain that can lead to feeling anxious, depressed, or hopeless" (Patz, 2016).
- **Anxiety and Specific Phobias**—Although men and women are affected equally by such mental health conditions as obsessive-compulsive disorder and social phobias, women are twice as likely as men to have panic disorder, generalized anxiety, and specific phobias. From puberty through age 50, women are more than twice as likely as men to develop an anxiety disorder, according to the Anxiety and Depression Association of America, with its symptoms of increased worrying, tension, exhaustion, and fear.

Again, so many factors come into play—including social and cultural norms and stressors, but how we react to them may be the biggest difference between men and women. That's the key finding of a 2012 study in the American Psychological Association's. Biology plays a role, too, of course, and researchers are increasingly looking at the effects of estradiol, a primary gonadal hormone in women.

- **Post-Traumatic Stress Syndrome (PTSS)**—Women are twice as likely to develop PTSS following a traumatic event (Hook & Marcellin, 2012).
- **Suicide Attempts**—Men die from suicide at four times the rate that women do, but women attempt suicide two or three times more often than men. Indian women have higher rates of suicide than women in most developed countries. Women in India also have a higher rate of suicide compared to men. The most common reasons cited for women's suicide are directly related to depression, anxiety, gender disadvantage and anguish related to domestic violence (Patel, Vikram, Rodrigues, Merlyn, *et al.*, 2002).
- **Eating Disorder**—Everyday Health estimates Women account for at least 85 per cent of all anorexia and bulimia cases and 65 per cent of binge-eating disorder cases. Large contributing factors behind eating disorders are the socio-cultural aspects. The sexualization of women plays a big role in females developing negative self-image as well as negative body image issues and poor self-esteem. Weight has and may always be an aspect of women's lives that is scrutinized and placed on a pedestal, so it is no wonder why females feel such pressure to be physically perfect. While eating disorders like anorexia nervosa and bulimia nervosa often develop during the teen years, the onset of such disorders can happen anytime of those affected by eating disorders.

Women's Symptoms are also different

Even when men and women share a common mental health diagnosis, the symptoms, and subsequently the treatment, can be different. For example, a man who is depressed is likely to report job-related problems, while a woman is more likely to report physical issues, like fatigue or appetite and sleep disturbance. Women are more likely to use religious and emotional outlets to offset the symptoms of depression compared to men, who often find relief through sports and other hobbies.

It was found that Indian women typically describe the somatic symptoms rather than the emotional and psychological stressors that trigger the symptoms of depression (Blum, Robert; Gates & William, 2015). This often makes it difficult to accurately assess depression among women in India in light of no admonition of depression (Blum *et al.*, 2015). Gender plays a major role in postnatal depression among Indian women. Mothers are often blamed for the birth of a female child. Furthermore, women who already have a female child often face additional pressures to have male children that add to their overall stress level (WHO, 2016). Women in India have a lower onset of schizophrenia than men (U.N., 2015[a]). However, women and men differ in the associated stigmas they must face (U.N., 2015[b]). While men tend to suffer from occupational functioning, while women suffer in their marital functioning. The time of onset also plays a role in the stigmatization of schizophrenia (U.N., 2015[a]). Women tend to be diagnosed with schizophrenia later in life, oftentimes following the birth of their children. The children are often removed from the care of the ill mother, which may cause further distress (U.N., 2015[c]). Women with schizophrenia more often experience depression and thought impairment, while men with schizophrenia are more likely to become apathetic and socially isolated. Women with schizophrenia typically respond faster to antipsychotic medication and need less personal care. Schizophrenic women also report more mood symptoms, which can complicate the diagnostic process and may require a prescription for mood stabilizers in addition to anti-psychotic medications.

Findings from the World Economic Forum indicate that India is one of the worst countries in the world in terms of gender inequality (Clancy, Carolyn, Massion and Charlea, 1992). Gender is one of the main social determinants of health—which include social, economic, and political factors—that play a major role in the health outcomes of women in India and access to healthcare in India (MacEachron & Allison, 2014). Therefore, the high level of gender inequality in India negatively impacts the health of women.

Studies have indicated that boys are more likely to receive treatment from health care facilities compared to girls, when controlled for SES status (Gronowski, Ann, Schindler and Emily, 2014). What goes on in the female brain and body to differentiate these responses to mental illness? The answers may lie in:

- **Biological influences**—Female hormonal fluctuations are known to play a role in mood and depression. The hormone estrogen can have positive effects on the brain, protecting schizophrenic women from severe symptoms during certain phases of their menstrual cycles and maintaining the structure of neurons in the brain, which protects against some aspects of Alzheimer's. On the less positive side, women tend to produce less of the mood stabilizer serotonin and synthesize it more slowly than men, which may account for the higher rates of depression. A woman's genetic make-up is also believed to play a role in the development of such neurological disorders as Alzheimer's.
- **Socio-Cultural Influences**—Despite strides in gender equality, women still face challenges when it comes to socio-economic power, status, position, and dependence, which can contribute to depression and other disorders. Women are still the primary caregivers for children, and it is estimated that they also provide 80 per cent of all caregiving for chronically ill elders, which adds stress to a woman's life. Isaac and Kapur (1980) showed that of the 313 cases of common mental disorders, only 14 were reported by families. Distress in the cases of women is more likely to be ignored. The decision about providing health care to the members of family usually rests with the male heads of families. In large joint families, where hierarchy and power equations are very strong, women usually reside in a very inferior place. In 2006 women accounted for less than 25 per cent of clinical trials published in 2004, (Geller, Stacie, Adams, Marci Carnes and Molly, 2006). A follow-up study by the same authors five years later found little evidence of improvement (Geller, Stacie, Koch, Abby, Pellettieri, Beth, Carnes and Molly, 2011).

Throughout our society, females have unfortunately been the object of sexualization, whether it be through magazines, movies, television shows, or peer relationships. This frequently negative sexualization can cause problems with the healthy development of self-esteem and self-image among females, as reported by the American Psychological Association. Both of these factors cannot only lead to unhealthy self-image but also to shame, depression, anxiety, and stress. In conjunction with the sexualization of women, violence and sexual abuse are two more important factors contributing to mental health issues in women. Reportedly one in five women is a victim of rape or attempted rape, and females also have a higher instance of experiencing sexual abuse. During civil unrest and violent conflicts, women make up an estimated 80 per cent of victims. Indeed, the prevalence of violence against women is cited between 16 to 50 per cent over the course of a lifetime (Katherine, 2000).

- **Behavioural Influences**—There is some thinking that women are more apt to report mental health disturbances than men and that doctors are more prone to diagnose a woman with depression and to treat the condition with mood-altering drugs. Women are more likely to report mental health concerns to a general practitioner, while men report tend to discuss them with a mental health specialist. However, women are sometimes afraid to report physical violence and abuse.

The illiterate, poor, refugees, unemployed and women in low paying work or sex workers, household maids and beggars are most vulnerable to mental distress. Bachrach and Nadelson (1988) write that two thirds of the chronically ill in the U.S. are the women. 30 to 90 per cent of homeless women in the West are mentally ill leading many mental health professional to address issues of poverty, mental health and homelessness. Studies in India have shown that even though fever women get admitted to mental hospitals for care, once there, they stay for a longer period of time. The reason for this range from the economics to the attitudes of the hospital staff toward 'appropriate feminine' behaviour. Lobbying for early discharge may be seen as a aggressive and assertive behaviour, which is an indication that the woman has not recovered fully. The ideal women patient is expected to be compliant, patient, passive, dependent and submissive.

Problems with India's Healthcare System

At the turn of the 21st Century India's healthcare system is strained in terms of the number of healthcare professionals including doctors and nurses. The healthcare system is also highly concentrated in urban areas. This results in many individuals in rural areas seeking care from unqualified providers with varying results. It has also been found that many individuals who claim to be physicians actually lack formal training. Nearly 25 per cent of physicians classified as allopathic providers actually had no medical training; this phenomenon varies geographically (Rao, Mohan, Rao and Krishna, 2011).

Women are negatively affected by the geographic bias within implementation of the current healthcare system in India. Of all health workers in the country, nearly two thirds are men. This especially affects rural areas where it has been found that out of all doctors, only 6 per cent are women. This translates into approximately 0.5 female allopathic physicians per 10,000 individuals in rural areas (Rao & Krishna, 2011).

A disparity in access to maternal care between rural and urban populations is one of the ramifications of a highly concentrated urban medical system. According to Government of India National Family Health Survey (NFHS II, 1998-1999) the maternal mortality in rural areas is approximately 132 per cent the number of maternal mortality in urban areas (Adamson, Paul and Krupp, 2012).

The Indian Government has taken steps to alleviate some of the current gender inequalities. In 1992, the Government of India established the National Commission for Women. The Commission was meant to address many of the inequalities women face, specifically rape, family and guardianship. However, the slow pace of change in the judicial system and the aforementioned cultural norms has prevented the full adoption of policies meant to promote equality between men and women (Doshi, Sonal, Gandhi and Bindi, 2008).

In 2005, India enacted the National Rural Health Mission (NRHM). Some of its primary goals were to reduce infant mortality and also the maternal mortality ratio. Additionally, the NHRM aimed to create universal access to public health services and also balance the gender ratio (Ministry of Health and Family Welfare, 2013). However, a 2011 research study conducted by Nair and Panda found that although India was able to improve some measures of maternal health since the enactment of the NHRM in 2005, the country was still far behind most emerging economies (Nair, Harish and Panda, Rajmohan, 2011).

Lack of social justice in women health can be seen as a risk factor for increased illness. It is a big challenge for us to create a healthcare system that is congruent with the goals of social justice in women health empowerment. Creating a healthcare system that is congruent with the goals of social justice – in particular framing women's health as a fundamental human right appears to have the potential to contribute to the improvement of women's lives. And yet, despite the fact that women's right to health is recognized, there is a lack of social justice in the Indian society. Even after succeeding in accessing healthcare, women have been discriminated (Thorat & Mangesh, 2012), numerous barriers exist which prevent women from enjoying the highest attainable standard of physical and mental health. Women continue to experience injustices and inequalities in their health status and in their interactions with the healthcare system. One can conclude that, "it does not suffice to just have rights. Neither is it enough that these rights be officially recognized. What is necessary is that there be conditions which permit these rights to be exercised." For attaining the goal of social justice in mental health issues, our society can take some steps listed below:

- To ensure that Health policies and programmes are responsive to sex and gender differences and to women's health needs.
- To increase knowledge and understanding of women's health and women's health needs.
- Support the provision of effective health services to women.
- Promote good health through preventative measures and the reduction of risk factors that more imperil the health of women.

- The establishment of a women's health equity Act.
- The development of a women's health model which incorporates bio-medical and social determinants.
- Analysing the relationship between gender mainstreaming and women focused holistic care, research and policy.
- Involving women consumers in the design, implementation and evaluation of all health policies and programmes.
- Estimating the significant costs of social injustice in responding to women's health.
- Disaggregating all health data by sex, age, and socio-economic status.
- Identifying innovative quantitative and qualitative methods to document gender inequalities in the health care system and other sectors impacting on women's health.
- Evaluation of all relevant health policies and research.
- Investigation of multi-sectoral responses to women's health as more efficient, effective approach than relying solely on the healthcare system as the policy area responsible for people's health and well-being.
- Build evidence on the prevalence and causes of mental health problems in women as well as on the mediating and protective factors.
- Promote the formulation and implementation of health policies that address women's needs and concerns from childhood to old age.
- Enhance the competence of primary healthcare providers to recognize and treat mental health consequences of domestic violence, sexual abuse, and acute and chronic stress in women.

References

Adamson & Krupp, (2012). "Are marginalised women being left behind? A population-based study of institutional deliveries in Karnataka, India", BMC Public Health, **12**: 30. doi:10.1186/1471-2458-12-30.

American Psychological Association (2012). "Men tend to externalize emotions while women tend to internalize them", *Journal of Abnormal Psychology.*

Astbury, J. & Cabral, M. (2000). *"Women's Mental Health: An Evidence based Review"*, Geneva: World Health Organization. Google Scholar.

Bacharach, L.L. & Nadelson, C.C. (eds.) (1988). *"Treating Chronically Mentally Ill Women"*, Washington: Americon Press.

Blum, Robert W. & Gates, William H. (2015). "Girlhood, Not Motherhood: Preventing Adolescent Pregnancy", (PDF). UNFPA. ISBN 978-0-89714-986-0. Retrieved 5 August, 2016.

Clancy, Carolyn M., Massion & Charlea T. (14 October 1992). *"American Women's Health Care. A Patchwork Quilt with Gaps"*, JAMA, 268 (14): 1918–1920. doi:10.1001/jama.1992.03490140126048. PMID 1404719.

Doshi, Sonal Gandhi & Bindi (2008), "Women in India: The Context and Impact of HIV/AIDS". *Journal of Human Behaviour in the Social Environment*, 17 (3-4): 413-442. doi:10.1080/10911350802068300.

Geller, Stacie E., Adams, Marci Goldstein, Carnes & Molly (December 2006). "Adherence to Federal Guidelines for Reporting of Sex and Race/Ethnicity in Clinical Trials", *Journal of Women's Health*. 15 (10): 1123-1131.

Geller, Stacie E., Koch, Abby; Pellettieri, Beth & Carnes (March 2011), "Inclusion, Analysis, and Reporting of Sex and Race/Ethnicity in Clinical Trials: Have We Made Progress?", *Journal of Women's Health*, 20 (3): 315–320. doi:10.1089/jwh.2010.2469

Gronowski, Ann M., Schindler & Emily I. (2014). "Women's Health", *Scand. J. Clin. Lab. Invest. Suppl. 244: 2–7.* doi:10.3109/00365513.2014.936672. PMID 25083885.

Hattie, J.A., Myers, J.E. & Sweeney, T.J. (2004). "A factor structure of wellness: Theory, assessment, analysis and practice". *Journal of Counselling and Development*, 82, 354-364.

Hook, B.D. & Marcellin, N. (2012). "Common Mental Health Issues in Women", *Everyday Health: Common Health.*

Isaac, M.K. & Kapur, R.L. (1980). "A cost-effectiveness analysis of three different methods of psychiatric case finding in a general population", *British Journal of Psychiatry*, 137, 540-546.

Katherine, W. (2000). "Promoting Mental, Emotional and Social Health: A Whole School Approach", London: Routledge Falmer, 8, 16, p. 12.

Loganathan, Santosh & Murthy, R. (2011). "Living with schizophrenia in India: Gender Perspectives". Transcultural Psychiatry. 48 (569), 569-584.

MacEachron, A. (2014). "Women's Health in the Post-2015 World: Ensuring No One is Left Behind" (PDF). *BCUN News*, Business Council for the United Nations. Retrieved 13 July, 2016.

Merton (1994). "Review Essay: Women and Health Research", *Journal of Law, Medicine and Ethics*, 22, 272-279.

Ministry of Health and Family Welfare, "About NHRM", National Rural Health Mission. Government of India, Web. 28 April, 2013.

Nair, & Panda (2011). "Quality of maternal healthcare in India: Has the rural health mission made a difference". *Journal of Global Health*, 1 (1), 79-86.

NLM (2015). "Women's Health", *Medical Subject Headings (MeSH)*. Retrieved 6 July, 2016.

Patel & Rodrigues, M. (2002). "Gender, Poverty and Postnatal Depression: A Study of Mothers in Goa India". *Am. J. Psychiatry. 159*, 43-47. doi:10.1176/appi.ajp.159.1.43. PMID 11772688

Patz, A. (2016). "4 Mental Health Issues that are More Common in Women", *Mind and Body Emotional Health.*

Pereira, & Andrew, G. (2007). "The explanatory models of depression in low income countries: Listening to women in India". *Journal of Affective Disorders*, 102, 209–218. doi:10.1016/j.jad.2006.09.025. PMID17074394.

Rao, M. & Rao, K. (2011). "Human resources for health in India". *Lancet*. 377: 587–98. doi:10.1016/s0140-6736(10)61888-0WHO (1948). "WHO definition of Health". Archived from the original (Preamble to the Constitution of the World Health Organization as adopted by the International Health Conference, New York, 19–22 June, 1946; signed on 22 July.

Shahmanesh, M. & Wayal, S., *et al*. (2009). "Suicidal Behaviour Among Female Sex Workers in Goa, India: The Silent Epidemic", *Research and Practice, 99*(7): 1239–46. doi:10.2105/ajph.2008.149930WHO (August 2016). Child, early and forced marriage legislation in 37 Asia-Pacific countries (PDF). WHO IPU. Retrieved 5 August, 2016.

Thorat, M. (2012). "Tackling breast cancer in India", *Lancet*, 379: 2340-2341. doi:10.1016/s0140-6736(12)61017-4.

World Health Organization (WHO) (2001a). *Strengthening Mental Health Promotion*, Geneva: World Health Organization. Google Scholar.

World Health Organization (WHO) (2001b). *Mental Health: New Understanding, New Hope*, The World Health Report, Geneva: World Health Organization. Google Scholar.

World Health Organization (WHO) (2016). *Women's Health*. Retrieved 8 January, 2017.

UN (2015a). *The Millennium Development Goals Report* (PDF). New York: United Nations.

UN (2015b). *Millennium Development Goal 3: Promote Gender Equality and Empower Women* (PDF), New York: United Nations.

UN (2015c). *Millennium Development Goal 5: Improve Maternal Health* (PDF), New York: United Nations.

17

Employment Status, Self-efficacy and Self-esteem among Women

Swaran Lata

Introduction

In recent years women from all corners have been employed in various organizations and this has brought changes in the status, personality and empowerment of women. Women are rising in economic status, and gaining greater social standing in the society. Employment provides them an opportunity to develop a sense of accomplishment, fulfilment and contentment by proving themselves in their assigned work roles. It raises their self-esteem and self-efficacy and, thus, in a way paves way for their empowerment.

Self-esteem

Morris Rosenberg (1965), defined self-esteem as a favourable or unfavourable attitude towards the self. According to Joubert (1990), self-esteem can be defined as a "person's judgement of general self-worth that is a product of an implicit evaluation of self-approval or self-disapproval made by the individual". According to Tesser (2000), "Self-esteem is a global evaluation reflecting our view of our accomplishments and capabilities, our values, our bodies, other's responses to us, and events, or occasions, our possessions". Emerging as common across most definitions of self-esteem is the component of self-evaluation and self-worth. One should have a positive view of the self.

The positive consequences of women's employment in large scale studies are likely to be obtained only for those women who regard their paid work role as a significant source of self-fulfilment (Paula *et al.*, 1987). The role of paid worker is not only a source of self-esteem; self-identity, social rewards, but, is also a source of stress for women under conditions of role conflict and role overload. Accumulated research suggests that unemployment is associated with increased depression and poorer self- esteem. Low self-esteem is there when self-regard and social position is devalued (Chodorow, 1974). However, even in less selective samples, employed mothers appear to be psychologically healthier than mothers who are not employed (Ross and Mirowsky, 1988). Mary and Good (2005) suggested that employment brings self-esteem and independence. However, low paid jobs contribute to oppression rather than independence.

Self-efficacy

Self-efficacy means one's belief in his ability to complete tasks in specific situations. It influences emotional, behavioural, and thought patterns in different human levels. Self-efficacy or belief-related ability is one of the most powerful characteristics associated with an individual's motivation, health, flexibility and capabilities to face difficulties of life (Bandura, 2001). Self-efficacy determines an individual's resiliency to adversity and his/her vulnerability to stress and depression (Bandura, Caprara, Barbaranelli, Gerbino & Pastorelli, 2003). General self-efficacy aims at a broad and stable sense of personal competence to deal effectively with a variety of stressful situations (Adeyemo, 2008; Schwarzer, 1994).

Self-efficacy has been found to be intimately associated with capacity to change one's situation and has been used as a predictor of behaviour, usually job seeking behaviour (Wenzel, 1993). In a study by Eden and Aviram (1993), self-efficacy levels were found to be associated positively with looking for work and with re-employment. According to Flammer (2001), people with higher perceived self-efficacy to fulfil job functions consider a wide range of career options. Valiante (2004) believes that efficacy contributes more heavily to occupational preferences. Perceived efficacy is a robust contributor to career development. According to Bandura's theory, people with high self-efficacy—that is, those who believe they can perform well—are more likely to view difficult tasks as something to be mastered rather than something to be avoided. A person with high self-efficacy is less concerned with failures and he is stronger in confronting difficulties (Lee, L., Arthur, A., and Avis, M. 2008).

Employment Status

The Government of India or a Government of States in India classifies public employees into Group A (Gazetted/Executive), B (Gazetted), B (Non-Gazetted), C and D. Group A is the highest rank class and the Group D is the least.

Group A (Gazetted)—These officials belong to the managerial or highest class of government servants for example—officers of the All India Services, i.e., IAS, IPS, IFS, IRS, IRTS, scientists from GSI, ISRO, DRDO, DAE, Assistant Professor and above in Central, State or in an Autonomous University etc.

Group B (Gazetted)—These officials belong to the Central Secretariat Services, Income Tax Officers, Asst. Audit/Accounts Officers of Indian Audit & Accounts Department, JCOs in Armed Forces, Principal/Headmaster of High School, Officers in State Civil Services etc.

Group C—These officials are public servants in non-supervisory roles, e.g. Naib Tehsildar, Head Clerks/Section Heads, Police Head Constables, Typists, Stenographers, Tax Assistants, Telephone operators, etc.

Group D—These employees belong to the lowest rank.

Methodology

Rationale

High self-esteem is very essential for the empowerment of women. Women with high self-esteem feel good, cope effectively with challenges and criticism, experience self-worth and does not feel herself inferior to anyone whereas those with low self-esteem, have a negative approach and are psychologically distressed and depressed. Review of literature has shown that employment raises self-esteem and independence.

Women also require high self-efficacy to perform well in their roles. They need to view difficult tasks as something to be mastered rather than something to be avoided. High self-efficacy helps in displaying appropriate behaviours and positive attitudes. It is important for employed women to have increased self-efficacy since this would pave the way for carrying out tasks with confidence and belief in oneself which would lead to success and goal attainment.

Against this background, the present study aims to investigate that whether employment status of women affects the self-esteem and self-efficacy among women?

Objective

1. To assess the group difference in self-esteem and self-efficacy among employed and unemployed women.

Hypotheses

1. There would be significant group difference in self-esteem and self-efficacy among Group B and Group C women employees.
2. There would be significant group difference in self-esteem and self-efficacy among Group B women employees and educated unemployed women.
3. There would be significant group difference in self-esteem and self-efficacy among Group C women employees and educated unemployed women.

Method

Participants

The present study was conducted on 150 educated married women with age range of 30-45 years from Varanasi city. Sample included equal number of Group B women employees (N = 50), Group C women employees (N = 50), and educated but unemployed women (N = 50).

Measures

Self-esteem Scale developed by Rosernberg (1965). This scale consists of 10 items, score ranging from 0 to 30. The internal consistency of the scale is 0.77.

General Self-efficacy Scale developed by Ralf Schwarzer and M. Jerusalem (1995). This scale consists of 10 items, score ranging from 1 to 4. The Cronbach's alphas ranged from .76 to .90.

Demographic Sheet

Demographic sheet was developed by researcher containing information about age, education, designation, and marital status.

Results

Descriptive statistics for means, standard deviations and t-value for Self-esteem and Self-efficacy are summarized in Table 17.1.

Table 17.1: Mean, SD, t-value of Self-esteem and Self-efficacy among Group B and Group C women employees

Variable	*Group B Women Employees (N = 50)*		*Group C Women Employees (N = 50)*		*t-value*
	Mean	*SD*	*Mean*	*SD*	
Self-esteem	24.12	2.66	20.02	3.54	6.61**
Self-efficacy	34.74	2.86	31.32	3.95	5.02**

**=0.01 level of significance.
*=0.05 level of significance.

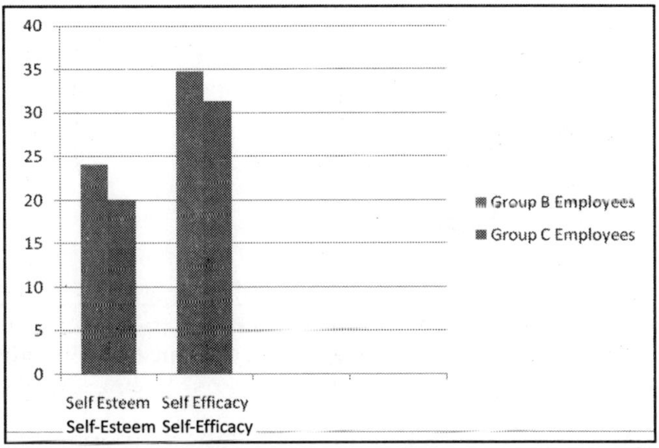

Fig. 17.1: Self-Esteem and Self-efficacy in Women Employees (Group B and Group C)

Table 17.1 and Fig. 17.1 indicates significant group difference in Self-esteem and Self-efficacy among Group B and Group C women employees

Table 17.2: Mean, SD, t-value of Self-esteem and Self-efficacy among Group B women employees and educated unemployed women.

Variable	*Group B Women Employees (N = 50)*		*Educated Unemployed Women (N = 50)*		*t-value*
	Mean	*SD*	*Mean*	*SD*	
Self-esteem	24.12	2.66	20.56	3.49	5.83**
Self-efficacy	34.74	2.86	31.04	4.65	4.86**

** = 0.01 level of significance.
* = 0.05 level of significance.

Table 17.2 and Fig. 17.2 indicates significant group difference in Self-esteem and Self-efficacy among Group B women employees and Educated unemployed women.

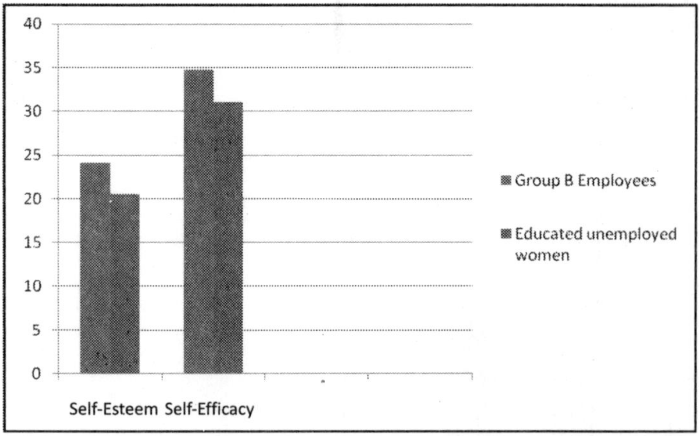

Fig. 17.2: Group Difference in Self-Esteem and Self-Efficacy among Group B Women Employees and Educated Unemployed Women.

Table 17.3 and Fig. 17.3 indicates significant group difference in Self-esteem and Self-efficacy among Group C and educated unemployed women.

Table 17.3: Mean, SD, t-value of Self-esteem and Self-efficacy among Group C women employees and Educated unemployed women.

Variable	*Group C Women Employees (N = 50)*		*Educated Unemployed Women (N = 50)*		*t-value*
	Mean	*SD*	*Mean*	*SD*	
Self-esteem	20.02	3.54	20.56	3.49	0.32
Self-efficacy	31.32	3.95	31.04	4.65	0.77

**=0.01 level of significance. *=0.05 level of significance.

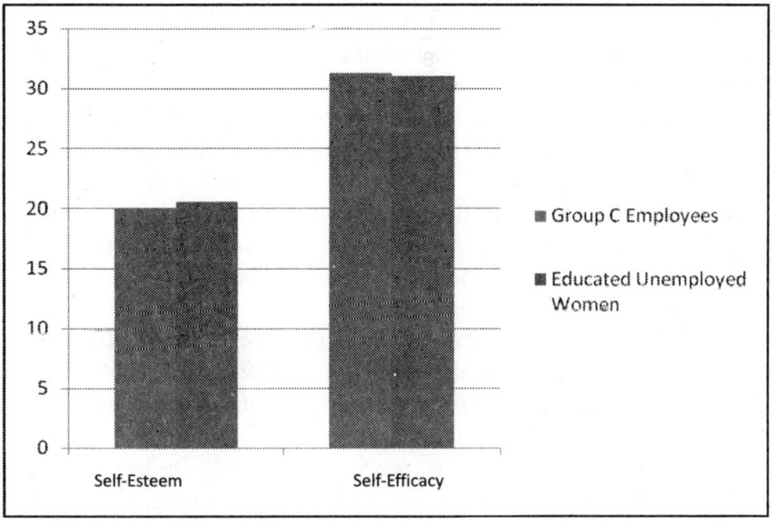

Fig. 17.3: Self-esteem and Self-efficacy among Group B and C Women Employees and Educated Unemployed Women

Discussion

The objective of our study was to assess the group difference in self-esteem and self-efficacy among Group B, Group C women employees and educated unemployed women.

Table 17.1 shows significant group difference in the self-esteem and self-efficacy among Group B and Group C employed women. The self-esteem means of Group B employees (M = 24.12) are higher than the Group C employees (20.02). The self-efficacy means of Group B employees (M = 34.74) are also higher than the Group C employees (31.32). Graph 17.1 shows the mean of self-esteem and self-efficacy among Group B and Group C women employees. Establishing oneself in a reputed and recognized career gives confidence, competence, and independence and changes the personality and lifestyle of the individual. Group B (Gazetted) employees are at high rank with high salaries and emoluments. They avail better facilities, autonomy, power and privileges as compared to the Group C employees. Thus, type of employment and status also brings difference in the self-esteem and self-efficacy among employed women, with Group B employees higher in self-esteem and self-efficacy than Group C employees. This finding is in accordance with the works of Messias *et al.* (1997). Multiple roles and challenges faced by women daily develop self-efficacy and self-esteem as they are better able to realise their abilities and potentials. They avail informational, instrumental and emotional support and deal with daily stresses of life. Bradburn (1969) also reported a consistent relationship between better education, higher income and happiness.

Table 17.2 shows significant group difference in the self-esteem and self-efficacy among Group B and educated unemployed women. The self-esteem means of Group B employees (M = 24.12) are higher than the educated unemployed women (20.56). The self-efficacy means of Group B employees (M = 34.74) were also found to be higher than the educated unemployed women (31.04). Graph 17.2 shows the mean of self-esteem and self-efficacy among Group B and educated unemployed women. The self-esteem and self-efficacy of well educated women were found to be less than the Group B employees. The employed women are economically independent and self-reliant and have greater access and exposure to the latest technologies, rules and policies as a result they have higher self-esteem and self-efficacy. They positively evaluate their abilities and competencies and develop a positive attitude towards themselves. They are able to take decisions and are respected, recognized and appreciated in the family and society. The educated women although literate still do not have knowledge about several tasks like saving policies, income tax, and insurance etc. and thus feel themselves dependent on someone and have a feeling of incompetence and insecurity. Economic dependence also lowers their self-esteem and self-efficacy as they are not respected for not doing a job. Highly educated women when unemployed appeared to be more disillusioned and frustrated and have low psychological well-being. The results can also be corroborated with the findings of several other researchers who found higher self-esteem among employed women than unemployed women (Wadhawan, 2016; Akram, 2017; Chaudhary, 1995; Baruch, *et al.*, 1987; Messias *et al.*, 1997; Mary & Good, 2005; Feld, 1963; Bernard, 1982; Coleman and Antonucci, 1983; Paula *et al.*, 1986).

Table 17.3 shows insignificant group difference in the self-esteem and self-efficacy among Group C and educated unemployed women. The self-esteem means of Group C women employees (M = 20.02) are lower than the educated unemployed women (20.56). The self-efficacy means of Group C women employees (M = 31.32) are higher than the educated unemployed women (31.04). Graph 17.3 shows the mean of self-esteem and self-efficacy among Group C and educated unemployed women. This is because women at lower occupational jobs have dual jobs to play (both at household and workplace). The work roles of Group C employees are monotonous and rigorous. Their salary structure is also low and hence witness low socio-economic status. They do not feel intrinsically motivated and rewarded. They work because of economic necessity and not out of choice. Thus, they do not feel any enthusiasm and pride of their job. As a result, the self-esteem and self-efficacy of Group C women employees is similar to educated unemployed women. Whereas women at home are at ease as they do not have to go to the workplace. They are satisfied with the household chores and enjoy the status of the husband. The obtained results are in accordance with the findings (Azhar & Vasudeva, 2006; Hartley, 1980; Tabatatabaei, 1999) who found insignificant differences between employed and unemployed women on self-esteem and self-efficacy.

Conclusion

Summing up, this study has explored self-esteem and self-efficacy among employed and unemployed women. On the basis of the results obtained from present research work, it has revealed that significant differences were found in self-esteem and self-efficacy among Group B and Group C women employees, among Group B employees and educated unemployed women, but, insignificant difference was found between Group C and educated unemployed women. Thus, employment is a factor which can raise the self-esteem and self-efficacy among women. Women should be encouraged for higher education and motivated to seek high rank jobs. This would enhance their self-worth, autonomy, confidence, power, dignity and scope to cherish their dreams and to be empowered.

References

Adeyemo, D.A. & Adeleye, A.T. (2008). "Emotional Intelligence, Religiosity and Self-efficacy as Predictors of Psychological Well-being among Secondary School Adolescents in Ogbomoso, Nigeria", *Europes Journal of Psychology.*

Akram, M. (2017). "Self-esteem and Psychological Well-being among Working and Non-working Women", *The International Journal of Indian Psychology,* Volume 5, Issue 1, 147-153.

Azhar & Vasudeva (2006). "Self-efficacy and Self-esteem: A Comparative Study of Employed and Unemployed Married Women in Iran", *German Journal of Psychiatry,* 111-117.

Bandura, A. (2001). "Social Cognitive Theory: An Agentic Perspective", *Annual Review of Psychology,* 52, 1-26.

Bandura, A., Caprara, G.V., Barbaranelli, C., Gerbino, M. and Pastorelli, C. (2003). "Impact of affective self-regulatory efficacy on diverse sphere of functioning", *Child Development,* 74, 1-14.

Baruch, G.K., Biener, L. & Barnett, R.C. (1987). "Women and Gender in Research on Work and Family Stress", *American Psychologist,* 42, 130-136.

Bernard, J. (1982). *The Future of Marriage,* New Haven: Yale University Press.

Bradburn, N.M. (1969). *The Structure of Psychological Well-being,* Chicago: Aldine.

Coleman, L.M. & Antonucci, T.C. (1983). "Impact of Work on Women at Midlife", *Developmental Psychology,* 19, 290-294.

Chaudhry, M. (1995). "A study of marital adjustment, role conflict, fear of success, general well-being and life stress amongst working and non-working married women", Unpublished Ph.D. thesis. Panjab University, Chandigarh, India.

Chodorow, N. (1974). "Family structure and feminine personality", In: Rosaldo, M. and Lamphere, L. (eds). *Women, Culture and Society.* Stanford: Stanford University Press.

Eden, D. & Aviram, A. (1993). "Self-efficacy training to speed reemployment: Helping people to help themselves', *J. Applied Psychology,* 78(3), 352-360.

Feld, S. (1963). "Feeling of adjustment", In: F.J. Nye & L.W. Hoffman (eds.), *The Employed Mother in America*. Chicago: Rand McNay.

Flammer, A. (2001). "Self-efficacy", *Encyclopedia* of *Social Behaviour*, 13812.

Hartley, J.F. (1980). "The impact of unemployment upon the self-esteem of managers", *J. Occupation Psychology*, 53(2), 147-155.

Joubert, C.E. (1990). "Relationship among self-esteem, psychological reactance, and other personality variables", *Psychological Reports*, 66, 1147-1151.

Lee, L., Arthur, A. & Avis, M. (2008). "Using Self-efficacy theory to develop interventions that help older people overcome psychological barriers to physical activity: A discussion paper", *Int. J. Nurs. Stud.*, 45, 1690-1699.

Mary, D. & Good, G. (2005). "Women and mental of cache", www.un.org /womenwatch/dcw/csw/mental.html

Messias, D.K., Im, E., Page, A., Regev, H., Spiers, J., Yoder, L., & Meleis, A.I. (1997). "Defining and redefining women's work: Implications for women's health", *Gender and Society*, 11, 296-323.

Paula, R., *et al.* (1986). "Psychological consequences of multiple social roles", *Psychology of Women Quarterly*, 10, 373-378.

Paula, R., *et al.* (1987). "The relationship of employees to self-perception and well-being in women: A cognitive analysis", *J. Sex Roles*, 17, 718.

Rosenberg, M. (1965). *Society and the Adolescent Self-image*. Princeton, NJ: Princeton University.

Schwarzer, R., & Jerusalem, M. (1995). "Generalized Self-efficacy Scale", In: J. Weinman, S. Wright & M. Johnston (eds.), *Measures in Health Psychology: A User's Portfolio. Causal and Control Beliefs*, pp. 35-37, Windsor: NFER-NELSON.

Schwarzer, R. (1994). "Optimism, vulnerability and self-beliefs as health-related cognitions: A systematic overview", *Psychology and Health: An International Journal*, 9, 161-180.

Tesser, A. (2000). *The Encyclopedia of Psychology Behavioural of Science*, 3, 213-216.

Valinate, G. (2004). Self-efficacy: The exercise of cost role (Albert Bandura). Emory University. www.emory.edu/education/mfp/leftbookII.htm

Wadhawan, K. (2016). "A Comparative Study of Self-esteem of Working and Non-working Women in Relation to their Psychological Well-being", *International Journal of Applied Research*, 2(6), 531-532.

Wenzel, S.L. (1993). "The relationship of psychological resources and social support to job procurement self-efficacy in the disadvantaged", *J. Applied Psychology*, 23(18), 1471-1497.

Yahya, A.S. (1999). "The effect of employment status on the self-esteem and mental health of Iranian employed and unemployed people", *Iran Labour Market*, Vol. 8, Ministry of Labour and Social Affair Publications, Tehran, Iran.

18

Empowering Social Status

The Psyche of Indian Women

Garima Singh

> "To call women the weaker sex is a libel; it is man's injustice to woman. If by strength is meant brute strength, then, indeed, woman is less brute than man. If by strength is meant moral power, then woman is immeasurably man's superior: Has she not greater intuition, is she not more self-sacrificing, has she not greater powers of endurance? Without her man could not be. If non-violence is the law of our being, the future is with woman."
>
> —***Mahatma Gandhi***

India is a multifaceted society where no generalization could apply to the nation's various regional, religious, social and economic groups. Nevertheless, certain broad circumstances in which Indian women live affect the way they participate in the society. A common denominator in their lives is that they are generally confined to home, with restricted mobility, and in seclusion. Other, unwritten, hierarchical practices place further constraints on women. History depicts the paradoxical situation of Indian woman where she was sometimes concurred as Goddess and at other times merely a slave. Despite major changes that have occurred in the status of women in some parts of the world in recent decades, norms that restrict women to the home are still powerful in India, defining activities that are deemed appropriate for women. They are, by and large, excluded from social life, which by its very nature takes place in a public forum.

The 21st century been marked as the century for women and so women empowerment is high on the agenda in development plans and policies. Even then after various efforts by government, institutions and social scientists the phenomenal women empowerment is not taking real shape due to ignorance by women themselves. Actually, women's empowerment is not just switching on and off women libido but it is more than this. Women empowerment is the vital instrument to expand women's ability to have resources and to make strategic life choices. The main component of empowerment, i.e., developing a sense of self-worth, a belief in one's ability to secure desired changes and the right to control one's life, is wholly absent in Indian women. Therefore, though the empowerment of women has become one of the most important concerns in India, but practically women empowerment is still an illusion of reality.

Social inclusion is the key to empowerment and therefore any attempt to assess the status and problem of women in a society should start from the social framework. Social structure, cultural norms, and value systems are crucial determinants of women's role and their position in society. In respect of the status there is a gap between the theoretical possibilities and their actual realization. The most relevant cause of this gap being that majority of the women are lacking in the psyche of rebellion and thus they are not acting as the active agents of the change.

The Psyche of Indian Women: Trapped in Social Chains

The empowerment of women has become one of the most important concerns today, but practically women empowerment is still an illusion of reality. We observe in our day to day life how women become victimized by various social evils. The prevailing social restrains of patriarchy essentially consigns women to the 'inside sphere'. Women are docketed with heavy work responsibilities but still they are dissatisfied with their roles as 'happy housewives'; what is fatiguing to them is not their daily demands of the house, but, the energy they lose in personal ambitions and thwarting the psychic need for larger purpose and meaning in life. Thus, the concrete details that trap women are easily viewed, while the chains that bind her in trap are the shackles in her own mind and spirit. The various social constrains imposed in lives of women and the relative self-imposed psychic confines are discussed below.

Gender Bias in Health Concerns in India: The health and safety concerns of women are paramount for the well-being of a country and are an important factor in gauging the empowerment of women in a country. However, there are alarming concerns where maternal healthcare is concerned. Women from infant stage to their old age get an unfair deal in the matter of health. Their health concerns receive a low priority resulting in women bearing pain and discomfort in silence for long periods of time without seeking relief. The sex-ratio in India speaks volumes about the neglect. It is not just the poor who for want of resources and with the inherent preference for a boy are guilty of bias. Even in well-to-do families parents tend to spend more on the healthcare of boys than on girls.

In India, the highest number of deaths in the age group of 16 to 25 is recorded among women. Anemia is one of the most commonly found deficiency among the women and it is also mentioned by several studies that they are often not too healthy when they bear the first child and none of them are physically ready to bear a second child. The available data says that in India about 20 per cent of the women in the age group of 15-49 years are at the risk of unintended pregnancy. Coming to anti-natal care only 10 per cent of the pregnant women receive it on an average in rural India. Female child mortality is at higher level in India as girls have unequal access to resources. Discrimination against girl children start even in the womb and untold number of female foetuses are aborted in prenatal sex-selection stage. This is, in spite of legislations, prevalent in many parts of India. In many communities, the mothers of girl children sometimes neither get nutrition nor do they care when they are pregnant. Even the women herself who embraces feminism chooses to abort a female child in her womb, with no concern of even her own health. The women herself has internalized social belief against a female child and in favour of a male child. Thus, the research evidences clearly depict noteworthy gender disparities in expenditure on health in Indian society.

***Poverty and Hunger*:** Women are identified, and identify themselves, as those responsible for the health, education, and well-being of their children, husband, and the family and home as a whole. Despite, women are very often unable to own land or property, lack inheritance rights, are particularly at risks of exploitation and violence if they are unable to bring a good dowry, and are often viewed as men's property in themselves. In India, girls are discriminated against in obtaining education on the grounds that they could not be spared from domestic labour or because education for boys was a better family investment. Lower rates of literacy leaves women disadvantaged, for example in awareness of government programmes or other services of their legal rights. Women tend to be financial losers from marital divorce, tended to avoid legal action, and as female heads of households with children are particularly vulnerable to poverty. In marriage, men dominated decision making, and women are dependent on men, have less choice, and are often the subject of domestic violence.

Poverty affects the woman most in as much as the female members in the family are denied education, healthcare, nutritious food, and good sanitation because of poverty. Poverty directly affects the future of women. Girl children are discriminated in the matter of feeding compared to boys. Studies have shown that girls in rural areas take a mean of 1,355 kilocalories/day in the 13-15 years age group and 1,291 kilocalories/day in the 16-18 years age group, which is much below the recommended levels. The disproportionate impact of poverty on girls is not an accident but the result of systematic discrimination.

Hungry people live in a social environment of traditional prejudices, unjust law, corruption, broken promises, and failed economic policies, leading to the severe subjugation of women, marginalization and disempowerment. It is a tragic irony that while the society holds women responsible for all the key actions required to end hunger: family nutrition, health, education, food production and increasing family income on the one hand, through laws, customs and traditions women are systematically denied the resources, information and freedom of action they need to carry out their responsibilities, on the other.

Narayan *et al.* (2000) focus clearly that despite widespread changes in gender roles, traditional gender norms have shown greater tenacity, which leaves families struggling to meet new demands. Men have often lost their traditional roles and women have taken on new ones. Thus, the psychological effects have been profound, which are rightly put by Narayan *et al.* (2000) as, "These changes touch core values about gender identity, gender power, and gender relations within poor households, and create anxiety about 'good woman' or a 'good man'. Values and relations are being broken, tested, contested and renegotiated in silence, pain and violence". Although this has brought those women greater independence and empowerment who fought and protested for it, still the changes mostly had limited impact on women's empowerment.

Low Literacy Rate

In spite of certain outstanding examples of individual achievements, and a definite improvement in their general condition over the years, it remains true that Indian women still constitute a large body of underprivileged citizens. Women of course do not form a homogenous group in class or caste terms. Nevertheless, they face distinctive problems that call for special attention. The educational, economic, political and social backwardness of women makes them the largest group hindering the process of social change. It is inevitable that when this 'backward' group has the major responsibility of bringing up future generations, the advancement of society cannot be rapid or take any significant form of development. In the report of the committee appointed by the National Council for Women's Education, it was emphatically stated that what was needed to convert the equality of women from *de jure* to *de facto* status was widespread education for girls and women and a re-education of men and women to accept new and scientific attitudes towards each other and to themselves.

A changing society and a developing economy cannot make any headway if education, which is one of the important agents affecting the norms of morality and culture, remains in the hands of traditionalists who subscribe to a fragmented view of the country's and the world's heritage. The differences between the positions of men and women in the society will not lessen; leave alone disappear, as long as there are differences between the education levels of men and women.

The low literacy among women brings down the national literacy. This gap which exists between the literacy rates of the two sexes also exists between the enrolment of girls and boys at all levels of education. Right from the primary school to the university, we find that the number of girl students is considerably lower than boys. According to Article 45 of the Constitution, universal compulsory and free education until the age of 14 was to be achieved by the year 1960. Looking at the present condition of primary education in villages, it is doubtful whether we can achieve 100 per cent enrolment of girls. It is unfortunately true of our society that children are sent to school not according to their intelligence or aptitude but according to their sex. The reasons for not sending girls to school are both economic and social. In rural areas, girls are required to help in household work. The resources of the rural poor are so limited that they do not have anything to spare for children's education. If resources are available, it is the boy who is sent to school first. Parents, even mothers, also do not see the value of educating especially a daughter who would get married and remain a housewife. Since they cannot see any direct relationship between education and economic betterment, they have very little motivation to send their children to school.

It is still not being realized by large sections of society, including the females, that there is definite connection between education, good motherhood and efficient house management. The management of millions of households and the upbringing of millions of children is thus in the hands of illiterate women. It is here that a change is required if our intensions of empowering women are not to remain a mere pretense.

The Inevitable Social Evil: Domestic Violence: Domestic violence can be described as when one adult in a relationship misuses power to control another through violence and other forms of abuse. The abuser tortures and controls the victim by calculated threats, intimidation and physical violence. Although men, women and children can be abused, in most cases the victims are women.

Globally, one out of every three women faces violence at the hands of their husbands, fathers, or brothers and uncles in their homes. In India, violence within the home is universal across culture, religion, class and ethnicity. The abuse is generally condoned by social custom and considered a part and parcel of marital life. Statistics reveal a grim picture of domestic violence in India. The National Crimes Bureau, Ministry of Home Affairs, Government of India reports a shocking 71.5 per cent increase in instances of torture and dowry deaths during the period from 1991 to 1995. In 1995, torture of women constituted 29.25 per cent of all reported crimes against women. Gracia (2004) draws attention to the 'hidden iceberg' of domestic violence against women, only a small proportion of which is reported to the authorities.

Provocative behaviour of women is one of the most prominent found causes of domestic violence in India. This indicates a high prevalence of victim-blaming attitudes and suggesting that the climate of acceptance of violence is among societal and traditional factors responsible for high rates of domestic violence. A report of the United Nations Population Fund (UNFPA, 2005) also showed that high proportions of women in samples in some countries (including India) believed that wife beating was justified for at least one of a number of reasons, which included: neglecting the children, going out without informing the partner, arguing with partner, refusing to have sex, not preparing food on time or properly, and talking to other men.

Perilla (1999) puts that there are certain basic cultural values held in common, like machismo and respect, which are relevant in understanding domestic violence. The question arises as to why women put up with abuse in the home or why do abused women stay in battering relationships? The answer lies in their unequal status and their belief systems of being a 'good woman' in society. The woman mostly tries asserting herself and coping by actively working on her own and her children's behalf; not protesting for what she goes through.

Women are often caught in a vicious circle of economic dependence, fear for their children's lives as well as their own, ignorance of their legal rights, lack of confidence in themselves and social pressures. These factors effectively force women to a life of recurrent mistreatment from which they often do not have the means to escape. The sanctity of privacy within the family also makes authorities reluctant to intervene, often leading women to deny that they are being abused. This is equally common in the higher as well as in the lower segments of the society. A woman who lodges a complaint of abuse is often forced to withdraw the complaint or drop the charges not only by her family and society but also by the authorities. Social prejudices reinforce domestic violence against women. They are treated as their spouses' property; husbands assume that this subordinate role gives them right to abuse their wives in order to keep them in their place.

Against this background is the traditional dowry, where the

father of the bride is compelled to give the groom/groom's parents substantial cash and/or other assets. In a majority of Indian families, a boy has inheritance rights while the girl is given a hefty sum at the time of marriage in lieu of her rights in the parental property. Official statistics show a steady rise in crimes related to dowry. More than 95,000 women are killed every year in India over dowry. While Bihar and Uttar Pradesh still record the maximum number of dowry crimes, Bangalore, India's fastest growing city also shows an alarming rise of dowry harassment and domestic violence. Cases of torture of women over dowry are the highest, accounting for 32.4 per cent of all crimes against women in the country. The evil of the dowry system has spread its tentacles in almost all parts of the country, all communities and all sections of the society. Women's physical and mental health is often permanently damaged and impaired resulting in 'dowry deaths'.

Domestic violence has devastating repercussions on the family. Mothers are unable to care of their children properly. Often they transmit to them their own feelings of low self-esteem, helplessness and inadequacy. Such women are often facing negligence towards the trauma that leaves her unable to make a decision, the lack of sympathy extended towards her by others, and even implications that she might have provoked the attacks. This negligence leads to the tendency to blame oneself and to carry shame and guilt about speaking to others about the abuse; and considerations such as her resources for subsisting financially and surviving by her own. Violence against women, the most pervasive human rights violation in the world today, has got to be stopped. It needs support not only from the government, but also from the civil society, and most significantly women themselves.

Delinquencies against Women: Crimes against women occur every minute; every day and throughout the year, though several such crimes go unreported. A total of 2,44,270 incidents of Crime against Women (both under IPC and SLL) were reported in the country during the year 2012 as compared to 2,28,649 in the year 2011 recording an increase of 6.4 per cent during the year 2012. These crimes have continuously increased during 2008-2012 with 1,95,856 cases in the year 2008; 2,03,804 cases in 2009 and 2,13,585 cases in 2010 and 2,28,650 cases in 2011 and 2,44,270 cases in the year 2012. The proportion of IPC crimes committed against women towards total IPC crimes has increased during the last 5 years from 9.2 per cent in the year 2009 to 11.2 per cent during the year 2013.

Rape is the fastest growing crime in the country today and as many as 18 women are assaulted in some form or the other every hour across India. Over the last few months cases of rapes and assault have made it to the headlines with alarming frequency. For an affected woman, it is an ordeal to lodge a complaint with the police, who, besides being reluctant to file a proper FIR, adopt a most unsympathetic attitude putting the complainant to further shame by asking her to give a graphic description as to how she was sexually abused.

Conclusion

Patriarchy is so deeply rooted in the Indian society that they manifest notions such as 'the good woman' and 'the good wife'. It is these social constrains and stereotypes that leads to social struggle of women and a challenge of life to those who move towards violation of such norms. Thus, the attainment of the real scenario of women empowerment seems to be comparatively poor. The need of the hour is to identify those loopholes or limitations which are observing the realization of empowerment of women and this initiative must be started from the womenfolk itself as well as more importantly policy initiative taken by the state and society. Women represent half the world's population and gender inequality exists in every nation on the planet. Until women are given the same opportunities that men have, entire societies will be destined to perform below their true potentials. The greatest need of the hour is change of social attitude of women and towards women.

References

Ali, A. (2002). *Islam in India–The Impact of Civilization*. New Delhi: Shipra Publications.

Baruah, B. (2013). "Role of Electronic Media in Empowering Rural Women Education of N.E. India", *ABHIBYAKTI: Annual Journal*, 1, 23-26.

Chandra, B. (1905). *"Essays on Contemporary India"*, Delhi: Har-Anand Publications Pvt. Ltd.

Deshpande, S., & Sethi, S. (2010). "Role and Position of Women Empowerment in Indian Society", *International Referred Research Journal*, 1(17), 10-12.

Duflo, E. (2011). *Women's Empowerment and Economic Development*, National Bureau of Economic Research, Cambridge.

Esposito, J.L. & Haddad, Y.Y. (1998). *Islam, Gender and Social Change,* New York: Oxford University Press.

Goswami, L. (2013). "Education for Women Empowerment", *ABHIBYAKTI: Annual Journal,* 1, 17-18.

Hazarika, D. (2011). "Women Empowerment in India: A Brief Discussion", *International Journal of Educational Planning & Administration,* 1 (3), 199-202.

Holmes, J. (2000). *Women and Ending Hunger: The Global Perspective,* New Delhi: Institute of Social Sciences.

Janaki, N. (1996). "Women and Law in Colonial India: A Social History, Delhi", *Kali for Women,* Bangalore: National Law School of India University.

Lalneihzov, J. (2007). *Women's Development in India: Problems and Prospects,* New Delhi: Mittal Publications.

Kadam, R.N. (2012). "Empowerment of Women in India: An Attempt to Fill the Gender Gap", *International Journal of Scientific and Research Publications,* 2(6), 11-13.

Koko, U. (1992). "Empowering People for Health and Family Planning", *IASSI Quarterly,* 11, 2.

Mahajan, V.D. (2010). *Modern Indian History,* New Delhi: S. Chand Co. (P) Ltd.

Mazumdar, M. (2004). *Social Status of Women in India,* New Delhi: Dominant Publishers and Distributors.

Mohanty, B. (2000). *Women and Political Empowerment,* New Delhi: Institute of Social Sciences.

Mokta, M. (2014). "Empowerment of Women in India: A Critical Analysis", *Indian Journal of Public Administration,* 9(3), 473-488.

Murthy, N.L., *et al.* (2007). *Towards Gender Equality: India's Experience,* Delhi: Serials Publications.

Nagaraja, B. (2013). "Empowerment of Women in India: A Critical Analysis", *Journal of Humanities and Social Science (IOSR-JHSS),* 9(2), 45-52.

Orford, J. (2003). *Community Psychology: Challenges, Controversies, and Emerging Consensus,* England: John Wiley & Sons Ltd.

Panucha, S. & Khatik, A. (2005). "Empowerment of Rural Woman", *Social Action,* 55, 349.

Sarkar, L. & Sivaramayya, B. (1996). *Women and Law: Contemporary Problems,* Delhi: Vikas Publishing House.

Shettar, R.M. (2015). "A Study on Issues and Challenges of Women Empowerment in India", *IOSR Journal of Business and Management (IOSR-JBM),* 17(4), 13-19.

Suguna, M., (2011). "Education and Women Empowerment in India", *ZENITH: International Journal of Multidisciplinary Research,* 1(8), 19-21.

19

Domestic Violence against Women in India

A Review

Priyanka Pathak and *Shobhna Joshi*

Today, violence against women is serious problem and most persistent violation of rights of women in the world. It is experienced by women of all ages, social classes and nationalities. Its effect on growth and development is profound and it is strongly related to cultures around the world. The term 'violence' derives from the Latin word **vis**, which means force and it refers to the forceful actions of one person which affects other person psychologically and physically and it also refers to use of physical superiority on the other person. Violence is abnormal behaviour and influenced by different circumstances.

Historically, violence against women is a manifestation of the unequal power relations between men and women, which have led to domination over and discrimination against women by men and to the prevention of *women's full advancement*. Poverty, discrimination, ignorance and social unrest are common and they are the predictors of violence against women in all societies. Culture plays important role in violence against women because in many cultures, traditions, cultural forces, cultural pattern aims to preserving male dominance and subdue women's dignity and status in family and society. In India, violence against women is considered a part of the natural order. In India, husband has right to beat his wife because certain amount of physical abuse as justified under certain conditions for women. Justification for violence stems from gender equality distorted views about the roles and responsibilities of men and women. Violence against women includes different forms such as intra-family or domestic violence and violence at work.

The goals of this chapter are to explore the presence of domestic violence, their physical and psychological effects on women and develop relevant policies/interventions to combat domestic violence effectively. These goals will be accomplished by identifying domestic violence among women, explore the effects of domestic violence on physical health and psychological health of victims and examine the possible treatment, prevention programmes and policies of Indian Constitution for women to overcome domestic violence.

In India, social, economical and psychological status of women has been changing from worst to better during different period. During Vedic period, women were regarded as useful and respective member of family and society and they enjoyed high status. After Vedic period, condition of women declined with the passage of ti ne and during the medieval period, women were given a position subordinate to man. In this period, law of the society did not recognize the equality and equal rights of man and woman. Later, in the British period, the status of Indian woman had deteriorated to the lowest level. Women were considered as completely inferior, having no significance. They had no right to express their thoughts and views. After Independence, women's position and status improved and it became further evident when immediately after the Independence, Indian women made their mark by acquiring higher positions in political as well as social arena. Government of India has taken several measures to assign equal status to women in the economic, political and social fields. More ways have been opened to them to show their talents and have a sense of participation in overall national activities. Despite of all these, mental and physical abuse of women has continued especially in domestic situation. Traditionally, an Indian woman had four fold status-role sequences. These were her role as a daughter, wife, housewife (home-maker) and mother. But, the position of women in many families is not good enough even when our country is growing in all the fields and contribution of women in this growth has been significant. In domestic situation, in all or most of the parts of India, women are treated as servant, they have no right to express their opinion and thoughts, they do not take any decision about her family because they are considered inferior and not eligible to take any decision of their own. The most important work for her is to manage their home and children. Even after performing their duties they are abused by their partners and other family members either psychologically or physically or in both ways. It is called domestic violence and it includes physical and psychological abuse. It is a serious problem across different countries, not only in India. But, here the main focus of this study is on domestic violence among women in India.

Domestic violence against women is the most prevalent form of gender-based violence. It typically occurs when male partner abuses his female partner, physically and psychologically, and in many cases the female partner is also abused by the male partner's family members and in some cases by other relatives also. Psychological abuse always accompanies physical abuse.

Domestic violence against women is not a new phenomenon. It is worldwide yet still hidden problem. It occurs in developed and developing countries both. According to UNICEF (2000) study, up to half the female population of the world is subjected to domestic violence. Indeed, domestic violence is tragically common place, but, it happens behind closed doors and victims fear speaking out. Even in a comparatively open society like the US, research shows that only 1 in 100 battered women ever reports the abuse she suffers (UNICEF, 2000).

According to the Protection of Women from Domestic Violence Act (2005) domestic violence as physical, sexual, verbal, emotional and economic abuse against women by a partner or family member residing in a joint family, disturb the lives of many women in India. Kishor and Johnson (2006) define domestic violence as violence against women. Women are generally perceived as the sole victims of domestic violence and men as the perpetrators (Abbot & Williamson, 1999).

Effects on Physical and Psychological Health

Many physical and psychological health problems can occur due to domestic violence. Many studies show that domestic violence can cause, many physical injuries, can occur which includes cuts, bruises, bite marks, concussions, broken bones, miscarriages, joint damage, migraines, permanent disfigurement, arthritis, hypertension, heart disease, and sexually transmitted infections which can be the reason of cervical cancer and eventually death (Abbot & Williamson, 1999; Coker, Hopenhayn, DeSimone, Bush, & Crofford, 2009; McCaw, Golding, Farley & Minkoff, 2007). In a study Coker *et al.* (2009) determined the relationship between domestic violence and cervical cancer. They expected that women who have been exposed to domestic violence to be at greater risk for cervical cancer. They also determined that 35.9 per cent of the women in the registry had experienced domestic violence in their lifetime and 1.3 per cent of the women in the registry had never experienced violence. Results showed that 3.5 per cent women with domestic violence reported having cervical cancer at some point and 1.3 per cent of the women who had never experienced violence also reported cervical cancer.

Physical injuries can be very harmful to a woman, but research has proven that psychological injury is more damaging to long-term health (Hill, Schroeder, Bradley, Kaplan, & Angel, 2009; McCaw *et al.*, 2007). Psychological health is more affected by domestic violence than physical health. Studies show that one or multiple mental health disorder is outcome of domestic violence. It includes stress, anxiety, depression, alcohol or substance abuse, personality disorders, post-traumatic stress disorder, sleeping and eating disorders, social dysfunction and even suicide (Abbot & Williamson, 1999; Gerlock, 1999; Howard, Trevillion & Agnew-Davies, 2010; McCaw *et al.*, 2007). In a study, Gerlock (1999) determined the health consequences of domestic violence on victims and their batterers. He found that 42 per cent of the victims visited healthcare centres due to physical health problems since six month and 29 per cent for mental health problems and 64 per cent believed that their health problems were related to the domestic violence. The women were also suffering from many health problems in which 16 per cent with musculoskeletal issues, 6 per cent pulmonary, 3 per cent dermatological, 6 per cent gastrointestinal, 2 per cent cardiovascular, 16 per cent neurological, 52 per cent with mood disorders, 58 per cent depression, 19 per cent anxiety, 3 per cent psychosis, 3 per cent with personality disorders and 10 per cent with substance abuse. The women also reported the short-term injuries (Gerlock, 1999).

Prevalence of Domestic Violence

According to National statistics, prevalence of lifetime physical, sexual and emotional domestic violence estimate that 40 per cent of women experience abuse at the hands of a partners (Yoshikawa, Agrawal, Poudel & Jimba, 2012). In 2006, the World Health Organization (WHO) organized a study to knowing the prevalence of domestic violence against women (Garcia-Moreno, Jansen, Ellsberg, Heise & Watts, 2006). The aim of this study was to estimate the prevalence of different forms of violence, to assess the health outcomes of domestic violence, to identify risk and prevention factors and to document the women's coping strategies at 15 sites in 10 countries. Total sample was 24,097 women, aged 15 to 49. It was found that in most sites, 30 per cent to 60 per cent of women had been the victims of domestic abuse; the absolute range was from 15 to 71 per cent, with physical and sexual violence being the most common. On the basis of this study it was suggested that domestic violence against women is common across the world, that most of women are abused by a partner than by an unknown perpetrator. According to Garcia-Moreno *et al.* (2006) large number of domestic abuse is considered to be severe and frequent. In 2013, World Health Organization (WHO) also suggests that women in South-East Asia (includes India, Maldives, Sri Lanka, Thailand and Bangladesh) are at a higher likelihood for experiencing partner abuse during their lifetime than women from Europe, the Western Pacific and potentially the Americas.

The studies also show that not only women but men also are the victims of domestic violence. According to estimation of The Domestic Violence Resource Centre, between 6,00,000 and six million women, and between 1,00,000 and six million men, were victims of domestic violence in 2003. In a survey conducted by National Violence against Women found that 25.5 per cent of women and 7.9 per cent of men self-reported having experienced domestic violence at some point in their lives (Tjaden & Thoennes, 2000)

In India, a survey conducted by National family and health (2005), shows that total life time prevalence of domestic violence was 33.5 per cent and 8.5 per cent for sexual violence among women aged 15-49 (NFHS, 2015). Another study conducted in 2014 reported that out of the large population of India, violence affects

27.5 million women over their lifetimes, The Lancet (as cited in Pahuja, 2011) more than 55 per cent of the women suffer from domestic violence, especially in the states of Bihar, Uttar Pradesh, Madhya Pradesh and other northern states (Pahuja, 2011).

In 2012 too National Crime Records Bureau record of India states reported crime rate of 46 per one lakh women, rape rate of 2 per one lakh women, dowry homicide rate of 0.7 per one lakh women and the rate of domestic cruelty by husbands or his relatives as 5.9 per one lakh women (NCRB, 2014). According to the latest report of National Crime Records Bureau, a crime has been recorded against women in every three minutes in India. Every one hour, two women are raped in this country and every six hours, a young married woman found beaten to death, burnt or driven to suicide (Pahuja, 2011).

Preventions and Policies

Preventing violence against women requires addressing causes and risk factors, which are complex and multiple, dependent on context and can shift with broader societal changes (Deshpandy & Chauthaiwale, 2017). Before prevention, it is important to know the main causes behind domestic violence against women. There are many reasons of domestic violence, such as, dominant behaviour of men, poverty and lack of basic amenities, alcoholism and use of other narcotics, lack of awareness among men about rights of women and constitutional punitive measures for crimes against women, financial as well as social dependence of women on men and abuse in the name of culture and tradition. The complexity of causes and multiple manifestations of violence against women suggest in themselves that multiple strategies are needed to successfully address this problem that is not only one preventive solution for all. Recent comprehensive global reviews show that there is significant evidence to recommend the following types of prevention interventions as effective or promising. Preventive violence against women can be addressed through different types of strategies:

It includes group or community based relationship-level interventions working with women and men, community initiatives to raise awareness and change attitudes about women's rights, men and boys' group education about the rights of women, protection for women escaping violence and protection orders and paralegal programmes and community based legal interventions (Deshpandy & Chauthaiwale, 2017).

An appropriate policy response including targeted legislation, appropriate resource and effective implementation, has been shown to help enable wholesale norm change by promoting non-tolerance of violence against women and girls (Deshpandy & Chauthaiwale, 2017). Other strategies involves such as intensive community-level work and awareness raising campaigns are also key in promoting changing attitudes and norms (Deshpandy & Chauthaiwale, 2017).

Victims of domestic violence need proper support of family as well as society. Most of the victims do not get adequate support in their efforts to overcome the consequences of domestic violence. Dedicated psychological, social, health and legal services tend to be at large to Indian women. In Indian society, social norms often blame the victim that is; they hold that they are responsible for their suffering. Thus, many victims find themselves socially marginalized and harmed by crippling health conditions. The justice system must also be accessible, responsive and effective for victims of domestic violence. The Constitution of India focuses on principle of gender equality in the form of fundamental rights. The Constitution of India not only grants equality to women, but also empowers the State to adopt measures of positive discrimination in favour of women for neutralizing the cumulative socio-economic, education and political disadvantages faced by them. The basis of the Constitution of India is democratic polity so our laws, development policies, plans and programmers have aimed at women's advancement in different spheres. In the Constitution of India, the main constitutional provisions for women are as under:

Article 14, confers on men and women equal rights and opportunities in political, economic and social spheres.

Article 15, prohibits discrimination against any citizen on grounds of religion, race, caste, sex etc.

Article 16, provides for equality of opportunities, matters relating to employment or appointment to any office under the State.

Article 42, Direct the State to make provision for ensuring just and humane conditions of work and maternity relief.

According to Protection of Women from Domestic Violence Act (2005)—This Act protects women from any act/conduct/omission/commission that harms, injures or potential to harm is to be considered as domestic violence. It protects the women from physical, sexual, emotional, verbal, psychological and economic abuse.

Five Year Strategic Plan (2011–2016) released by the Ministry of Women and Child Development discusses a plan for victims called "one-stop crisis centres for women", which would include medical, legal, law enforcement, counselling, and shelter support for themselves and their children. The significant differences in women's empowerment and domestic violence experience by region and population within India (Kishor & Gupta, 2004) underscore the need to culturally and regionally tailor the screening and support services provided at such centres. For example, in resource-limited states where sexual forms of domestic violence predominate, priority should be given to the allocation of healthcare providers to evaluate, document, and treat associated injuries and/or transmitted diseases. In settings where financial control and neglect are common, legal, financial, and educational empowerment may need to be given precedence.

Discussion

In Indian society, domestic violence originates from perpetual thought of gender inequality, which involves distorted thoughts about the roles and responsibilities of women. This sense of inequality starts with the birth itself; in case of birth of a baby boy, the birth is celebrated in many ways but in case of birth of a baby girl no celebration takes place. In Indian society most perpetraters are influenced by the societal messages that say that violence against women are acceptable. Freedom from violence is an imagination of victims' because in our society, many women who are victimized of any kind of violence feel that they are at guilt. The experience of domestic violence affects the lives of millions of women worldwide, in all socio-economic classes cutting across boundaries of wealth, race, religion and culture, thus, impeding the right of women to participate fully in society. Any kind of violence limits the ability of women to make choices about their lives. Violence against women violates as well as impairs or nullifies the enjoyment by women of their human rights and fundamental freedom. Physical violence is nearly always accompanied by psychological abuse and *vice versa,* which can be just as demeaning and degrading as physical abuse. Domestic violence increases fear and insecurity in women's life and are obstacles to their achievement and development. The fear of violence is a permanent obstacle in the growth of women and limits their access to resources and basic activities. Domestic violence against women is one of the crucial social process by which women are forced into a subordinate position as compared to men.

The present study aims to explore different aspects related to domestic violence against women. Violence against women is a serious issue in India. Domestic violence is a pattern of behaviour which involves violence by a person against another person in domestic situations. Although, development of women has remarkably increased in different areas since few decades, but unfortunately incidences of violence against women of rural areas as well as urban areas is still a burning issue. The majority of women are harassed physically as well as mentally by their partner and family members. Negative effects of violence on psychological health are more dangerous than physical health. It can lead to depression, anxiety and even suicide. The past 10 years have been an incredible period of growth in domestic violence research in India and South Asia. Our systematic review contributes to the growing body of evidence by providing important information about the physical and psychological effects of domestic violence, its prevalence, prevention, policies of Indian Constitution. WHO also emphasises that frequency of domestic violence is more in Asian countries than other countries. Review of research shows that there is indispensable need of measures to be taken to address the main causes of domestic violence in Indian society. Domestic violence against women can lead to distorted future of our society as women at domestic level are the one who provide their children a robust platform to build their future.

Conclusion

In India half of the population are women. Indian Constitution provides fundamental rights and privileges to women, but women always treated as inferior and deprived. They considered as physically and psychologically weaker than men. In the present time, women proved themselves in different areas of life affirming that they are no less than men at any field. But unfortunately all across our country, behind closed doors of homes, women are tortured and even killed. It is hidden problem, because women not expressed their problems with any one or society due to different reasons such as their children, financial dependency, attachment with family, loneliness, traditional thoughts of society about women that they can not live without any man. It is not happened only in rural areas, urban areas are also witness of domestic violence. It is becoming a bequest which being passed from one generation to another generation. But criminal offence against women reflects the miserable reality that women are not safe and secure at any place. It is not a problem of any special group, caste, gender and age rather it is beyond all social classes, gender, cast and age. Despite efforts made by various sections of society and the government to curb the threat of domestic violence against women, there is a rise in domestic violence. This can be curbed by educating women about her rights, providing adequate assistance and support, providing interventions, prevention programmes and providing punishment to offence of domestic violence. There is need for women to understand their rights and their benefits as well as every woman should be empowered and responsible for themselves. Education about gender equality and violence should be started in early stage of life for both boys and girls and promoting respectful relationship.

References

Abbott, P. & Williamson, E. (1999). "Women, health and domestic violence", *Journal of Gender Studies, 8*(1), 83-102.

Coker, A.L., Hopenhayn, C., DeSimone, C.P., Bush, H.M., & Crofford, L. (2009). "Violence against women raises risk of cervical cancer", *Journal of Women's Health, 18*(8), 1179-1185.

Deshpandey, V. & Chauthaiwale, J. (2017). *Tackling Violence against Women: A study of state intervention measures* (Unpublished report). Bharatiya Stree Shakti, Goverment of India, New Delhi.

Garcia-Moreno, C., Jansen, H., Ellsberg, M., Heise, L., & Watts, C.H. (2006). "Prevalence of intimate partner violence: Findings from the WHO multi-country study on women's health and domestic violence", *The Lancet, 368*(9543), 1260-1269.

Gerlock, A.A. (1999). "Health impact of domestic violence", *Issues in Mental Health Nursing, 20*, 373-385.

Hill, T.D., Schroeder, R.D., Bradley, C., Kaplan, L.M., & Angel, R.J. (2009). "The long-term health consequences of relationship violence in adulthood: An examination of low-income women from Boston Chicago, and San Antonio", *American Journal of Public Health, 99*(9), 1645-1650.

Howard, L.M., Trevillion, K., & Agnew-Davies, R. (2010). "Domestic violence and mental health", *International Review of Psychiatry, 22*(5), 525-534.

Kishor, S. & Gupta, K. (2004). "Women's empowerment in India and its states", *Economic and Political Weekly, 39*(7), 694–712.

Kishor, S. & Johnson, K. (2006). "Reproductive health and domestic violence: Are the poorest women uniquely disadvantaged?" *Demography, 43*(2), 293-307.

McCaw, B., Golding, J.M., Farley, M., & Minkoff, J.R. (2007). "Domestic violence and abuse, health status, and social functioning", *Women and Health, 45*(2), 1-23.

National Family Health Survey (2015). Ministry of Health and Family Welfare, Government of India.

Pahuja, D. (2011). "Domestic violence against women in India", *Legal India.* Retrived from https://legalindia.com

Tjaden, P., & Thoennes, N. (2000). *Extent, nature, and consequences of intimate partner violence: Findings from the National Violence Against Women Survey*. Washington, D.C.: Department of Justice, Publication No. NCJ 181867. 1-69. Retrieved from http://www.ncjrs.gov

UNICEF (2000). *Domestic Violence Against Women and Girls.*

WHO (World Health Organisation). (2013). *Global and Regional Estimates of Violence Against Women: Prevalence and Health Effects of Intimate Partner Violence and Non-partner Sexual Violence*, Geneva:WHO.

Yoshikawa, K., Agrawal, N.R., Poudel, K.C., & Jimba, M.A. (2012). "Lifetime experience of violence and adverse reproductive outcomes: Findings from population surveys in India", *Bio Science Trends, 6*(3), 115–121.

Index